UNCLE FRANK

UNCLE FRANK
The Biography of
FRANK COSTELLO

by LEONARD KATZ

with a foreword by
ANTHONY QUINN

DRAKE PUBLISHERS INC
NEW YORK

Published in 1973 by
Drake Publishers Inc.
381 Park Avenue South
New York, New York 10016

© Leonard Katz, 1973

Library of Congress Cataloging in Publication Data
Katz, Leonard, 1926-
  Uncle Frank
  1. Costello, Frank. I. Title.
HV6248.C67K38   364.1'092'4 (B)   73-5943
ISBN 0-87749-549-1

Printed in the United States of America

Table of Contents

Dedication

The old man died on December 5, 1971. Except for his family the event could hardly be called a tragedy. Just an old man who died at the age of 79. The old man was my father, Joseph Katz, a New York City cab driver for most of his life. During the Great Depression he was called Transfer Joe by the other cabbies because late at night he would promote calls by taking two-cent trolley car transfers as part-payment from groups of card-playing women waiting at transfer points. He had a zest for life that never ceased to amaze those who knew him. The last time I saw him alive, he performed a little dance in a hospital — just as if he was at a Jewish wedding — on his spindly legs to prove he was ambulatory enough to be discharged to a nursing home. I miss him very much and lovingly dedicate this book to his memory.

Leonard Katz

New York, N.Y.
July 18, 1973

Author's note

A book of this sort is never possible without the generous help of many. Law enforcement agencies have opened their records, friends of Uncle Frank have spoken with candor, and many of the countless people from all walks of life who knew him have shared what they know. I am most grateful for their help.

Throughout my research — even when dealing with local, state, and federal police officials on the higher levels — I was often faced with the problem of declining the interview or guaranteeing the anonymity of my source. I chose the latter course, naturally, even though I much prefer to name where any particular bit of information comes from.

In dealing with Costello's friends, acquaintances, and business associates, I was faced with the same problem. Writing a biography about a man who was known as the "Prime Minister of the Underworld" is not the same as writing a biography about a prime minister. As Costello readily acknowledged during his life: "I embarrass people." By this he meant that his notorious reputation caused his legitimate friends discomfort. In death he is still apparently embarrassing people. Many of those I interviewed would talk about him privately, but not publicaly.

The stolid, broad-shouldered figure of Frank Costello casts a giant shadow over the entire history of organized crime in America since the days of prohibition. His life span ran from the small, unaligned, violence-filled gangs that flourished at the turn of the century to the large, highly-organized Mafia families of today that run on modern, business-like principles. Uncle Frank had a great deal to do with this metamorphosis, and as a result, I think, his life represents a unique bit of Americana and has something to say about us as a people and a nation.

His strong, masculine face is hardly the traditional face of evil. He abhored violence, calling it "ignorance," and was as different in outlook and life style from the popular version of a Godfather or Mafia boss as one of our primate ancestors is from modern man. He was — given the setting of his background — an affable, articulate, immensely likeable individual with an old-fashioned sense of values. During his time he was the most powerful political force in the nation's largest city, and virtually no one was made a judge, held high political office, or became mayor without his approval. He understood and respected power and instinctively never abused it.

This is not to say he was just a political force and a gambler. He was also a Mafia chief. There is no question about that. For a number of years he was head of the old Lucky Luciano family, and his influence was so great that he had a seat on the "commission," organized crime's national board of directors. But what he yearned for most was "respectability," and he never tired of speculating what his life might have been like if fate had decreed he be born in a different environment.

"Do you want to know what kind of man Frank Costello was," an old-time Tammany Hall politician asked rhetorically during an interview. "Well, I'll tell you. He was a prince of a fellow."

This is how the vast majority of people I interviewed: business associates, politicians, show business personalities, lawyers, newspapermen, underworld figures, and even police and law enforcement officials felt about him. Yet he was often depicted in the press as a monster, a killer who could press a button and have someone blown away, a financer of the heroin trade, and the most powerful man in organized crime.

The truth lies somewhere in between, and that is what this book is about.

Foreword

I was staying at the Carlyle Hotel in New York City during the cold month of January in 1971. Not only had the weather turned cold but the project I was working on was getting colder by the minute. 'The project' was a motion picture I was trying to produce.

The launching of any motion picture is difficult enough, God knows, but ours had more built in problems than most. It dealt with the power struggle going on in Harlem between the white mob and the blacks.

First of all, since the picture dealt with police corruption, the police didn't want it made. The black mob didn't want it made, and the 'organization' didn't want it made.

Ralph Serpe, the co-producer of the picture, and I had gotten the message loud and clear. We were about to throw in the towel. One year's time, effort, energy, and investment was about to go down the drain.

Ralph and I sat in my suite, chain smoking and crying in our beer. I take defeat very badly. Ralph Serpe is an Italo-American who learned about survival on the East Side of New York, and he, too, hates defeat.

"Son-of-a-bitch," he shouted, as he got up and started to put on his heavy winter coat. He started for the door.

"Where the hell you going?" I called after him. Misery hates to be alone.

"I've got an idea," he said at the door and was gone before I could ask him what the idea was.

Outside, the wind was howling, and no matter how often I pounded the pillow, sleep refused to be my mate. Finally, after torturous hours of coercion, she begrudgingly acquiesced.

I was holding on for dear life when the phone rang. I didn't want to let go. I didn't want to return to the land of reality, but the phone insisted. I finally reached out for it.

"Tony?" I heard Ralph's familiar voice.

"Yeah?"

"Wait a minute, somebody wants to talk to you."

I turned on the light and waited. I glanced at the clock on the night table. It was eight o'clock.

"Hello, Tony. How are you?" a strange raspy voice was saying on the phone. I was sure it was a gag. Years before, I'd played a broken down prize fighter in a picture called *Requiem for a Heavyweight*. I had used that voice as the fighter. There after on the street or in restaurants people would greet me imitating that hoarse sound. I had gotten to resent it and now was sure that Ralph had put on one of his friends to pull the cheap joke.

Angrily I wheezed back into the phone, "I'm fine, pal, and why don't you go and screw yourself?"

There was a pause at the other end.

"Hey, Tony, this is Frank Costello."

Now I was sure it was a joker.

"Yeah? Well, I'm Tom Dewey." I wheezed as if my vocal chords were in shreds. Tom Dewey was the former Governor of New York who had sent many gangsters to jail and several to the electric chair.

I heard some angry voices at the other end of the line. Finally, Ralph came back on the phone.

"What the hell did you say to Frank?"

"Come on, Ralph, cut out the cheap jokes. I've got enough problems."

"Listen, *stronzo* (Italian for dumb shit), I'm here having breakfast with Frank Costello, and I've asked him to have lunch with us."

The name of Frank Costello conjured up all sorts of images. I, among millions of others, had been hypnotized by his hands on television during the Kefauver investigations twenty years before.

He had been described as the "czar of crime," the "king of the underworld," and all sorts of other princely titles, but most importantly, Frank Costello had been the cause of a broken "friendship" between a beautiful actress and myself.

We were watching the Kefauver and Costello encounter from a comfortable couch in Chicago.

"Boy, I'd hate to run into him in a dark alley," I said, running my hand through her long blond hair.

She said very quietly, "He's a very nice man, honey."

I jumped as if someone had touched me with a live electric wire.

"What do you mean he's a nice guy? You mean you know him?"

She got that terrible "I confess" look one dreads in women. "He's been very sweet to me."

I was appalled. This beautiful, innocent, near-virginal girl I was holding in my arms had consorted with the leader of the underworld! I pushed her away as if she'd suddenly been spattered by some terrible, offensive offal.

"You went to bed with *that* man?" I exclaimed disgustedly, pointing at the swarthy man on television.

She became indignant. "I didn't go to bed with him, and he didn't make a pass at me. He's one of the finest men I've ever met in my life."

My God, she had not only gone to bed with him but was still in love with him!

The more she defended him, the angrier and more righteous I became.

I dressed quickly and went to some southside bar to drown my disappointment.

Months later, I met her in New York and allowed her charms to sway my better judgment. She could be most persuasive. She finally almost convinced me that she and Costello had only had a platonic friendship.

One night, however, she tentatively asked me if I would mind if she had dinner with Frank Costello. She had run into him on the street, and he'd been very hurt that she hadn't called him. After all, he had paid for her acting lessons years before and had helped her with her career. She apparently told him about me, and he said, "Fine, bring him along, I'd like to meet him."

I had looked at the girl incredulously. Did I look like a sucker? Did she think she could pull the wool over my eyes? Never! Not only would I not go to meet her former lover, but I absolutely forbade her to have anything further to do with him. He was evil.

The girl shook her head sadly.

"He's a lonely man, and I can't hurt him."

With that I rushed out of the door, and the relationship was never again the same.

Now I heard the voice of that former ogre on the phone.

"Okay, wise guy, let's start all over again. Ralph thinks we should have lunch together."

"Fine," I heard myself saying, "where would you like to meet?"

"Where are you staying?"

"At the Carlyle Hotel. Do you know it?"

"Know it? I used to own it. See you there at one o'clock." The line went dead.

As I put the phone slowly down in the cradle, I wondered why in the hell I'd accepted the date. Now it so happens I have a peculiar frailty. Anybody named Frank has a big headstart in my affections. My grandfather's name was Frank, my own father was Frank Quinn, and I have a son named Frank. St. Francis of Assisi is my favorite saint, San Francisco is my favorite city, and I'm sure the Mexican revolution would not have been the same if it hadn't been for Francisco Villa. The only Frank I'd ever had trouble with was Frank Costello, and now I was going to break bread with him!

Around eleven o'clock, Ralph called and told me that there would be several other people joining us for lunch. It seemed that Frank had forgotten a very important luncheon date, and so as not to disappoint anyone he was combining the two dates.

The maitre d' at the restaurant didn't have a table big enough to accommodate our party, so he suggested we lunch in a private alcove just off the main dining room.

At one o'clock sharp the phone rang in my suite. It was Ralph.

"We're in the lobby, Tony. Hurry down."

When I walked into the lobby I saw Ralph and his party. I searched for the familiar face of Costello, whom I had never seen except on television and in bad newspaper clippings. I had expected to see a big six-foot bruiser with shoulders like Muhammed Ali's. Instead I found myself shaking hands with a man of average height and wearing a well cut English sports jacket that made his shoulders look quite normal.

The image I had lived with for twenty years shattered before my eyes. As we shook hands I felt a message being transmitted from my former rival. "Let's start from scratch — all former notions about each other forgotten."

Still, it was not easy to do that. Not for me. I had expected to meet a different type of man. I knew about Frank Costello's East Harlem background and what a jungle that was. I had read a great deal about what he'd done during his youth to survive. I knew that at one time he'd been considered a king of that jungle. I hadn't taken into account that I would be meeting an old lion now — a man who was in his late seventies or eighties. The only evidence of a predatory existence was in his eyes. They were the eyes of a man who had known all about the hunted and the hunter. Now he was the old lion who wants to be left in peace, who does not want to fight, but all around him the fight is still going on. Other foolish animals still want to challenge the old king.

As we shook hands, I realized we were not proving masculinity or phoney sincerity. We were making a pact to start from scratch.

I noticed, as the maitre d' led us into the small side room, that my 'guest' had created quite a stir, not only with the luncheon crowd but among the waiters. It did not surprise me. Frank had an aura of magnetism most star personalities would envy. He took over center stage without trying. Maybe that was his secret — not trying.

During lunch he told me how his vocal chords had been "burned" by an X-ray treatment for his "nodules." He talked freely and amusingly about Joe Kennedy and dozens of other famous people. He seemed to know a little about everyone — and a lot about everything.

The story that had me doubled up with laughter was an anecdote about Harry Truman. At one time the President had lived in Sand's Point, Long Island, and was visiting his daughter who still lived in the area. Frank and Truman had known each other quite well.

"You know, I used to like to walk in the morning. I didn't like to walk during the day because I knew people were watching me and so forth and saying there's Frank Costello, the gangster. I don't want to bother nobody. I want to be left alone. So I'd get up at five in the morning, and I'd take my walk. That morning as I came out of the house, I see guys up in the trees. I know they are cops and F.B.I. men keeping an eye on me, but I go about my way. Let them look all they want. So I'm walking, and way down at the end I see a little figure walking towards me. He's getting closer, and suddenly I realize it's Harry Truman! He starts to say, 'Hello Frank,' and just as he's about to say it, I say, 'Keep your mouth shut, you dumb bastard. They're watching us. Don't louse us both up.'

So he smiles and keeps walking, and I smile and keep walking!"

He was full of stories like that, and we kept the waiters around until four o'clock. They, too, were laughing.

Finally, he asked me what I was doing in New York.

"I'm trying to produce a picture," I said.

"What's the title?"

"*Across 110th Street*."

"What's it about?" he asked.

Now I didn't want to say, "Frank, it's about the white Mafia and the black Mafia and the struggle for power," because to me it wasn't about that, anyway. So I said:

"Frank, the story is basically about a minority — in this case, the blacks. They are not only suffering the usual indignities all minorities go through but are being squeezed by 'the mob' and victimized by their own people. Three guys pull a heist on the numbers racket and get caught, but in the end the money goes back to the people. That's what the picture is about."

"I see. Well, good luck, kid."

He didn't say, "Don't worry," or "I'll take care of it." All I know is that a couple of days later, all the flack stopped. The picture was made with the complete cooperation of Harlem and everyone else. We had no trouble from anybody.

I've read a great deal about Frank Costello's life. I know that at one time he had been a gangster, but I found him a warm, generous, gentle human being. The young lady had been right.

Frank and I both came from a world where a handshake was not merely a social gesture — but a commitment. We became friends. Whenever I went back to New York we'd get together.

I saw him last a few months before he died. We had lunch at Toots Shor's, where he once more regaled me with his never ending anecdotes.

"Frank," I pleaded, "I'd give anything to play 'the life of Frank Costello.'"

He turned to a friend sitting with us and said, "If my life is ever done, see that Tony does it. I know he would treat me nice."

We shook hands.

"You've got my word, Frank."

"You know, kid, where I come from — you shake hands, you keep your word. If you don't, send back the hand."

I won't have to. I'll treat him fair. He was a nice man.

Anthony Quinn,
New York, 1973

The hit

A man of ingrained habits, Frank Costello rose promptly at five A.M. on May 2, 1957. Putting on slippers and a red-silk bathrobe, he padded silently towards the large, eat-in kitchen in the seven-room apartment he shared with his wife and her two dogs at 115 Central Park West.

It was a cool morning, cool for this time of year in New York, with the temperature in the mid-forties. Traffic was almost nonexistent, with only a few cabs and delivery trucks breaking the early hour's silence. Scarcely anyone could be seen on the street.

In just fifty-six minutes, at 5:56 the sun would rise, making Central Park reasonably safe again, slowly transforming it from a shadowy, dangerous jungle into a pleasant green oasis in the center of one of the most highly urbanized areas in the world.

Once in the kitchen, Costello turned a handle to ignite one of the stove's gas jets. A maid had prepared and placed a coffee pot with the necessary ingredients on the stove the night before. All that was needed was heat and a few minutes before the smell of fresh-brewed coffee would fill the kitchen. A slice of packaged white bread was popped into the toaster.

With these rituals out of the way, he walked to his front door, opened it, and picked up *The New York Times* that had been delivered that

morning. He then walked back to the kitchen and began to read while
waiting for the coffee to percolate.

Although he preferred the *Daily News,* New York's morning tabloid
newspaper, Costello dutifully plowed through the *Times* every day. He
found the pictures and succinct writing characteristic of the *News*
easier to digest than the long, gray columns of America's best newspaper.

On this Thursday morning there was a great deal in the *Times* that
would interest Costello. The lead story concerned an old and intimate
friend and colleague, Joseph (Socks) Lanza, a swarthy, bull-faced
racketeer who was known as the "czar" of the Fulton Fish Market because he controlled the unions there.

Lanza had been transported from Sing Sing Prison, where he was
serving time, to the city to testify before the state Joint Legislative
Committee on Government Operations. The Committee, also known
as the Watchdog Committee, wanted to know how Lanza's wife could
tell him he was going to be paroled two days before the Parole Commission had considered the matter.

The thought that Lanza's parole was the result of a political fix did
not escape those who were concerned with such things. The Committee
was endeavoring to discover if his release was indeed the result of a
political favor and if so, who did the fixing. As a result, a major scandal
was brewing, and Lanza's parole had been revoked through the personal intervention of Governor Averell Harriman.

The Watchdog Committee questioned Lanza at a hearing held at
the Bar Association Building on West Forty-fourth Street. But the
tough Lanza chose not to cooperate. He took the protection of the
Fifth Amendment to all pertinent questions.

The story featuring a one-column picture of a smiling Lanza, with
his round, well-nourished face looking like that of a beefy football
coach snapped at the moment of victory, held no mysteries for Costello. The man who had once held Tammany Hall, the regular Democratic political apparatus of the city, in the palm of his hand was quickly
able to figure out how Lanza was able to find out decisions before
they were made.

He knew the political ins and outs of the city as well as any man,
and he knew that Socks, an affable and reasonable Mafia leader, had
many strong connections. Costello didn't need the *Times,* for instance,
to point out that Lanza' brother-in-law was P. Vincent Viggiano, Tammany leader of the Second Assembly District, located in Lower Manhattan. He knew from personal experience that Lanza had for years
wielded considerable political clout with a behind-the-scenes role.

For Costello, the man who could once place judges on the bench, elect district leaders, place his own man as the head of Tammany Hall, and even take credit for electing a mayor of the City of New York, it was all quite elementary. He knew how Lanza operated and how certain parole commissioners, who were appointed by the Governor, were controlled by the mob. The wonder was not that Socks Lanza could predict his future but that he had ever gone to jail in the first place.

There was another story on page one of the *Times* that interested Costello. The story concerned a championship fight on which he had bet heavily and won. Sugar Ray Robinson, one of boxing's immortals, at the age of thirty-six had regained the middleweight championship for the fourth time in his career by knocking out Gene Fullmer in the fifth round in Chicago Stadium.

Costello had always liked the class of Robinson. He considered him to be one of the greatest fighters he had ever seen pound-for-pound, but because he was generally regarded to be over the hill, Robinson was the three-to-one underdog in the fight. The experts didn't give him much of a chance against the young and bull-strong Fullmer.

Costello disagreed with the opinion of the fight experts and had taken the odds. He had bet $50,000 with a midwest bookie and $25,000 with a bookie in New York. His profits amounted to $225,000.

Although he had known the results the night before, he took pleasure in reading the fight details. Fullmer had been floored by a left hook and counted out one minute and twenty-seven seconds into the fifth round.

The *Times* was thick that Thursday, chock full of Mother's Day ads. It may have reminded him that he needed to buy a gift for Loretta, his wife of forty-three years. Although they were childless, he remembered to buy her something each Mother's Day.

Mrs. Costello, called Bobbie by all their friends, usually rose somewhere between nine and ten to personally prepare breakfast for the miniature Doberman and toy poodle she loved dearly. Her husband would often remark good naturedly that she would fix breakfast for the "damn dogs" while he had to get his own.

Breakfast was always a simple affair for Frank Costello. He habitually would drink his coffee black without sugar, and the slice of toast would receive a thin smear of margarine. (The dogs would get butter with their morning toast.)

He took pride in the fact that he had complete control of himself and — except for his cigarette habit — never indulged himself in any way. At the age of sixty-six he was in reasonable good health and carried his weight of 168 pounds easily on a compact frame that measured just one-quarter-of-an-inch short of five-foot-nine. He was a little thick in the middle, but not noticeably so for a man of his years. He watched what he ate because he cared about the way he looked — cared very much.

Costello lingered over the sports pages because that's what interested him most. He loved to gamble and habitually bet on horses and sports. He was a pretty astute baseball handicapper, and he knew the pitchers (because that's what baseball odds are based on) as well as any kid who collected baseball cards.

He noted that the Milwaukee Braves had beat the New York Giants by the score of five to one. The other New York teams had fared better: Don Drysdale had pitched a neat seven hitter for the Dodgers at Ebbets Field, winning seven to two; the Yankees in Detroit had beat the Tigers seven to four.

The race results also interested Costello. Before the days of the pari-mutuel machines, he had once been a handbook at the track, and he still kept tab on things even though he had been ruled off the turf as an "undesirable." He read that at Jamaica Race Track, the Youthful Stakes was won handily by a two-year-old named Bolero U, a favorite paying $4.50.

Although it was a chilly morning, the weatherman promised that things would warm up during the day, with a high of sixty-five or seventy expected. By night temperatures were expected to plunge into the forties again.

By eight A.M. he was dressed and ready to take the dogs for their morning walk in Central Park. As always, he was impeccably dressed, wearing a superbly-tailored, light-brown suit, white shirt, and matching tie. On his head he wore a light grey fedora.

To anyone who didn't know him, he appeared to be a successful businessman — which was just the impression he wished to convey. There was nothing in the manner he walked, talked, or dressed that suggested anything to the contrary.

This impression he projected for the outside world was not, of course, an accident. Above everything else, Frank Costello coveted respectability. It was a subject that crept into his conversation often, and he would tell friends that the "quest for respectability" was one of the motivating forces behind life.

Newspaper stories branding him as a top Mafia leader who was both a killer and involved in the heroin traffic terribly upset him and his wife. Under her goading he had sought the advice of one of his lawyers, Edward Bennett Williams of Washington, to see what he could do about this defamation of his character. Williams convinced the

Costellos that a libel suit would only result in more publicity and more "heartbreak."

"It just isn't fair. They shouldn't be allowed to print those awful stories about Frank," Mrs. Costello would complain to friends.

Costello's attitude was more philosophical. "It's all a racket," he would say. "I'm good circulation."

"Heartbreak" was one of his favorite words, and he used it to describe everything from a busted romance to the anguish felt by the Lindberghs after their child was kidnapped. It was a word he had a-dopted from the Broadway columnists whom he read avidly.

The Costellos had lived in the Majestic apartment building for many years. It is a huge, buff-colored high rise which occupies all of Central Park West between Seventy-first and Seventy-second Streets. They had an elevator-talk acquaintanceship with many of the residents and took pride in the fact that they were not only accepted but liked by their neighbors. Sometimes Costello discussed the weather with a neighbor and sometimes the rising crime rate.

"It just isn't safe to walk the dogs in Central Park anymore," he would say in his raspy voice.

On many mornings, after walking the dogs, a variety of men he had business dealings with would appear in the lobby of the Majestic. After being announced, they would take the elevator to the eighteenth floor.

These morning visitors were often some of the best-known names in New York. They included a department store magnate, Wall Street leaders, politicians, judges, lawyers, famous show business personalities, favored newspapermen, and occasionally men from Costello's other world — the underworld.

The rule was that you never appeared at the Costello apartment without first making an appointment. Costello saw almost anyone who had a legitimate reason to want an audience.

By ten or ten-thirty A.M., "Mr. Schedule," as he liked to call himself, would leave for the place that had been his hangout and business office since the late twenties — the Waldorf Astoria Barbershop. Everyone in the city who wanted to see "Uncle Frank," as he was referred to by Tammany politicians, favor seekers, and young friends, knew that he could be found there every morning he was in town.

The world famous Waldorf, located on Park Avenue, was a protective cocoon he had wrapped around himself. It was also Costello's idea of class. Police tailing him, for instance, knew better than to follow him into the Waldorf. They knew that as soon as they set foot into its plush, old-world lobby, word would be flashed down to the barber shop of their presence. Costello had everyone — bellhops, elevator operators, telephone operators, and even house detectives — either on his payroll or anxious to do him a favor.

Unlike other Mafia chiefs, men like Albert Anastasia and Vito Genovese, Costello took pains to avoid the trappings of the "Men of Respect." He never had a cadre of hard-eyed men around him or a bodyguard-chauffeur driving a long, black limousine to transport him from place to place. In fact, he never had a bodyguard in his life except for one imposed upon him by the police. When he went about town, he would walk or use cabs.

Each day at the barber shop he would be shaved and manicured, have a few hairs snipped, and have his shoes shined. He took great pride in his hands, and the manicurist would buff each nail until they could reflect overhead lights. While he was being tended to, those waiting to see him would sit on a nearby plastic covered bench or stand in the corridor.

His visitors came from all walks of life. Frank Erickson, the nation's top bookmaker, was often there. So were men who were well known at Manhattan Police Headquarters because they were linked to organized crime — men like Meyer Lansky, Joe Adonis, Little Augie Pisano, Anthony (Tony Bender) Strollo, Socks Lanza, and Costello's business partner, Dandy Phil Kastel.

Mixed in with the Mafia figures were Tammany politicians seeking to make a deal or to ask a favor, businessmen or aquaintances seeking a loan, and messengers there to make reports to Costello on his many business investments.

It was not unlike the days when kings ruled and subjects crowded the courts seeking boons. With each one, Costello walked slowly up and down the long corridor that separates the barber shop from the rest of the hotel. He talked freely because he was secure in the knowledge that his conversations couldn't be bugged under those conditions.

Police assigned to keep a watch on Costello never ceased to comment on the wide range of people that this rather ordinary looking man knew.

"If you watched the Waldorf long enough you'd see goombahs from all over the country," an Irish detective assigned to tail Costello recalled.

On that morning of May 2, 1957, one of the visitors Costello received handed him a small piece of paper on which a list of figures were written. He slipped the paper inside his jacket pocket, unmindful that before the day was over that piece of paper would cause him a great deal of grief.

By noon the parade of business associates and supplicants ended. The corridor, which had temporarily served as his court, was abandoned. It was time for lunch. Usually Costello would be joined by some of the more important names who had received an audience with him that morning. Often they would eat in the Waldorf's Norse Grill.

After lunch, Costello went to the Biltmore Hotel. The Biltmore, located on Madison Avenue, had an excellent Turkish bath. This was another of Mr. Schedule's ingrained habits. Three times a week he would go to the Biltmore's baths because he believed in the thera-peutic value of a steam room.

"It's good for ya'," he would solemnly advise friends. "It gets all that poison out of your system."

He also conducted business at the baths. Frank Erickson often ac-companied him there. So did many of the highly respected business leaders of the city. Department store tycoon Bernard Gimbel was seen in conversation with Costello at the baths on occasion. Another steam-room friend was Jim Farley, National Democratic Chairman under Franklin D. Roosevelt.

That day he left the Biltmore at about five P.M. and took a cab to Chandler's Restaurant on East Forty-ninth Street. He had an apppont-ment to meet Tony Bender to discuss family business. Bender, a tough, wily Mafia boss who ruled Greenwich Village and was a confident of Vito Genovese, had made the appointment. Genovese, a killer with an insatiable lust for power, was reputed to be the most powerful man in the Cosa Nostra.

Costello didn't know it at the time, of course, but the appointment was the beginning of a carefully orchestrated plan that would result in his being shot in the head and deposed from his throne.

Chandler's was still another of Costello's many meeting places. It was owned by the right people and was considered safe. At the time, police had reason to believe that its real owner was Joe Cataldo, also known as Joe the Wop, an intimate of Bender's. Costello would often meet some of the top underbosses of his family there — men like Tommy (Tommy Ryan) Eboli and Jerry Catena.

The story of the events of May 2, 1957 have never appeared in print. Since that fateful day, police have ascertained that Bender was al-ready there when Costello arrived. With him was his top lieutenant, Vincent Mauro, better known as Vincent Bruno.

They both greeted Costello with a good deal of warmth. As is the custom at such gatherings, the formalities were preserved.

"I hear you bet the nigger real good to beat Fullmer," Bender said.

"Hey, Frank knows what he's doing," Mauro cut in. "He doesn't get up five in the morning for nothin'."

"His pride was on the line," Costello answered in explanation of why he picked Robinson. "It meant a lot more than just another fight to him."

The purpose of the meeting was then brought up by Bender, and all three men talked quietly for a few minutes. Then Bender left, leaving Mauro for Costello's company.

Mauro, who at a future date would be arrested, convicted, and sent to prison with Genovese on a heroin rap, was quite welcome so far as Costello was concerned. The two men liked each other and in recent weeks had become very friendly. The initiative for this sudden closeness was Mauro's. He had gotten into the habit lately of showing up wherever Costello happened to be.

Costello reciprocated. He liked Vinnie. He was his kind of Italian: straight forward and gregarious with an infectious laugh. Costello liked everything about Mauro including his principles and his way of thinking (which was straight down the line and not too different from the way Costello thought).

Mauro was about five-foot-ten, husky, and with a paunch that only a fool would mistake for soft. He spoke with a marked New York-Italian accent and sprinkled his conversation with a lot of Italian words. Mauro could be described as an Italian's Italian who was unabashedly proud of his heritage. Costello liked that about him too.

Although their friendship had recently blossomed, they had known each other for quite a number of years. One time, in fact, Costello had mediated a problem that the hot-headed and impulsive Mauro had become involved in.

It dealt with a situation that had developed some years back in the Gold Key Club. The Gold Key, an after-hours joint on West Fifty-sixth Street, was frequented by show business personalities and many of the men of the secret society. It was sort of a common meeting ground, and they all rubbed shoulders in a sometimes not-so-happy, big family way. The Gold Key, for instance, was one of Frank Sinatra's stamping grounds when he was in town.

One night, singer Billy Daniels, who made the song, "That Old Black Magic" his trademark and who was then doing an engagement at the Copacabana, came into the Gold Key with his wife, a beautiful blond. Unhappily for Daniels, Mauro was there that early morning with Tony Bender and Jerry Catena.

Mauro didn't like the idea of a black man being with a white girl and kept his eye on Daniels. His interest became more pronounced when the couple began to argue. It was a family tiff, but Mauro didn't know they were man and wife and probably wouldn't have cared. From his point of view, blacks and whites shouldn't even be together, much less become involved in the intimacy of a heated discussion.

Daniels slapped his wife, and Mauro became an enraged bull. He was suddenly the defender of white womanhood and, despite his bulk, was at Daniel's side in the blink of an eye. He then picked him up bodily and threw him out of the second floor window of the Gold Key.

Needless to say, quite a commotion was caused. Daniels was hurt badly enough to require hospital treatment. As for Mauro, even in the racial climate of the early fifties, everyone who was sane agreed that he had stepped badly out of line.

The situation called for the talents of the underworld's great mediator. By delicate maneuvering, Costello found out that: (1) Daniels just wanted an apology; (2) was afraid that he was in trouble and would be killed; and (3) wanted most of all to be able to go to the Gold Key again without fear of being maimed.

Mauro wasn't about to apologize. He felt he had done the right thing. Besides, he said, he thought the blond was just one of the Copa girls that Daniels used to bring to the Gold Key all the time. Furthermore, he added, to apologize would be to lose face in very important circles.

Costello talked to Mauro like a father to an errant son. He pointed out that the incident could cause a lot of problems for a lot of people, and besides, just because Mauro didn't know it was Daniels' wife, the facts remained the same. They were married and that was that. You were out of line, he told Mauro, and you should be man enough to admit it.

The incident was finally smoothed over, and everyone continued to go to the Gold Key for fun and games. As for Costello, both sides felt that he had played the role of the honest broker.

While Costello and Mauro were gabbing at Chandler's, Phil Kennedy, a tall, handsome male model who was then managing the Huntington Hartford Model Agency, happened to walk in for a drink. Despite his profession, he was no pansy. He liked to hang around the underworld characters the same way some men like to hang around athletes. He was a close friend of Frank Erickson — in fact, he confided to friends that he was Erickson's adopted son. He was also an intimate of Costello whom he used to call "Uncle Frank."

Kennedy was having marital problems and, when Costello mentioned that he was having dinner with Bobbie and a party of friends at L'Aiglon, said he would go along for a drink or two before going home. Mauro was invited to join the dinner party but declined, saying that he had some business to attend to and would join them later if he could get away.

Costello and Kennedy arrived at the restaurant on East Fifty-fifth Street a little after six. The group that would make up the dinner party was already there: Bobbie; Generoso Pope Jr., youngest son of the publisher of the Italian-language daily, *Il Progresso* and publisher in his own right of the *National Enquirer; Enquirer* columnist John J. Miller and his wife, Cindy; and Al and Rose Minaci, Al being the owner of the Paramount Vending Company, one of the largest, independently-owned juke box outfits in the country.

The Costellos, Miller, and Pope dined together on the average of twice a week. Each would take turns playing host, and this evening it was Miller's turn. He had invited the Minacis because his boss, Gene Pope, had asked him to. Al Minaci was anxious to get to know Costello better.

Costello walked into L'Aiglon in an absolutely ebullient mood. He was happy about the betting coup he had pulled off in the Robinson-Fullmer fight and during drinks told why he was so certain Robinson would win. For a winning gambler there is no greater pleasure than talking about his big score.

"My luck is going good," he said at one point and then reached over and patted Cindy's stomach. She was in the ninth month of pregnancy and was absolutely enormous. It was good luck to pat a pregnant women on the stomach he explained, and everyone laughed.

Costello was also full of news of national importance. He had just received word that Senator Joseph McCarthy of Wisconsin had died.

"All that booze finally got him" he said. "Like I always say, too much of anything is no good. You gotta do things in moderation."

Costello had been an admirer of McCarthy's at one time. Recently, however, he was convinced that his judgement had been wrong on that score. During the years that McCarthy was finding Communists under every bed, Costello had arranged to meet him and had been impressed with the man's sincerity.

"He was going after the Commies, and that was a good thing, right?" said Costello, "But then he started doing wrong things and accusin' everyone of being a Commie. Christ, for a while there I was afraid he was gonna accuse me."

Everyone laughed at the joke.

As a newspaperman, Miller wondered how Costello had gotten the news of McCarthy's death so fast. He knew it hadn't been announced as yet. Costello's ability to find things out before they became general knowledge never ceased to amaze him.

As always, Costello dominated the subject matter of the conversation. He was like a good talk show host who had the finesse to pose a question and then draw everyone out on the subject, furthermore, if someone went off on a tangent, he had a way of bringing everyone back to the topic he was interested in.

After listening he then gave his views on the subject. He leaned forward to get everyone's attention, his blue-grey eyes sparkled, and his normally taut, expressionless face came alive. Everything to Costello had several angles, and he delighted in telling how he figured those angles.

The Costello party sat in the first booth on the right as you entered the well-known French restaurant. The booth contained a large, round table that could comfortably seat eight or ten. Whenever Costello dined at L'Aiglon, even if it was just he and Bobbie, he was given that table.

A handsome and well-dressed group, they sat and chatted, sipping drinks, laughing at small jokes. Costello had a little fun at Cindy's expense. As she had ballooned from 108 to 160 pounds during the pregnancy, he speculated whether it would be a multiple birth. Kennedy kept mentioning that he was in trouble at home and that he might as well go and face the music. He never did that night.

Costello was a moderate drinker and, as was his custom, had two scotches before dinner. It was obvious that he was in an expansive mood, and everyone listened as he dipped into his seemingly inexhaustible fund of stories, always so rich in detail. Cindy, who had to visit the bathroom frequently because of her pregnancy, remembers patiently waiting until he would come to the end of one before excusing herself. She knew that Costello was a sensitive man and didn't want to risk offending him by leaving the table before he reached the punch line.

Bobbie, who had a weight problem, looked especially attractive that night in a light blue dress. She had a mink jacket around her shoulders.

After about forty-five minutes or so, they ordered dinner. Waiters hovered over them, cleaning ash trays, refilling drinks, constantly checking the table to make certain that everything was in order. The service, as it usually was when you were with Costello, was superb.

Costello made one telephone call from L'Aiglon. It was to Jake Kossman, a tall, heavyset Philadelphia lawyer who drove Costello to distraction because his clothes were always rumpled and because when he ate he had a great deal of difficulty in finding his mouth.

"He's a good lawyer, but if ya' go into court with him, one look and ya' lose the case," he explained to friends.

Kossman was working with Edward Bennett Williams in trying to keep the Government from sending Costello back to jail.

When dinner was served, the waiters carried the plates on towels and solemnly warned: "Hot! Don't Touch!"

Costello, whose insistance on being served burning hot plates was well known in L'Aiglon, touched his plate lightly with his hand. It was hot enough to satisfy him.

The dinner was disturbed by a number of phone calls. Kennedy called his wife, apparently trying to make peace. Mauro called the restaurant twice and each time asked to speak to Miller whom he knew quite well. He apologized for not being able to join the party and said he would try and get there in time for dessert.

In 1954, after a long trial in which he was charged with income-tax evasion, Costello was convicted and sentenced to serve five years in a federal penitentiary. He had served eleven months of that sentence and was released in March, 1957, following some nifty legal footwork by his attorneys. However, he was only out until the higher courts decided the legal questions raised by his lawyers. If the higher courts didn't reverse the conviction, he would have to go back to serve the remainder of the time he owed.

Costello was calling Kossman because a court decision was expected that day on a case that was similar to his. The way Costello's lawyers explained it, his hopes for a reversal rested with what the court did with that case.

"You don't stand a chance," Kossman told Costello over the phone. "The court found for the Government."

Costello thanked him and went back to join the group. No one realized he had just received a crushing legal blow that would almost certainly mean he would have to go back to prison. His facial expression betrayed nothing.

During coffee, Bobbie suggested that since it had been such a pleasant evening, they should all go to the Copa to catch the show. Costello immediately vetoed the idea. The Copa would mean a late night, and he didn't like to stay out late. It was already ten o'clock, and he was usually home by then.

Bobbie's face showed her disappointment, and Costello suggested that they all go to Monsignore. It was on the same street as L'Aiglon, and they had strolling musicians for entertainment. Everyone agreed.

❊   ❊   ❊

By ten P.M., two black limousines — one facing north and the other south — had already been waiting near the Majestic apartments for thirty minutes. The one facing south was parked near a public phone booth and contained just the driver. The one facing north was parked directly across the street from the Majestic — alongside Central Park — and contained two men, the driver and a passenger.

❊   ❊   ❊

Just before they left, Miller received a third phone call from Vinnie Mauro. Again, he was full of apologies for not being able to make it, but this time he wanted to know if Frank was going home. Miller answered that they were all going to Monsignore. Mauro said that was great and that he'd try to catch Frank there. Then he made, in view of what was discovered by the police about that evening, a strange request. He told Miller he was at El Borracho, a night club, and that if Frank left Monsignore before he got there, he'd appreciate it if Miller gave him a call. He didn't want to dash over only to be disappointed at finding Frank gone. Miller promised he would do just that.

The gaiety of the evening continued at Monsignore. Costello asked the strolling musicians to play an Italian folk song having to do with a couple having their first child. He patted Cindy's stomach again for luck and proposed a toast that the coming child be a boy. Other Italian songs were requested.

They were joined at Monsignore by Frankie (Mario) Bonfiglio, an old friend of Costello's. The club was a hangout for Mario, as everyone called him, and he came over to pay his respects. Mario, who had a substantial police record, was in the laundry business and supplied the linen to every mob-connected and many legitimately-owned restaurants and clubs from Harlem to Greenwich Village.

    ❖   ❖   ❖

For those at Monsignore, the minutes slipped by quickly. Time dragged, however, for the men sitting in the limousines double parked near the Majestic. They kept looking at their watches and checking the entrance.

    ❖   ❖   ❖

At approximately ten forty-five, Costello checked his watch and rose to leave. He was receiving a very important phone call at his home from Edward Bennett Williams, he explained, but as everyone was having such a good time, he didn't want the party to break up. He said he would grab a cab and that everyone should stay.

Phil Kennedy said he would go with Uncle Frank and drop him off. He lived only a few blocks away from the Majestic, and they could go together. He had to go home sometime, he remarked.

As they left, Miller remembered that he had promised to call Mauro. He dialed the number of El Borracho and contacted him immediately. He explained that Frank had to go home and had just left.

    ❖   ❖   ❖

The phone rang in the public telephone booth near where one of the limousines waited. The driver answered the call then climbed back into the car and blinked his lights on and off. Both cars then made U-turns and changed positions.

    ❖   ❖   ❖

Costello and Kennedy hopped a cab in front of Monsignore. The driver sped west to Sixth Avenue and then turned right to head north. At Fifty-ninth Street he turned left, again heading west, until he picked up the beginning of Central Park West. Another right turn and it was just a straight run north to the Majestic. When he reached West Seventy-second Street, the cabbie made a U-turn and stopped in front of the building.

※   ※   ※

It was 10:55, and even before the cab had stopped, the limo containing the two men pulled up behind. A tall, fat man, young and vigorous, jumped out and rushed into the building. He preceeded Costello by a few seconds. The doorman tried to stop him, but the fat man just brushed him aside. Costello, in a hurry, paid no attention.

※   ※   ※

Rushing for the elevator, Costello passed the waiting fat man. He stopped short and whirled around as he heard a voice say: "This is for you, Frank!"

In that very instant, just six to ten feet away, he saw the fat man's right arm extended and a gun pointing directly at his face. There was a loud bang as the pistol's firing pin slammed down on the cartridge.

Hard times

At a time in life when a man his age could reasonably expect to be looking forward to grandchildren, Don Luigi Castiglia's wife gave birth to their sixth child — a boy. The mildly unusual event took place on January 26, 1891 in Lauropoli, an obscure hill town near the ancient city of Cosenza, in continental Italy's southern-most province of Calabria.

"Buon augurio del bambino," the villagers of Lauropoli shouted as the entire Castiglia family walked to church in their Sunday best for the infant's baptism.

Don Luigi accepted the shouts of "good luck" with a slight bow of his head and pursed lips. Under the circumstances the birth of another child (even a man child) at this stage of his life could be considered something other than good fortune. He was forty-five, a desperately poor farmer. Maria, his wife, was thirty-eight. Poverty forced her to hire out as a midwife whenever anyone called on her. They had four daughters — two of them old enough to marry. Then there was Eduardo, already being called upon to work with his father in the fields even though he was only five.

The Castiglia family wasn't merely poor. That, after all, was true of virtually everyone in Southern Italy then. It was a condition of the times. Even among the people of Lauropoli, though, the Castiglias were considered poor. Often the growing family didn't have enough food.

Maria, a deeply religious woman, offered the thought that this infant that had come so late was a gift from God. Perhaps, but Don Luigi knew that the task of providing for such gifts fell upon him.

"What is the child to be called?" the priest at the church asked.

"Francesco," was the answer.

❊　　　❊　　　❊

Thirty-five years after he had left, in 1927, Frank Costello once again laid eyes on the church he was baptized in. He had narrowly missed a jail sentence when a federal jury in Brooklyn failed to agree on whether he was guilty or innocent of breaking the prohibition laws. He decided it was a good time to take a little vacation and returned to Lauropoli. One of his sisters still lived there, and she insisted that he go with her to church on Sunday. He reluctantly agreed.

While walking to church she explained that the entire village knew that he had made good in America. There are still many poor people in Lauropoli, she said, and it is expected that you will help them.

Following services every man, woman, and child formed a line on the church steps to greet Don Francesco Castiglia. One by one Frank's sister introduced them, and for each one she had a tale of woe.

"His wife needs an operation."

"Five thousand lire. Next."

"He wishes to send his son to school to learn a trade."

"Three thousand lire. Next."

"A landslide destroyed his crops."

"Two thousand lire. Next."

"Her husband died suddenly and left her with two small children."

"Eight thousand lire. Next."

And so it went until the line was exhausted.

❊　　　❊　　　❊

Hard times was a condition endemic to all of Calabria. Each year bore witness to fresh disasters: landslides, crop failures, disease. Still the short, swarthy men of Calabria continued to cling to the land, cling with a tenaciousness that earned these strange, backward people the reputation of being hard-headed. In Italy the people of Calabria are noted for this quality just as the people of Bologna are noted for the excellence of their cuisine.

Calabria was a lean land of ignorance and superstition in which the church was supreme and the lowly goat the main source of meat.

❊　　　❊　　　❊

Frank Costello never lost his taste for good meat. In the early twenties a bootlegger associate was arrested, and he received word that federal agents were out to do the same to him. He decided to hide out at his brother's home in Astoria, Queens. At the time Astoria still contained many little farms in which the Italian inhabitants created an old-country atmosphere. Some even kept a few goats as pets.

One day Costello and a few visiting cronies spotted the pet goat of his brother's neighbor. "Let's have a barbecue," Costello suggested. In no time at all the goat was slaughtered, cleaned, and dressed. Then a barnfire was built, and it was slowly roasted. It was the first goat he had since he was a little boy. When the neighbor found out what had happened to the goat he loved, he threatened to punch Costello in the mouth.

✻   ✻   ✻

Yet it was a wildly beautiful land of high mountains, green hills, plateaus, and valleys. The old, crumbling, picturesque towns seemed to adhere to the mountainsides and hilltops like huge grapes on a vine. Wherever land was fertile, grain was grown, and where it was arid, the silver leaves of the eternal olive trees glistened in the sun. Grapevines grew everywhere.

If you look at the map, Calabria is the toe of the Italian boot. Sicily lies directly across the Strait of Messina, just seven miles away. With the Sicilians, the Calabrese shared not only abject poverty but also an ancient infusion of Greek blood.

Calabria, as well as Sicily, had been a stepping stone over the centuries for invaders seeking to plunder Italy's heartland. The Byzantine Greeks, Visigoths, Saracens, and French had all passed through, weaving a history of cruelty, murder, and rape to be repeated in Calabrese folktales of resistance and vengeance.

This was the world that Francesco Castiglia was born into on January of 1891. It was a world that he left at the age of four. Its code of honor and its legacy of hardship, ignorance, and squalor, however, would stay with him for the rest of his life.

Don Luigi Castiglia left Lauropoli for America about 1893. He could only afford to take part of his family with him, leaving behind his wife, two of his daughters, and little Francesco. The cost of deck passage on one of the filthy steamers that hauled the immigrants was only eight dollars, yet the Castiglia family couldn't raise enough money to travel together. Don Luigi confidently expected to be able to earn money quickly in America and send for the rest of his family.

Maria had to wait two years until her husband could save enough to buy the steamship tickets. He was finding things in New York, where he was staying with relatives to save money, to be as difficult as in Lauropoli. He was a quiet, self-effacing, ineffectual man who had a good deal of difficulty adjusting to the new environment. He had merely exchanged rural squalor and hopeless poverty for the urban variety.

Maria worked like a dog to keep her portion of the family alive. There was seldom enough food to eat. One time, though, a grain merchant befriended her by advancing two sacks of flour on the promise of future payment. Often when it seemed all hope was lost, a bit of money arrived from Luigi. Sometimes she prayed to the Virgin Mary that all the married women in the village would become pregnant so there would be work for her as a midwife.

❖   ❖   ❖

One day during his return visit to Lauropoli, Don Francesco was approached by a timid, little man who handed him a piece of paper. The paper, the man explained, was an IOU signed by his mother. He had advanced her two sacks of flour, and she had left for America without paying him.

Don Francesco looked at the paper and recognized his mother's mark. He paid the debt plus interest that more than made up for the years the man had waited.

"I never wanted a piece of paper so bad in my life," he explained to a friend years later. "The old bat nagged me to death all my life. It was always: 'Frank, why don't you get out of the rackets?' or 'Frank, why don't you go straight?' She always swore she never did anything wrong in her life. I wanted that piece of paper to show her how she had beat this poor old guy out of two sacks of flour."

❖   ❖   ❖

Maria was a clever, tenacious woman who was easily more capable than her husband. It was through her strength and determination that the family was able to survive those years. The children instinctively recognized this inner strength she possessed and turned to her for sustenance. Don Luigi was ignored.

In 1895, two steamship tickets finally arrived. After two years of working, this represented all the money her husband was able to save. It meant that one of the girls would have to be left behind. (Little Francesco presented no problem because he was young enough to travel free.) Relatives were found who promised to take care of her until a ticket could be sent.

❖   ❖   ❖

Costello liked to reminisce about his humble beginnings and would tell close friends about his first Atlantic crossing. "It was just the three of us: my mother, my sister, and me. All we took with us from the old country was this huge iron pot my mother liked to cook in. They just fixed up the pot like a bed by lining it with a blanket, and that's where I slept for the entire crossing."

New world

The virtually intact Castiglia family began life in the New World by moving into a three-story tenement at 236 East 108th Street, a solidly Italian ghetto in the East Harlem area of Manhattan. They lived in four rooms in what was commonly called a railroad flat — each room behind the other in a straight line — and shared the bathroom in the hall with the other family living on the same floor.

The sights and smells of Italy were all around them as the people of the neighborhood tried to recreate the familiar atmosphere of their beloved homeland. Many of the residents were Calabrese — part of the great migration of Italians to these shores between 1880 and 1900. One could walk the streets of East Harlem in any direction and, except for the Irish cop on the beat, hear only Italian spoken.

The streets throbbed with life. A wandering blind man would know when he entered an Italian neighborhood. Sweating, tireless men dragging pushcarts could be found on every block selling fresh tomatoes. Everyone agreed the ones grown in *bella Italia* were better, had more taste. In nice weather, old men sat in the sun and spun tales of their youth or rolled bocce balls in the gutter. Small groups of short, fat women dressed in ankle-length black dresses gossiped in front of every building. Gangs of vigorous, dark-haired youths roamed the streets, restless and menacing. Shouts of joy or disappointment came from the seemingly endless crap game being held in the middle of the block. You had to bounce the dice off the curb or the roll didn't count. The hangout was a pool hall on East 108th Street between Third and Second Avenues. On the corner stood a spaghetti factory where the women could buy fresh-made pasta. On the opposite corner an Italian bakery did a brisk business.

The men did the dirty work of the city. They could be seen in all neighborhoods hauling garbage or digging up the streets with a pick-axe or shovel. Others traveled north to the Bronx or east to Queens to lay bricks for the tenements springing up everywhere. Many labored twelve hours a day in factories. Wherever there was a mean, hard, low-paying job, you could find a Southern Italian or Sicilian.

Don Luigi Castiglia went into business. He opened a hole-in-the-wall grocery, just a few doors away from his home, on East 108th. However, because of conditions or his incompetence, he couldn't make a go of it. Maria and the children helped him wait on customers, stack the produce, and wrestle with the milk cans. His store opened early in the morning and closed late at night. Yet all he could do was eke out a bare living.

There was never enough to eat for the animal-like hunger of the growing boys. At dinner time, Francesco would check his plate against those of the rest of the family to make certain he was getting his fair share. Eduardo taught him how to supplement his diet by stealing from pushcarts.

✻   ✻   ✻

"When you dined with Frank with any regularity," recalls columnist John J. Miller, "one of the things you learned was to never touch the food in his plate. I mean, you know how good friends will nibble at each other's food. That was a cardinal sin with Frank. If someone did it he would just push his plate to the side. You could see by his face that he was just furious. Then he'd call the maitre d' over and order two more portions — one for whoever touched his plate and one for himself. It wasn't a germ phobia. He just hated anyone eating his food. I think it had something to do with being so poor when a kid — he was subconsciously still protecting everything he had on his plate."

✻   ✻   ✻

Because he was slow in learning English, Francesco didn't start school until he was nearly nine. In October of 1909, according to an Immigration and Naturalization Service report, Frank Castiglia was placed into the first grade of Public School 83, located on East 109th Street. This is the first known instance of his first name being anglicized. A year later, for some unknown reason, he was transferred to another school in the neighborhood.

✣ ✣ ✣

In later years, Costello told friends that he had hated school. He liked to run the streets where he had a chance to earn money. When he was seven or eight he wandered into a Jewish neighborhood in West Harlem. It must have been a Saturday because a man with a beard offered him a penny to light his stove. He later discovered that orthodox Jews believed it a sin to light a fire on Saturday. He began hanging around the Jewish neighborhood and soon had a good business going as the local Shabbas goy. When he got a little older, he upped the price on Jewish holidays to a nickel. It was, he said, his first organized scheme to earn money.

✣ ✣ ✣

The hot-house, ghetto environment did more than change Francesco's first name. It weakened the structure of his ties to his family. How could Don Luigi demand obedience and respect when his sons were able to earn more in a day running a crap game then he could sweating in the grocery?

"Go to school, my son."

"I go to school, Father. I go to school everyday."

"Francesco, I don't like the friends you have. They are no good and will amount to nothing."

"I will amount to something, Mama. Something better than spending my life in a grocery store."

"Don't talk that way. You must have respect for your father. Understand me now. Respect."

"Yes, Mama."

✣ ✣ ✣

When he himself was about sixty, Frank Costello visited a psychiatrist. He told him how he had hated his father, despised him. Despised him for his humility and inadequacy. Loathed the way he was willing to settle for a life that amounted to nothing, just poverty and drudgery.

✣ ✣ ✣

Frank Castiglia quit school when he was in the fifth grade. He was thirteen. By now he openly defied his parents and was indistinguishable from the groups of young hoodlums that roamed the streets of East Harlem. He completed his education in one of the best finishing schools for racketeers this country has ever seen — a New York ghetto during the first twenty years of the twentieth century.

In *Gang Rule in New York* by Craig Thompson and Allan Raymond, the geographical and racial divisions of these turn-of-the-century gangs are succinctly described:

"The pre-prohibition gangs of New York as classified by their natural or racial antecedents were principally made up of Irish, Italians and Jews. They hung together partly by national and partly by neighborhood ties. The Irish pretty well controlled the West Side and most of the West Side gang leaders were Irish. The East Side belonged to the Italians and Jews..."

East Harlem was ruled by Ignazio Lupo, also known as "Lupo the Wolf." He was head of the Mafia, a secret society of native-born Sicilians which had its roots in the tortured history of that island. It was founded to protect the people of Sicily from the pillage and rape of its many conquerors over the centuries and evolved into a government within a government. The leaders of the Mafia were known as "Men of Respect."

As an imported product, the Mafia in the United States was called by non-Italian outsiders the "Unione Siciliana." That name stuck until the middle thirties when "Mafia" came into popular use. In the early sixties, Joe Valachi came up with still another name for the organization — the "Cosa Nostra."

When Lupo the Wolf was running things in New York, the patriotic motivation for the Mafia had long disappeared. Its members preyed mostly on Italians and specialized in extortion and terror. Businessmen were assessed a tax. If they refused to pay, they were beaten up or their business set fire to. If they still refused — or committed the cardinal sin by complaining to the police — they were killed. In return for payment, the Mafia guaranteed protection and an order to things. The Mafia bosses adjudicated disputes. Wrongs were set right.

Each shakedown note bore the imprint of the society's symbol — the Black Hand. Those who received one became terror stricken. An elderly Italo-American with a long memory recalled for writer Frederic Sondern Jr. the effect a note bearing the imprint of the Black Hand had on his Sicilian-born father:

"Then my father would pay. He would say, 'Guiseppe, you see, it is the same here as at home. The Mafia is always with us.' Then I would plead with him to go to the police. After all, we were in America. 'No, Mother of God, no!' he would shout. 'The police here cannot do even as much as the police at home. They do not know the Mafia. We get put out of business or killed and no one will ever know why. They do not understand the Mafia and never will.'

On East 107th Street, just around the corner from where the Castiglia family lived, one of Lupo the Wolf's chief lieutenants had his headquarters. He was Ciro Terranova who became known as the "Artichoke King" when he cornered the market in the twenties. The headquarters had an infamous reputation and was dubbed the "Murder Stables" by police. In 1920 the building was torn down and the bones of twenty-three different men were found in its walls and under its floors.

Southern Italians had their own secret society called the "Camorra." It operated much the same as the Sicilian Mafia and even adopted the symbol of the Black Hand. A man by the name of Enrico Alfano, alias Erricone, ruled the Camorra in the early 1900s.

In the streets of East Harlem, Frank Castiglia absorbed the lessons of his environment, its morality, its ideals. All important was the code of *omerta* or *silence*. Whoever did not adhere faithfully to this code was less than a man. Contemptible. To be spat upon. To be ostracized and killed. No matter how you were threatened, no matter how you were cheated, robbed, maimed, you were less than a man if you went to the police. You took your own revenge. No matter how long it took, you kept your silence and waited for the right moment.

❀   ❀   ❀

After the gunman hired by Vito Genovese had bungled the job, Frank Costello was taken before a New York County grand jury. He was asked the meaning of the slip of paper found by detectives in his jacket pocket. Assistant district attorney Al Scotti didn't even bother to ask Costello if he had seen or could identify who had shot him. He knew better than to waste his breath. The paper, however, was another matter. Costello had it in his pocket and couldn't deny knowledge of it.

Costello refused to talk. He took the protection of the Fifth Amendment on self incrimination. Scotti offered immunity and warned he would go to jail unless he talked. Costello still refused. He was then given time to confer with his attorney, the famous criminal lawyer Edward Bennett Williams.

They talked quietly in an anteroom, close to where the grand jury sat. Williams, who had used all of his legal skills to keep Costello out of jail on a number of other charges, understood that if Costello talked he would have to implicate others, nevertheless, he pleaded with his client to tell what he knew. He told him that they had come to the end of the line. He was absolutely frantic because he liked Costello, considered him a warm, compassionate human being who never went back on his word, and he didn't want him to go to jail.

"For God's sake, Frank," he said, "you've got to answer their questions now. Don't you realize that if you don't you're going to jail, and there's nothing in the world I can do about it?"

Costello spread out his hands, palms up in a gesture of frustration and helplessness. He had a world of respect and affection for Williams and knew that he was upsetting him by his obstinacy. Finally, he looked at the ceiling of the grand jury anteroom and spotted a fly walking.

"I can no more answer those questions than I can walk on the ceiling," he answered in an anguished voice, meaning that to break his code and inform on others was something he was literally physically incapable of doing.

✿   ✿   ✿

"Perche non vai lavorare?" (Why don't you go to work?) Don Luigi asked his youngest son in exasperation after he quit school and began hanging around the streets all day.

Frank decided he had better follow his father's advice. He found a job in a piano factory as a helper. Within a year he left because he found the job hard and dirty and the pay beneath contempt. His father's anger was easier to take than twelve hours a day of muscle-aching work.

He went back to hustling on the streets. He began to steal, to break into stores, and to bust open vending machines to loot them of the handful of pennies they contained. One day a cop caught him red handed as he was rifling a busted machine. The cop was about to run him in when one of the local politicians came by and recognized Frank as a neighborhood boy. The politician and the cop were Irish, and a wink and a joke passed between them.

"I'll take care of the little dago," the politician said. The cop shrugged his shoulders and walked off.

Before being turned loose, Frank was given a short lecture on the facts of life. "I've just done you a favor," he was told. "Now remember that when I need a favor."

The incident impressed young Frank Castiglia. It gave him an insight into how things worked in the world. Doing someone a favor was like making a deposit in the bank. You could draw against that deposit when you needed it. Obviously the bigger your bank account, the better off you were.

It was around this period of his life that he began calling himself Frank Costello. The reason probably has to do with the fact that he was taking chances and figured out that if he was arrested and gave a different name, there was less chance of his parents finding out. What's interesting is that he gave himself an Irish name. One can only speculate as to how his youthful mind arrived at the name of Costello. Psychiatrists recognize that the choice of a name reflects a person's inner longings and ambitions. If a Jew named Ginsburg, for instance, changes his name to Gordon, it is obvious that he is anxious to be accepted and become successful in the "WASP" world. It follows, then, that an Italian who adopts an Irish name is motivated in the same way. He could have, after all, adopted a phony Italian name, and it would have served as just as useful a shield.

One of Frank's good friends in those years was a small, thin, neighborhood youth who seemed to always be around. Sometimes he would act as a lookout during a stickup or keep a storekeeper busy while his merchandise was being looted. He was three years younger than Frank and only about five-foot-four. He had all the guts in the world, though, and wouldn't hesitate to take on someone twice his size.

Frank liked Willie Moretti, liked his good-humored, wise-cracking personality. It was a relationship that lasted throughout their lives. As Frank rose in the world, so did Willie until he was recognized as Frank's top lieutenant in New Jersey, the man who ruled the Mafia in the Garden State.

Sometime between his fifteenth and sixteenth year, Frank began to be noticed by the local racketeers. He had attained his full height and had developed into a tough, brawling street fighter who could methodically chop down an opponent while outwardly maintaining his calm. More important, he seemed to have a head on his shoulders and was reliable. When he was sent on an errand he did exactly as he was told.

One of the mobsters began to use him to collect rent in a few of the tenements he owned in the area. Frank collected the rents faithfully, turned in every cent, and was thrown a few dollars for his trouble.

One of the tenants was a middle-aged blond of about forty or so. She had obviously once been pretty but now was beginning to show her age and had put on weight, the type Costello called in later life a "broken valise." Her rent was seventeen dollars a month, and when she didn't have the rent one time he decided to carry her and told the mobster-landlord that he had knocked on her door several times and no one was home. She must be away, he said, and promised to collect for both months next time.

When he showed up the following month, the blond answered the door wearing a slip. She invited him in, and as he sat down on a couch he realized two things: she didn't have a damn thing on underneath the slip, and he was going to be given the opportunity to lose his virginity.

As he sat there thinking things out, he decided the blond wasn't worth it. She offered him coffee and, when he refused, offered wine. He said sure, why not. As he drank the wine, she began to look better and better to him. Her lumpy body began to appear taut and desirable, the wrinkles in her face disappeared, and her blond, frizzly hair seemed to become long and silky. He tumbled her on the couch and left.

When the time came to turn the money in, he told the mobster that the blond had given him thirty-four dollars in an envelope. Somehow or other he had lost that envelope. Without a moment's hesitation the mobster beat him unmercifully on the street, knocked him to the ground, and stomped him in full view of his friends. It was the worst beating he ever received in his life.

❊   ❊   ❊

Frank never forgot the lesson he learned that day. He delighted in telling friends, in detail, of losing his virginity and then getting the shit kicked out of him. His friends knew the story so well that the expression "her hair is getting longer and silkier" became a code when he was tempted to go into a business deal with someone who his common sense told him was a loser. He'd look at the guy offering the deal and say in a loud voice: "His hair is getting longer and silkier," and everyone would get the message.

❊   ❊   ❊

Frank Costello's first arrest occurred on April 25, 1908 in the Bronx. According to the charge, he and two other youths followed Giuseppe Dionisia, twenty-one, a coal dealer, into the cellar of his business address on Washington Avenue. They demanded money, and when Dionisia refused, all three began to beat him. He fought back tenaciously, but all resistance ceased when Costello struck him on the head with a hammer. A total of $17.50 was taken from Dionisia's pockets. The trio were charged with assault and robbery.

Costello was arrested by a cop named Wesser and taken before General Sessions Judge Kernochan where he pleaded "not guilty." On May 8, the charges against him were dismissed.

Despite the fact that the charges against him were dismissed, the New York City Police Department kept on file the mug shot taken at the time of his arrest. Looking at the photograph of the young Costello, one sees a hard-eyed youth with close-cropped hair and a fuller face than he had in later life. Except for the large nose and general expression, it really doesn't look very much like the man whose face became known nationally as a real-life "Godfather."

His second arrest occurred on October 16, 1912. This time the complainant charged that the crime took place in his own neighborhood, on the corner of Third Avenue and East 108th Street. He and two others were accused of assaulting and robbing Mrs. Philomena Sorgi, a housewife described as being over twenty-one. The attack took place at eight thirty A.M. when, according to her testimony, Costello and two others pinned her from behind and relieved her of $1,635 in cash and $220 worth of jewelry. All three were charged with assault and robbery.

At this arraignment he again pleaded "not guilty" and gave his name as *Castello,* apparently in an effort to conceal from the court that he had been arrested before. The charges were dismissed. How he was able to walk away this second time is unknown. Perhaps his parents went to the complainant who lived in the neighborhood and pleaded with her not to press charges. Whatever the case, the youngest son of Don Luigi Castiglia and Maria Aloise Saverio was rapidly earning a reputation for being a holdup man. Unless he mended his ways, he would eventually see the inside of a jail. There was no question of that. His methods were too crude and amateurish for him to get away with the stuff he was pulling for very long.

He was no longer a kid even by the standards of America where adolescence lasts a lot longer than in Italy. At the time of his second arrest, he was closing in on his twenty-second birthday. It was obvious that the two robbery charges he walked away from were merely the tip of the iceberg. Even the most stupid, inefficient criminal pulls many more jobs than he is called to account for.

In Costello's salad years he didn't like to be reminded that he had once been a cheap, two-bit hoodlum. He'd explain it all away by talking about the ghetto environment and saying: "Tough times make monkeys eat red pepper."

At both arrests he gave his occupation as a "pipefitter," yet there is no record that he ever worked at that trade. He was an accomplished liar and was cunning, vicious, and streetwise.

Between the two arrests he and his brother Eduardo, who by now called himself Edward Costello, hooked up together. They traveled downtown to Greenwich Village where Frank became friendly with Owney (Killer) Madden, a short, thin, young man who had the reputation of being absolutely fearless and a little crazy. Madden, who came here as a child from England, was a feared killer by the time he was sixteen. He was head of a notorious West Side gang called the Gophers. In the twenties, Madden would win the reputation of being the mob's top torpedo and become a celebrity gangster in his own right.

Frank and Eddie also began hanging around the West Side docks where for a time they succeeded in muscling themselves in as steve-

dores, for stevedore hiring. The way it worked, you had to pay the
Costellos to get a job.

In 1914, Frank became friendly with Dudley Geigerman. Through
him he met the rest of the family which included three more brothers
and a sister named Loretta whom everyone called Bobbie. She was a
pretty brunette with a quick wit, high spirits, and a little girl's voice
that stayed with her through the years.

Frank was attracted to Bobbie immediately. He began frequent-
ing the Geigerman apartment on Seventh Avenue in West Harlem.
What the parents, Jacob and Cecelia Geigerman, thought of his interest in their daughter is unknown. The Geigermans were Jewish, and it
is probable they looked upon the growing romance with mixed emo-
tions. Not that Don Luigi and Maria — if they knew what was going
on — would likely have been joyous at the prospect of having a
Geigerman for a daughter-in-law.

They were married on September 23, 1914. Just how old Bobbie
was at the time of their marriage is in dispute. She gave her age on
the marriage license as nineteen, but an Immigration and Naturalization Service investigative report says she was only fifteen. Frank
obviously didn't worry too much about the accuracy of the information
he filled out on the license. He gave his occupation as a "plumber"
and listed his birthplace as "New York City."

The ceremony took place in the home of friends, Saverio and Pauline
Cassoto, who had an apartment on West End Avenue. To join them in
holy wedlock they chose an Episcopalian Minister, the Reverend Thomas
McCandless of St. Michael's on West Ninety-ninth Street, probably
because it was neutral ground — a priest or rabbi might tend to ask
too many questions.

Marriage didn't reform Costello. He continued to frequent his old
haunts and mix with the same hoodlum company. If anything, marriage
put money pressure on him that he didn't have before. The couple
moved into an apartment in West Harlem. Bobbie stayed home in her
role as housewife while Frank hustled on the streets. He also began
carrying a gun.

On March 12, 1915, he was arrested in Manhattan on the charge
of carrying a concealed weapon. At the booking he gave his name
as Frank Saverio, borrowing from his mother's maiden name. The
records of the time show that he wrote the letter C then stopped and
crossed the letter out and wrote Saverio. Later he assured investigators that his real name was Stello.

He pleaded "not guilty" at the arraignment, but this time the charges
against him weren't dismissed. He was held in high bail, which he

couldn't raise, and spent a month in the Tombs waiting to go on trial. While he waited, his lawyer, a man named Goldstein, did a little plea bargaining with the district attorney's office. The DA agreed to reduce the charge against Costello to a misdemeanor if he agreed to plead guilty. The lawyer explained that if he was convicted on the weapons charge as a felony, he could receive up to seven years. This way the most he could receive was a year. Furthermore, the chances were he would get off with a suspended sentence or maybe probation, since there was no record of prior convictions. Costello didn't like the idea of pleading guilty, but he decided to take a chance. Sitting in the Tombs was beginning to get to him.

On May 15, he stood before General Sessions Judge Edward Swann for sentencing. Before imposing sentence, the Judge read Costello's probation report, based on information supplied by the defendant. It read:

"This defendant is 22 years of age, born in New York, has been married for six months, and at the time of his arrest, was living with his wife and parents at 222 East 108th Street, in four rooms. Defendant's wife states she is in a delicate condition."

✻   ✻   ✻

(Except for the amount of time he had been married, everything in the first paragraph of the report is false. Costello had passed his twenty-fourth birthday, he was born in Italy, he did not live with his parents, and Bobbie was definitely not pregnant.)

✻   ✻   ✻

"Defendant states that he has worked for his father who has been in the grocery business at 232 East 108th Street, for a number of years. Mr. Castello states defendant always worked for him as a clerk. This business has been sold, and they run a small business now at 222 East 108th Street. Neighbors verified defendants statement regarding his working for his father."

✻   ✻   ✻

(Costello hadn't worked in his father's grocery store in years, and he had even lied to the probation officer about his real name, insisting it was Castello.)

✻   ✻   ✻

"Defendant states that when he left his father's employ, he went to work for the Interboro Rapid Transit (IRT subway) as a pipefitter's helper at 148th Street and Seventh Avenue. I called at the office of this company at 98th Street and Third Avenue and interviewed Mr. Beancheau who states they have no record of defendant under the name of Castello or Saverio.

"Defendant states that when he left the IRT Company, he went on a visit to his brother Edward in Wisconsin and remained there some time. When he came home, he became engaged, and was married six months ago. He started in a liquor business at 239 East 109th Street and was in this business four months, when arrested for having a revolver."

D. P. Conway

Probation officer

❉   ❉   ❉

(The reason that there was no record of Costello at the IRT was because he never worked there. He insisted he was gainfully employed because he knew the courts took a dim view of someone accused of a crime who has no record of steady, gainful employment. It is doubtful that he ever visited Eddie in Wisconsin or had ever been in Wisconsin at that time. So far as the liquor business goes, it was probable that Costello had an interest in an East Harlem ginmill.)

❉   ❉   ❉

The clerk of the court, addressing Costello as Saverio, asked him if he had anything to say before the court passed judgment on him. Before he had a chance to reply, Judge Swann cut in:

Judge Swann — "Now Saverio, what is your real name?"

Costello — "Stello."

Judge Swann — "You didn't know that, did you Mr. Berra?"

Mr. Berra — "No your honor. He says his father's name is Stello, his name is Stello, and his mother's name is Saverio."

❉   ❉   ❉

(Berra was an Italian interpreter brought into the court at the request of Costello. Why he should ask for an interpreter, since he spoke English perfectly well, staggers the imagination. He obviously was trying to pose as a poor, dumb immigrant who didn't know the laws of this country. It was a charade that didn't quite go off as planned.)

❉   ❉   ❉

Goldstein (Costello's lawyer) — "He has been known by that name for a number of years. He has been recently married, and he has a mother of sixty-five years of age, and his father is seventy-two, and

they have no other means of support except this defendant. Furthermore, he was in business in a neighborhood, which, I understand,
quite some few bad characters are around there, and he had this revolver for the purposes of protection in his place of business. These
are the facts which have been told to me."

           ✻   ✻   ✻

*(Note that the lawyer has added on three years to the ages of both
Don Luigi and Maria.)*

           ✻   ✻   ✻

Judge Swann — "I find that in 1908, that is, seven years ago, he
was arrested for assault and robbery, and in that case he was discharged. I find that in 1912 he was again arrested for assault and
robbery, and he was discharged in that case. In those cases he gave
the name of Frank Castello. (Even Judge Swann was becoming con-
fused.) In this case he gives his name as Frank Saverio, and I have
looked him up, and I find that, while there are a good many letters
in regard to him, nevertheless, I find his reputation is not good. On
the contrary, it is bad."

Goldstein — "He informs me that one of these cases was where a
pocketbook was stolen while he was in the presence of his family,
and both were on cases of suspicion. I feel, your Honor, that the young
man was probably not up to the mark in his younger days, but since
he has been married, he has started in business."

Judge Swann — "What is his business?"

Goldstein — "They started a cafe."

Judge Swann — "What is his business?"

Goldstein — "He is a pipefitter."

Judge Swann — "He has not been a pipefitter for some time, has
he?"

Goldstein — "He was a pipefitter up to two years ago, your Honor."

Judge Swann — "And he tells the probation officer that he has been
in the grocery business for a number of years. That is, his father said
that he, the father, was in the grocery business for a number of years,
and the defendant worked for him as his clerk."

Goldstein — "Yes, sir."

Judge Swann — "What have you to say now why the judgment of
the court should not be pronounced against you, and you be committed to the penitentiary for one year?"

Goldstein — "May I ask your Honor this: of course, my information
is simply what the young man and some of his friends have told me.
I have not since last Saturday had time to properly investigate this

case. His father and mother consulted with me. As I said, this young
man in his younger days has not led the life he should have led, but
now, since he is married and started to make a living, he is willing to
go with his brother, and his brother will give him employment, and
I ask your Honor to be as light with him as you can."

Judge Swann — "I find that appeals were made for him even in
those assault and robbery cases. One case he assaulted and robbed
a woman going to the bank with sixteen hundred dollars. Now I commit him to the penitentiary for one year, and this is about the last
time appeals will do him any good. In other words, appeals have ceased
to do him good up to this time."

Costello — "Will your Honor give me another chance?"

Judge Swann — "You have had chances for the last six years, and
those chances have to cease some time."

Costello — "You could put me on probation for as long as you like."

Judge Swann — "I have not spoken about something which I have
here among the papers and which I need not speak of. I have got it
right from his neighbors that he has the reputation of being a gunman, and in this particular case, he certainly was a gunman, and he
had a very beautiful weapon, and he was thoroughly armed, prepared
to do the work of a gunman, and he was charged on two other occasions with doing the work of a gunman and, somehow or other, got
out of it."

Costello — "Your Honor, I took the plea just because I was in prison for one month and wanted to avoid trouble, being I was a married
man. But the revolver wasn't found on me. It was found one hundred
feet away from me."

Judge Swann — "That is right, and they saw you throw it there.
The officers followed you and saw you throw the gun away, and they
first captured you and then took you back and got the gun. In other
words, your actions were those of a guilty man in every particular.

"I sentence you to the penitentiary for one year. The law says
seven years in state prison."

Costello served his time, eleven months because of one month off
for good behavior, in the City Penitentiary on Welfare Island. He
came out with the resolve never to do another day of time.

Opportunity
knocks

The national binge began as a dull party at midnight on January 16, 1920, when the Eighteenth Amendment, known as the Volstead Act, went into effect. Across America, sentimental drinkers hoisted their the nation's largest city alone. Converted brownstones, cellars, hideevent had all the drama of an obituary notice set in agate type.

It was the beginning of a wild, wet, incredibly lawless decade. Only no one realized it. What began as a dull party ended in the biggest hangover in the history of the world.

The Eighteenth Amendment had been passed late in 1917 while we were in the midst of the war to "make the world safe for democracy." Drinking interfered with this national commitment. Besides the manufacture of whiskey used up grains needed for the war effort. The solution, obviously, was to put an end to liquor.

By January of 1919, aided by the religious ferver of zealot reformers who visualized an America cured of all its ills once the curse of alcohol no longer blighted the land, the necessary thirty-six states ratified the amendment, and a year later it became law.

The reformers, however, made one mistake. They failed to correctly gauge the difference in the temper of the American people during wartime and peacetime. Sacrifice during wartime was acceptable, but during peacetime it became an outrageous imposition. Yet when the law went into effect, no one could guess that the American people would ignore its provision.

Prohibition became the catalyst for organized crime as we know it today. It was the chemical reaction that changed freelance, unorganized, penny-ante gangs into tight-knit organizations grossing millions and run on modern business principles. Gangsters-turned-bootleggers became national heroes as they opened the spigot that assuaged the thirst of the American public. At stake was undreamed of wealth with enough profit for everyone: rum-runners, bootleggers, gunmen, speakeasy owners, graft-seeking politicians, corrupt judges, and bribe-taking cops.

If the Mafia were a religious organization, their patron saint would be Saint Andrew, in honor of Representative Andrew Volstead of Minnesota.

Prohibition provided the American people with a drama reminiscent of the world's first morality play. Liquor was the apple, a speakeasy was the Garden of Eden, and the smiling bootlegger was Eve who promised unspeakable delights.

New York became the premier stage for the reenactment of these dramatics. An estimated thirty-two thousand speakeasies operated in the nation's largest city alone. Converted brownstones, cellars, hideaways in Greenwich Village and Harlem, legitimate-looking nightclubs, and whatever else the ingenuity of man could devise or disguise served as a speakeasy. There were only fifteen hundred prohibition agents in the entire nation to stem the tide and enforce the law. A fifty dollar bill could induce most of them to become blind.

Men and women from every level of society frequented these speakeasies. Breaking the law became the great leveler. You knocked at the door of a brownstone, and some muscle-bound ex-pug dressed in a tuxedo looked you over through a peephole. "Joe sent me," became a national expression. We had become a nation of guys named Joe.

The seedier and more lethal action of the drama took place off stage as the gangs fought each other for control of the lucrative trade. Gun battles on land and sea erupted daily as Darwin's law of survival of the fittest came into play. Police estimate that more than one thousand gangsters died in the bootleg wars of the twenties in the New York area alone.

Frank Costello, unaware of the future that awaited him, was released from prison in 1916. The year away taught him a lesson he never forgot. He never again carried a gun as long as he lived.

He returned to the East Harlem neighborhood he knew so well and resumed hustling on the streets. He appears to have prospered somewhat because the former Mary Fata, now a woman of sixty-five but than a child of eight or nine, remembers seeing him often on East 108th Street. She recalls that he was well dressed, and that everyone in the neighborhood looked up to him.

What she remembers best is her mother yelling from the window, telling her to come upstairs. "I'd yell back, 'all right, I'll be right up, just wait a while.' Frank Costello would hear me, and he'd come over and give me a little tap on my backside and tell me, 'Get up to our mother. Your mother is calling'. He chased me many times."

Costello's number came up in the draft during World War I, but he never went into service even though his claim of exemption as an alien was turned down. His draft record dated June 5, 1917 reveals he said he was self-employed as a fruit dealer and gave his business address as 222 East 108th Street, the location of his father's grocery store. He gave his home address as 125 West 116th Street.

How he was able to beat the draft is unknown. An Immigration and Naturalization Service investigation of him in the fifties, when the government was seeking to deport him, says: "Costello never did serve in the military forces of the United States, although he was apparently called for induction. The exact circumstances surrounding his near-induction are still shrouded in the enigmatic cloth of the past and this investigation has been unable to pierce that veil of obscurity. It has been ascertained, however, that notwithstanding his attempt to gain exemption by virtue of his alienage, Costello, was actually called for induction by his local draft board. How he avoided induction is still a mystery."

An incident that occurred in May of 1919 shows that besides still being an accomplished liar and schemer, he was also still a petty thief. Costello and two others were arrested and charged with robbing one Peter Moreo of one hundred dollars in a park in Queens. The trio, according to the indictment, were observed by a police officer removing the one hundred dollars from Moreo's pants pockets.

The grand larceny charge against Costello was eventually dismissed. A point of interest in the small-time holdup is that one of the men accused with him was Vincent Rao, who later became a Costello lieutenant and a power in the Mafia in his own right. Rao, who grew up in East Harlem with Costello, was one of the invited guests at the famous gangland Appalachin meeting in upstate New York in 1957.

In August of 1919, Costello and Harry Horowitz formed the Harry Horowitz Novelty Company. The fly-by-night venture was started with a total of three thousand dollars in capital to cash in on the punchboard craze that was sweeping the city. To play the punchboard cost anywhere from a nickel to a quarter, depending upon the size of the prize being offered. The player made a choice from a large, cardboard card which contained several hundred covered holes. Inside each hole was a tiny piece of rolled up paper. If the player punched out a piece of paper with a lucky number or name he was a winner. The prize was a kewpie doll. The Harry Horowitz Novelty Company manufactured the kewpie dolls.

After reporting a gross business the first year of somewhere between eighty thousand and one hundred thousand dollars, the company went bankrupt in July of 1920. The punchboard craze was over, and the partners decided it was more profitable to go bankrupt than pay creditors.

Frank and Eddie Costello appear to have plunged into the bootlegging business in the latter part of 1920 or the early part of 1921. Frank supplied the brains, and Eddie the brawn. Although Frank was every bit as tough as his brother and millions of brain cells smarter, he watched his step because he feared going back to prison. He knew that most beefs — as long as violence wasn't involved — could be squared with the cops or a friendly judge.

Eddie was heavier and more powerfully built than Frank, but he had the same generous Castiglia nose, and when you saw them together the family resemblance was obvious. The resemblance ended there, though. Eddie was a crude, ignorant thug who police say was a hit man for the mob in the late twenties.

The Costellos were't the only ones who saw an opportunity of turning a quick profit in illicit booze. The East Side gangsters leaped into the breach. There was Benjamin (Bugsy) Siegel and Meyer Lansky, the heads of the Bugs and Meyer mob; Salvatore Lucania, later to win fame as Lucky Luciano; Joe (the Boss) Masseria, one of the powers in the Unione Siciliana; Umberto Valenti and Tommy (the Bull) Pennochio, both powers in the Unione also; and Louis (Lepke) Buchalter, Jacob (Gurrah) Shapiro, and Jack (Legs) Diamond. Brooklyn contributed Joseph Doto, better knows as Joe Adonis, and Albert Anastasia. Up in the Bronx you had Arthur Flegenheimer who everyone called Dutch Schultz, and across the Hudson in New Jersey, there was Abner (Longy) Zwillman.

There were others — many others — enough names to pad out a phone book: Arnold Rothstein, the underworld's financial genius and banker; William (Big Bill) Dwyer, who went from a longshoreman to a millionaire in less than two years; Irving Wexler, called Waxey Gordon an East Side pickpocket who dealt in narcotics as well as booze; and Larry Fay, an ex-cab driver who parlayed a hit at the track into a fleet of cabs and a string of successful nightclubs.

Prohibition provided Frank Costello with his golden opportunity. It gave him the chance to develop his inherent abilities which were perfectly matched to the jungle-dangerous world of the bootlegger. He was judicious, wily, and had an instinct for taking a chance at the right time.

Though outwardly generous, he was a ruthless, driving businessman who watched every buck. He also was imaginative and took credit for being the first one to think up the idea of using a seaplane to protect his ships from hijackers. He also claimed it was his idea for the famous, electronically-controlled, disappearing bar in one of his prohibition hangouts, the swank Club Twenty-One.

People trusted him instinctively. In the early years, some who did regretted it, but although he began the era as a thief and swindler, he ended it as a man of wealth who commanded respect and could say with justification that his word was his bond.

Prohibition also gave him the opportunity to enlarge his world. He met and became friends with people in all walks of life: legitimate businessmen, other racketeers, killers, politicians, gamblers, newspapermen, show business personalities, judges, city officials, and everyone else who counted on the New York scene.

The Costello brothers were strictly small timers when they started out. They began by briefly working for Arnold Rothstein, using his capital to finance their operation and splitting their profits with him. They then became wholesalers on their own, dealing in a few dozen cases at a time. Wholesalers sold to the small army of retailers who supplied the speaks and general public. Even housewives bought liquor by the case in those days.

In the first year or so of prohibition — before the establishment of Rum Row off the Long Island and New Jersey coast — much of the demand for liquor was met with Federal Government supplies. In the New York area alone, millions of gallons were stored in Government-owened-and-guarded warehouses along the waterfront. Much of the liquor was still legally owned by legitimate merchants who had to turn over their supplies when prohibition arrived. A trickle of liquor was allowed to be sold for medicinal purposes to drug companies with authorized permits.

The trick was to get the booze out of the warehouses, and the gangsters-turned-businessmen used two methods: forged permits and hijacking. Both methods achieved unusual success, turning the trickle into a flood.

The next step was to get the liquor into the hands of the public. This, however, presented problems because what was hijacked or

drawn out with phony permits wasn't always what the customers wanted.
Fifty cases of gin didn't do a wholesaler any good if his retailers wanted
scotch. To solve this problem, the wholesalers established a curb exchange for bootleg liquor in the Little Italy section of Lower Manhattan. The exchange, ironically, ringed police headquarters and ran along
Kenmare, Broome, Grand, and Elizabeth Streets. There they traded
among themselves, swapping to suit their individual needs.

The makeshift marketplace also served another need, as explained
in *Gang Rule in New York* by Thompson and Raymond:

"The curb exchange also was a clearing house for territorial allot-
ment so far as any arrangement could be made to stick. Wise, silent
old Tommy (the Bull) Pennochio, a Unione power but never the boss,
adviser to Joe Masseria and later Lucky Luciano, another Unione
leader, was acknowledged by many as the boss of the bootleg exchange.
Tommy the Bull believed in peace and quiet, but he never could enforce it very well. In addition to being a meeting place for the trans-
action of business, the curb exchange became also a battleground,
mostly between the unimportant small time operators who murdered
in retaliation for encroachment on their territory, but occasionally
among the higher-ups. The exchange encircled New York City Police
Headquarters with gunfire, and fledgling detectives did not have far
to walk to practice investigating."

The exchange became a melting pot for the gangs involved in the
bootleg trade. Italian, Jewish, and Irish mobsters mingled together and
did business with each other for the first time. Amidst the erupting
violence and bloodshed, alliances and friendships were formed that
lasted anywhere from a day to a lifetime.

Costello was a daily visitor to the exchange. That is where he became
close to Joe (the Boss) Masseria and Lucky Luciano and where he developed lasting friendships with Meyer Lansky and Bugsy Siegel and
many other household names in the history of gangland.

The Italians were divided into two camps. Many of the old timers
who were in positions of power and authority looked with suspicion
on anyone who wasn't Sicilian, much less not even Italian. Suspicion
had been bred into the bones of the older Sicilians, referred to as Mustache Petes. The young and ambitious new breed, represented by the
attitudes of Costello and Luciano, disagreed. They talked incessantly
about how times had changed and the need for cooperation instead of
bullets. The young Lansky agreed. He saw eye to eye with Costello
and agreed that the rackets should be treated like a business. What
were they doing, after all, except catering to the needs of the people.

The social club on Mulberry Street became one of the hangouts for members of the Masseria gang, and Costello slowly formed alliances with its leaders, earning a position of respect and influence.

"Even in those days, Frank had the reputation of not liking violence," recalls a member of the old exchange. "He didn't even carry a gun. Lucky was another story. He had a pretty bad reputation."

Years after Luciano had been deported to Italy, Costello told friends that he thought the younger, volatile, violence-prone Luciano regarded him as a father figure during their relationship. He described Luciano as being "just a punk kid" in those days and told how they had quarreled one time in a speakeasy in Little Italy. Luciano pulled a knife on him, Costello said, but he talked him into putting it away, telling him that "violence was ignorance." Finally Luciano came to his senses, and they resumed their friendship.

*   *   *

(Don Luigi Castiglia, aged seventy-five, died on December 12, 1921. The family buried him quietly in Queens. It must have been a difficult time for Frank Costello for reasons other than those a son faces on the death of his father. Reverence for the one who has given you life is a very real thing for Italians. It's part of their culture. Yet knowing how Frank really felt about Don Luigi, it is not difficult to imagine him laden with guilt, not willing to admit, even to himself, until many years later, the true state of his feelings. In retrospect, his friends recall that he never spoke about his father. Some even thought he had been left fatherless as a child and had been raised by his mother and an older sister.)

*   *   *

Joe the Boss was short, thick necked, built like a fireplug, and shrewd. He was also hungry for complete control of the Unione and the power it represented. His chief rival was Umberto Valenti, head of what might be loosely described in those days as a rival family. On August 9, 1922, Valenti attempted to settle things by eliminating Masseria. Joe the Boss was cornered in a millinery shop on Second Avenue by a gunman. Fritz Heiney, owner of the millinery shop, later described the incident to police.

"The man with the revolver came close to the other fellow and aimed," he said. "Just as he fired, the man jumped to one side. The bullet smashed a window of my store. When the man fired again, the fellow he aimed at ducked his head forward. The man with the gun fired again; and again the other man ducked his forward. The third shot made a second hole in my window."

The incident didn't hurt Joe the Boss's reputation. He became known as the man who could literally dodge bullets. In the future it would be proven that he couldn't.

Joe the Boss had no problem figuring out who had hired the gunman. He immediately sent out peace feelers to Valenti. He said he wanted to talk things over, work things out. It was a little like the general of one army saying he wanted to surrender to the general of an opposing army. Valenti sensing victory, agreed. The peace conference was held in an Italian restaurant on East Twelfth Street on August 11. Bowls of pasta were consumed. Glasses of wine were lifted in toasts of friendship and undying loyalty. Joe the Boss agreed to everything his rival demanded. It was a complete capitulation. At the end of the conference they shook hands, and Valenti left. Outside the restaurant several of Masseria's men shot him to death. Joe the Boss became unrivaled head of the Unione Siciliana.

✳   ✳   ✳

In prohibition's early years, many businessmen who enjoyed a reputation of respectability saw an opportunity to make a great deal of money and joined forces with the mobster-bootleggers. They were the fronts and bankrolls for the early operations and reaped half the profits. When the streets of New York became a shooting gallery, many of them got out. However, by that time the racketeers didn't need financiers. They had all the capital necessary.

One of the Costello brothers' early partners in illicit liquor was Emanual (Mannie) Kessler, a Jewish businessman on the fringe of the mob without any real contacts or alliances. Kessler, then sixty-three brought in a shipment worth about one hundred thousand dollars. He asked the Costellos to get rid of the twenty-five hundred cases for him, for a share of the profits, naturally. They agreed. Terrible things happened to that shipment. It was stored in a warehouse in Queens, and a raiding party of police found and confiscated the entire lot.

Kessler, who was convicted of violating the Volstead Act and sent to Atlanta Penitentiary in 1923, accused the Costellos of robbing him. In a statement given some years later to Federal law enforcement officers, he said that the Costello brothers had stolen one thousand cases of the shipment, worth about forty thousand dollars. They then tipped off the District Attorney's office to the location of the remaining liquor in the hope that this would obliterate any trace of their disloyalty.

In the Machiavellian world of the bootlegger, acts of treachery went on all the time. It was not unusual for a small-timer, for instance, to notify the authorities about a rival merely out of jealousy or pique.

Other times a squeal was made to square an arrest. A bootlegger who was collared was a good bet to turn informer and to tell the authorities about bigger fish in order to be let off the hook.

In those early days, Frank Costello, the up-and-coming mobster who preached peace, had a man killed for informing on him if the story of a bootlegger named Henry Thiele is to be believed. Thiele said he learned about the incident in Freeport, Long Island in 1923, from the lips of the apostle of peace himself. What follows is Thiele's statements upon being questioned by an Immigration investigator:

Q. "What was the occasion of this meeting in Freeport?"

A. "About liquor."

Q. Do you remember anything that transpired at that meeting?"

A. "He says he got this sonuvabitch and put him where he belongs with six bullets shot through his body."

Q. "Who was he talking about?"

A. "Louie DeMar."

Q. "Who was Louie DeMar?"

A. "He was a double-crossing guy."

Q. "Was he a rumrunner or bootlegger?"

A. "Yes he was."

Q. "This is what Frank Costello told you?"

A. "Yes."

Q. "Did Frank Costello tell you in what manner DeMar had double-crossed him?"

A. "For being a double-crosser and doing things. That one time he had a load of alcohol, and he gets me to ride through to New York City. I damn near hit a car. I was driving the car, and he sat quiet in case of a pickup. It was his (DeMar's) alcohol."

Q. "Did Frank Costello tell you why DeMar had been bumped off?"

A. "He said he squealed on him."

Q. "Did Frank Costello indicate who did the actual killing?"

A. "No."

Q. "And that story was told to you in Freeport around 1923?"

A. "That's right."

Q. "Did you have any conversation with Frank Costello in the 1923 meeting?"

A. "He told everybody that a boat of his had been knocked off up in Bayville (Long Island) and that he had been double-crossed and that he would take care of the party who did it."

Whether Thiele's tale is accepted or not, it points out that the business of bootlegging was definitely not for timid people. A don't-treadon-me reputation was necessary to survive in the shark-infested waters in which the bootlegger had to swim.

The fact that Costello bragged openly about killing a double-crosser is reason enough to suspect that he had nothing to do with the death of Louie DeMar. He was not the type of man who allowed his tongue to create possible problems. DeMar may very well have been blown away by someone else who had a score to settle, and Costello — ever the opportunist — may have decided to take advantage of the situation. Talking about the killing openly was a good way to serve notice on other bootleggers that double-crossing Costello was not smart.

In July of 1921, according to a *New York Times* article, the first ships appeared off Rum Row laden with whiskey picked up in the Bahamian port of Bimini. At first the rumrunners stayed just beyond the three-mile limit. They were forced out an additional nine miles, however, when Federal lawmakers got busy and made twelve miles the legal limit of American territorial waters.

The Rum Row coast off Long Island and New Jersey was hardly the only one. Every major city off the East and West Coasts had a Rum Row, but the one sitting outside of New York was by far the biggest and most famous. Large ships anchored right outside the Coast Guard's jurisdiction, and the bootleggers came alongside with fast speedboats capable of carrying hundreds of cases. Some of the Rum Row captains even had signs listing the price of their wares.

Deals would usually be made by shouts and hand signals, and the bootleggers would throw a wad of bills encircled with rubber bands aboard the rumrunner. Then the whiskey bought was lowered, and the speedboat made a dash for the shore.

In *Rum Row*, a book about the rumrunning exploits of Captain Bill McCoy of the *Arethusa*, the most famous rumrunner of the period, author Robert Carse tells how the Rum Row fleet operated in those early days:

"The *Arethusa* had as many as fifteen customers at a time. No engine was shut down; the boat skippers were ready for instant flight. The boats clunked hull to hull around the schooner, pitching, yawing, settling to their loads. The motor concatenation made a shout hard to hear on deck, and the men were under extreme tension as they swung the burlocks from the hatch to the rails, across the rails to the cockpits being stowed. But McCoy's mate was at the mainmast crosstrees with a pair of nightglasses; he kept the deck informed of any Coast Guard movement.

"Men known to McCoy made their own cargo transferral. They put the money in his hand or tossed the rolls of bills and told him the amounts, the brands taken. 'Here's three grand for five hundred Johnny Walker Black . . . I got four hundred of Dewer's Bill, and I'll top off with a hundred of Booth's High and Dry. Pay you the next time I'm on deck . . . Got Golden Wedding and the count is right and this squares for it. So long, Bill.'"

This changed when gangsters figured out that the Rum Row ships were easy to hijack. Posing as customers, they would pull alongside in their fast speedboats, hold up the captain and crew, loot all the whiskey they could carry, and zoom away. They became infamous as the "go-through guys", and when hijacking increased in intensity, the Rum Row ships armed themselves. Raging gun battles were fought at sea. Sailors who resisted were killed and dumped overboard. Some Rum Row captains put cannons aboard their vessels to defend themselves. Soon no one was allowed on board. Bootleggers seeking to do business were covered with guns from the moment they came into view.

The Federal Government didn't take long to find out that Bimini was being used as a bootlegger base of operations and moved to shut off the flow of booze. The British Government cooperated, and the pipeline was pretty well pinched. The action shifted next to Saint Pierre et Miquelon, French islands off the coats of New Foundland.

The really big money in bootlegging was made by the big operators who had the capital to load a ship with alcohol, bring in the entire load, and then sell it to the wholesalers. This entailed a good many risks, but it was worth it. One successful voyage meant a minimum of $250,000 in profit to the importer.

The problems were immense. An organization consisting of a small army of men had to be recruited and supervised to smuggle in a load of that size. First a ship had to be bought or chartered, then a competent ship's captain and crew had to be hired. When the ship arrived for a secret rendezvous off the coast, speedboats had to meet it and unload the precious cargo while keeping an eye out for hijackers and the Coast Guard. The speedboats then had to make a run for some little inlet — Oyster Bay, Montauk, Freeport, East Hampton, or Deal, New Jersey, to name just a few. There were hundreds of little docks where the speedboats could unload.

The trip by land was even more treacherous than the one by sea. Split-second timing between the speedboats and men on shore had to be developed so the load of liquor would be exposed as short a time as possible. The booze was loaded into international trucks while the local police were paid to look the other way. Once loaded, the trucks rumbled on the narrow, deserted highways into the city. The run resembled an army convoy during wartime. Two cars loaded with men armed with shotguns and machine guns preceded the convoy. Everyone was on edge watching for hijackers or police. Another armed car protected the rear.

One of the importers or a trusted agent usually rode in the lead car armed with a huge bankroll, prepared to buy himself out of trouble. Cops and prohibition agents in Nassau and Suffolk Counties constantly patrolled the roads looking for the convoys. Stopping one meant a big pay day.

Hijackers were feared the most. The East Side gangsters would set up roadblocks to stop the convoys or conduct lightning-fast raids on the flanks. Pitched gun battles occurred often enough to make a convoy run seem like a patrol behind enemy lines. The dead were dumped. The wounded carried along until a doctor could be conveniently summoned. Sometimes innocent bystanders were caught in the crossfire, and there would be headlines in the newspapers. Citizen groups protested, but no one did anything about it. Too many people were making too much money.

Each of the small, sleepy towns of Long Island has its favorite story of the prohibition years. Oldtimers can point out the spot where battles took place and can tell you how many were killed and wounded. Only memorial plaques are missing.

Even when the load of liquor was safely in the warehouses, the problems and dangers continued. The liquor first had to be cut and then needed to be put in bottles with authentic looking labels so that the customers would think they were getting the "real thing." (Double the booze, double the profit.) Gunmen also had to guard the warehouse from the ubiquitous hijackers, and local police had to get their share. Only then could the liquor be finally sold to the wholesalers.

The profits were enormous. The best scotch could be bought for $45 a case on St. Pierre et Miquelon. The cost of shipping it to Rum Row added $10 to the price of each case. Overhead, labor, and bribes added another $10, making the cost to the importer $65 a case or $325,000 for the entire 5000 lot. After the whiskey was cut and repacked, it was sold to the wholesalers for $85 a case. Multiply $85 by 10,000, and you come up with a figure of $850,000. Subtract the $325,000 total cost from the total gross, and you have a net profit of $525,000.

This is the sort of instant wealth a successful importer who bought his booze in by the shipload could look forward to. The great risks were matched by the great profits.

Frank Costello may have quit school in the fifth grade, but this didn't impair his mathematical ability. He didn't need an accountant to tell him that the big money was in being an importer, not a wholesaler.

Sometime in 1923, Big Bill Dwyer and he joined forces and became partners. Why Dwyer — already an importer — agreed to the merger is open to speculation. Police theorize that it was simply Costello pointing out that hijacking made the business quite precarious. With him as partner, his friends in Little Italy could guarantee that they wouldn't have to be concerned with such things. The friends, of course, would get a piece of the action. But why not? There was enough for everybody, and with the kind of protection he could guarantee, a greatly expanded operation was inevitable. Nobody would lose. Everybody would make more money than before.

Dwyer, the theory goes, didn't rise to his position in life by being stupid. He accepted the offer he couldn't refuse.

The Dwyer-Costello partnership proved to be one of the most successful syndicates to operate during the prohibition years. Federal investigators estimate the combine brought in forty million dollars worth of alcohol a year, and during that time, they were the only importers never to lose even a truckload of whickey to the hijackers.

William Vincent Dwyer was known as Big Bill, not for his physical size but for the enormity of his bankroll and the reach of his political influence. He was a New York-born Irishman with an easy way about him and a fine sense of humor.

In the forties, when the Internal Revenue Service had gone through him like mineral water, leaving him ostensibly broke and certainly owing them more than he could ever hope to pay back, he said:

"Always remember America is the finest country in the world, the greatest ever created, and the fairest and most reasonable too. I owe them eleven million dollars in taxes, they've just agreed to settle the claim for one million dollars."

He claimed to be penniless at the time.

Dwyer was born in 1883, grew up in Hell's Kitchen, and as soon as he was old enough began working on the docks as a longshoreman. When prohibition came along, he didn't hesitate — he plunged right in like a claim jumper rushing to the gold fields. By 1923, Big Bill was part of the New York scene with an office in the Times Square area, a piece of several restaurants, an expensive home in an exclusive suburb, and a reputation as a stand-up guy. He earned the reputation when he was arrested one time and paid two cops twenty-five hundred dollars to let him go. The cops were caught, but Dwyer refused to testify against them. After that Big Bill was strictly A-okay with the men in blue.

With the money he made bootlegging, he bought the Mount Royal

Race Track in Montreal and had a partnership in the Coney Island
Race track in Cincinnati. He later became the head of Tropical Park
in Florida.

He loved sports and was the original owner of the football Brooklyn
Dodgers. In 1925, a friend told him about "a game being played up
in Canada on skates." Dwyer dispatched another friend north to investigate.

"I said to Bill Halpin to go up and see what this hockey is about,"
Dwyer told sportswriter Jimmy Cannon. "Halpin went up and looked
at it and came back and said it was a helluva game. I said go back
and buy me a team and we bought one."

Dwyer spent two hundred thousand dollars for the Americans and
brought them to New York. He claimed he never made a dime out of
hockey, but he never regretted the purchase "because I got someplace
to go nights when the hockey season starts."

Physically he was a medium-sized, fleshy man with a lop-sided face
and a good gambler's calm. His face was rearranged when he broke
his jaw in an auto accident, and it never healed properly. He dressed
in the height of fashion, and a huge ring that adorned his finger was
made in the shape of a swastika with a large ruby in the center and
diamonds decorating the four bent arms.

During the years from 1922 to 1925 and 1927 to 1929, the tax
people said his income was in excess of eight million dollars. Quite a
bundle to go through when you consider that he died broke in 1946.
Hopefully he had a lot of fun spending it.

Although he stayed in the background, Costello gradually took over
the operation. Dwyer was like a fighter who is no longer hungry and
was content to allow his partner to attend to all the details. Costello
hired the crews for the ships, equipped the speedboats with war sur-
plus Liberty engines so they would be the fastest things afloat, bribed
cops, Coast Guard crews, and prohibition agents, paid off the politicians, assembled a small army of gunmen to protect his interests,
made deals with other importers, and set the price of the merchandise
with the wholesalers.

He was the outside man and indefatigable as he watched every buck
that came in. Often he would be seen during loading operations at
various spots on Long Island. He would go from Oyster Dock in Oyster
Bay to Fusaro's Beach in Huntington then dash to Freeport or to the
tip of the island, Montauk.

Frederick Charles Pitts, an ex-coastguardsman who was part of a
Costello speedboat crew, had reason to remember how his boss
watched every dime. One time he had personal problems and asked

Costello to advance him two hundred dollars. He wanted it sent to his wife, and Costello agreed. After thinking it over, however, Costello only sent one hundred dollars because he decided two hundred dollars was too large an advance.

As the money rolled in, Costello began to hedge his bets. He invested in other businesses and real estate. Some of the enterprises bore his name and could be traced. Others didn't and couldn't. He advanced his brother Eddie the money to buy a trucking company, then used it to transport liquor; he founded the Koslo Realty Company and built houses in the Bronx; he opened the Frank Costello Auto Company, also in the Bronx; the Dainties Products Company was formed with his old business partner Harry Horowitz to manufacture chocolate-covered ice cream pops; with other partners he opened the Club Rendezvous, where Gilda Gray was the featured attraction. People came to him with deals, and if it looked good he invested.

Success opened up the world for Costello. It was hard to believe that as late as 1919 he had been arrested over a one hundred dollar misunderstanding. He gained confidence in himself and his judgment and acquired a sense of self worth. Unlike men such as Joe the Boss and others of the family who kept their own company in Little Italy, there was nothing menacing about Costello. He was soft-spoken, quiet, and friendly. Respectable businessmen didn't feel threatened in his company; politicians and city officials didn't fear being seen with him. Most people didn't even know there was a Mafia, much less that he was involved. Neither did the police. He was looked upon simply as an extremely successful bootlegger and businessman who liked to gamble. That wasn't a cause for social ostracism. On the contrary, everyone drank and gambled.

As his contacts broadened, so did his influence. He became known as the man to see in New York for anything connected with bootlegging. Top bootleggers in other cities, men like Charles (King) Solomon in Boston, Max (Boo Boo) Hoff in Philadelphia, and Johnny Torrio and Al Capone in Chicago, became his friends.

New York's night life in the twenties, as writer Lloyd Morris pointed out, was fabulously rich and varied. Costello was also a part of this scene. He went to the clubs for both business and pleasure. The clubs attracted all types. Bootleggers, well-heeled businessmen, gangsters, scions of high society, con men, celebrities, city officials, and even judges. They all rubbed shoulders together in the speakeasy-nightclubs. On any given night one could see such disparate characters making merry as Dutch Schultz, appearing deceptively mild mannered despite his reputation as a killer; Aimee Semple McPherson, the Hollywood evangelist; Mae West, star of the hit Broadway play called *Sex*; Jimmy Walker, the up-and-coming politician and soon to be Mayor of New York, charming everybody with his light-hearted Irish wit; Stephen Graham, the British author; Bill Fallon, the famous criminal lawyer, dubbed the "Great Mouthpiece," who had an unquenchable thirst; Owney Madden, recently released from prison and claiming he was reformed; and Lord and Lady Mountbatten.

West 52nd Street between Fifth and Sixth Avenues was famous throughout the nation. Literally every building on both sides of the block contained a speak. The top joint was the ornate Club Twenty-One, Costello's favorite nightclub. It attracted the biggest names in New York society and those with social pretensions from the hinterlands. The food was exquisite and the booze right off the boat.

Other night attractions in town included the Dutch Schultz-owned Embassy Club, featuring singer Helen Morgan who made everyone weep when she hoisted her tiny, vulnerable figure on top of the piano and sang the torch song "Bill;" racketeer Big Bill Duffy owned the Silver Slipper which featured the madcap comedians Clayton, Jackson, and Durante; Jack (Legs) Diamond was the sponsor of the Hotsy Totsy Club, famous for its brassy bands and anything goes attitude; entertainer Harry Richman owned the Club Richman, where the emphasis was on beautiful girls who wore a little less than the law allowed. There was also British comedienne and song stylist Beatrice Lillie at the Sutton Club, blues singer Libby Holman at the Lido, and dancers Fred Astaire and his sister, Adele at the Trocadero.

But despite the plethora of entertainment offered, the most famous entertainer in town was a blond, brash, big-bosomed broad from Waco, Texas who caught the spirit of the decade and was featured in the swank El Fey Club. She didn't have much of a voice, and she couldn't dance. She just acted as the mistress of ceremonies and insulted the customers. Her real name was Mary Louise Cecelia Guinan, but she won fame as Texas Guinan. She and the age were made for each other as she wisecracked her way into the affections of everyone with her raucous greeting to customers: "Hello, sucker."

Racketeer Larry Fay, a sadistic, over-dressed, little man, horse-faced and stricken with a touch of meglomania, was her backer. He put her into a series of his clubs including — besides the El Fey — the Del Fey, the Three Hundred Club, Club Intime, and Texas Guinan's.

Writer Edmund Wilson described her in this way: "This prodigous woman, with her pearls, her glittering bosom, her abundant, beautifully-bleached yellow coiffure, her formidable trap of shining white teeth, her broad bare back behind its grating of green velvet, the full blown peony as big as a cabbage exploding on her broad green thigh..."

She presided from atop a piano with a small gold police whistle in one hand and a noisemaker in the other, trading quips with customers, reigning over the bedlam she created. She was busted so often that she had a routine all worked out: the band played the "Prisoner's Song," and she marched away like Joan of Arc being led to the pyre. In spite of all the arrests, she never spent a day in jail — any judge who dared sentence her would have been hung in effigy. She married three times, earned a king's fortune during her reign, and died in 1933 at the age of forty-nine, leaving an estate valued at $28,173.

New York was an all-night town in the twenties. The real revel rousers headed uptown to Harlem after two A.M., and slumming soon became the in thing for high society. The white swells swarmed into the Cotton Club, owned by Arnold Rothstein and Owney Madden, where blacks weren't allowed as customers. Ethel Waters was often featured at Harlem's premier nightclub. Connie's Inn, Small's Paradise, and the Nest in Jungle Alley featured miniature, fast-paced revues and jazz orchestras headed by stars like Duke Ellington, Cab Calloway, Fletcher Henderson, and Louis (Satchmo) Armstrong.

Frank Costello often took Bobbie with him when he made the nightclub circuit. She loved the excitement generated by live entertainment and still begged to catch the latest show at the Copacabana in the later years when her husband had tired of it all and preferred to be home by eleven.

Arnold Rothstein was one of Frank Costello's close associates in those days. He was a thin, sallow-faced man who started out as a gambler and became the financier of the underworld. Rothstein worshipped money. It was his personal god. He would do anything for money and had his finger in loansharking, bootlegging, phony securities, gambling, drugs, fencing stolen Liberty Bonds, and anything else that promised a pay off.

He was New York's biggest racketeer in the twenties and put together the largest gambling empire in the nation. He is remembered chiefly as the man responsible for the "Black Sox" scandal, the attempt to fix the 1919 World Series between the Chicago White Sox and the Cincinnati Reds. According to his biographer, Leo Katcher, who detailed Rothstein's life in the excellent book, *The Big Bankroll,* the fix was one of the few dirty things he was falsely accused of.

Rothstein was a financial genius of sorts who ran his empire pretty much out of his hat. Yet he kept track of every dime ever owed him. If he loaned a man money, he would insist that a life insurance policy be taken out for the amount advanced. This way, if death prevented the pay off, he would collect anyway.

He was a compulsive gambler who hated to gamble. He played cards methodically, showing no passion. Often he played in games where the turn of a card meant winning or losing $250,000. His lawyer, Bill Fallon, said of him: "Rothstein is a man who dwells in doorways. A mouse standing in a doorway, waiting for his cheese."

Rothstein was born in New York in 1882, the son of a highly respected, middle-class, Jewish textile merchant. He quit high school after two years and became a pool hustler. After opening up a series of gambling houses, he hit the big time and set up a clearing house for bookies. Through Rothstein, a bookmaker who felt himself overextended could lay off his bets with bookmakers across the country.

On Rothstein's payroll at various times were the Costello brothers, Waxey Gordon, Larry Fay, Owney Madden, Philip (Dandy Phil) Kastel, and many others. Kastel, an owlish-looking, dapper little man, was one of Rothstein's lieutenants. He ran a bucket shop for his boss, a fly-by-night brokerage house that sold phony stock securities. Near the end of the decade, Kastel went to work for Costello and became his partner in the slot machine racket.

Costello and Rothstein frequently were involved in business deals with each other. They also often borrowed from each other. When Rothstein was murdered in 1928 for welching on a gambling debt, a Costello I.O.U. for forty thousand dollars was found among his papers.

Rothstein was an unpleasant man, but even his enemies gave the devil his due: he possessed a cunning mind, and no one ever got the best of him in a business deal.

There's no question that the younger, less sophisticated Costello admired Rothstein's shrewdness and learned from him many things not taught in Harvard's School of Business. Many years after Rothstein's death, Costello told a newspaperman during an interview:

"All I know I stole. If I saw you hold a cigaret a certain way, and I liked it, I would steal it from you."

Rothstein wasn't the only man he said he admired in those days when he was rising in wealth, power, and prestige. Another was a hard-driving Irishman from Boston named Joseph Kennedy. According to Costello, the future ambassador to the Court of Saint James and the father of the thirty-fifth president of the United States, approached him for help in smuggling liquor. A deal was worked out in which Kennedy had the liquor dumped at Rum Row, and Costello then took over.

Costello told the story of being in business with Joe Kennedy to a number of close friends, including columnist John Miller.

"The way he (Costello) talked about him," Miller said, "you had the sense that they were close during prohibition and then something happened. Frank said that he helped Kennedy become wealthy. What happened between them I don't know. But the way Frank talked you had the feeling that in later years he had tried to reach Joe Kennedy for something and that he was completely ignored. Frank didn't mind if someone said no to him. He could understand that. But nothing made him angrier than to be just ignored, as if he didn't exist."

Costello also told writer Peter Maas, shortly before he died, that he had been in business with Kennedy during prohibition. Maas said that Costello had agreed to tell his story to him for a book. After the old Mafia chieftain died — causing Maas' book also to die — the story of the alleged Costello-Kennedy relationship appeared in the *New York Times* and created quite a flap.

Stephen Smith, a Joe Kennedy son-in-law who has often acted as a Kennedy family spokesman, said that a check of the family patriarch's business records reflected no such business relationship and that his father-in-law had never imported liquor illegally into the United States.

"I can't say he never talked to Costello," Smith said, "but I never heard of it, and I'm sure it would come as news to anybody in the family."

Nevertheless, when I was in New Orleans researching this book, I interviewed a lawyer who worked for Frank Costello in the late forties. The lawyer, who asked that his name be withheld, said that one time it was necessary for him to fly to New York to see Costello on a business matter.

"When I arrived in his apartment," he said, "Costello was on the phone. He waved to me and continued talking. He was in the midst of cussing someone out like I never heard before. This went on for a few minutes, and then he hung up.

"I was curious. Since he hadn't made any secret about the phone call, I decided to be a little impolite and asked him, 'who were you talking to like that?' He looked at me and gave this little laugh and said, 'Oh, just that Kennedy fella from Boston.'"

Rackets
is business

The speedboat had been wandering around in the morning fog for more than an hour, darting in and out among the anchored ships of Rum Row, while the city-born sailors searched for the rumrunner they wanted. Suddenly a powerful, gleaming white cutter pulled alongside. The stars and stripes fluttered in the breeze on the stern, and the inscription "CG 126" was clearly visible on the bow.

"Who ya' lookin' for," shouted the chief boatswain who was the captain on the Coast Guard boat.

"The Vincent White," *one of the sailors on the speedboat shouted back.*

"Sonuvabitch, you're the ones we've been searching for," the chief boatswain said. "She's anchored further south. Just follow us and we'll take ya' to her. Do ya' happen to have some scotch on board? We're fresh out."

"Throw the lushes a couple of bottles," the skipper of the speedboat ordered in a low voice.

A grinning Coastguardsman caught the two bottles as neatly as an outfielder in a baseball game. Then the CG 126, on official patrol looking for rumrunners, made a neat 180 degree turn and showed the way to the Vincent White.

The pier on South Street, near the Fulton Fish Market, was nearly deserted at two a.m. All that was visible was a truck parked near the pier and two cops. Soon from the water came the muffled roar of a speedboat traveling at low speed. It became clearly visible at about a hundred yards and was heading directly for the pier. Less than a minute later the speedboat tied up, and its crew began loading cases of liquor into the truck. It was a hard job, and the loaders cursed as they sweated.

"How about giving us a hand?" one of the loaders finally asked the cops who were watching like foremen at a construction site. "We're all on the same payroll, you know."

The cops looked at each other, shrugged their shoulders, and finally slowly walked over and took a place in the loading line. Within twenty minutes the truck was loaded and on its way. The speedboat pulled out. The cops resumed their beat.

❖   ❖   ❖

The speedboat Klip *roared into New York Harbor with its powerful Liberty engine under strain. Directly in back of her was a Coast Guard cutter in full chase.*

The skipper of the Klip *was at the wheel, and he noted that the cutter was gaining on him. He began to dodge in and out of the river craft that early morning in October of 1925.*

"Peg a few shots and see if you can scare them off," he ordered.

Members of the Klip's *crew began firing rifles. The cutter returned the fire. Passengers aboard a Staten Island ferry, watching the chase with pop-eyed interest, dropped to the safety of the deck as the* Klip *cut across its bow in order to use the ferry for cover.*

❖   ❖   ❖

In the middle twenties it seemed everyone was on the payroll of the bootleggers: Coast Guard, cops, prohibition agents, politicians, and anyone else who could hinder the flow of liquor pouring into the country. That's why the gun battle between the *Klip* and the Coast Guard cutter upset Costello so much. It was dumb. Stupid. People could get hurt that way. Furthermore, if it was discovered that the *Klip* was one of his boats, there could be a good deal of trouble.

Frank Costello firmly believed in keeping a low profile and avoiding trouble. His agile mind constantly went over every aspect of the giant bootleg operation he ran. Lists of everyone needed to be taken care of were reviewed and updated regularly.

He didn't feel that what he was doing was *really* illegal. Christ, the public wanted liquor, and he was supplying it — good whiskey that was properly aged and that would never cause anyone to go blind or become sick like that home-brewed rotgut being sold when prohibition first started. You couldn't force people not to drink anymore than you could make them stop gambling. He knew that. Everyone knew that. Everyone, that is, except the Government.

Despite the dramatic upswing in his fortunes, Costello continued to live simply, a marked contrast to his flamboyant partner who flashed his wealth like he owned the mint. His only concession to his prosperity was when in 1925 he moved out of Harlem and into a modest home in an attractive, quiet, middle-class neighborhood in Bayside, Queens. He dressed conservatively and took great pains in choosing his suits — nothing flashy to cheapen the image he had of himself in his mind's eye, most often blues and grays with white shirts and maybe a red tie for a dash of color.

He and Bobbie were often seen in the popular restaurants and nightclubs around town. It was all part of his carefully nurtured image of being a prosperous businessman (which, in fact, he was). He owned real estate, an ice cream factory, and a car agency and could account for his style of life. Dwyer, on the other hand, lived like he owned General Motors. No wonder everyone thought Costello merely worked for him.

Toots Shor, the well-known restaurant owner whose establishment in New York is a popular hangout for the sporting fraternity, became a good friend of Costello's during prohibition. He has nostalgic memories of the times.

"Jiminy Cricket, it was a different era then," he said. "In those days you'd walk into Moore's Restaurant, and you'd see all the politicians, men like Jimmy Walker and Jim Farley. You'd see all those guys. You'd see Frank sitting at one table and Charley Sherman, who was supposed to be a tough guy, sitting at another. You'd see them all sitting around talking to one another.

"Then you'd go to the Plaza Theater, and you'd see Owney Madden and those fellows, all those judges and politicians and the other side. There was no difference; they all dressed alike. They'd say hello to each other. Or not you'd go to the Palace Theater. It was a vaudeville house, and it was a big thing to go on Sunday nights. Then you'd go to the Cotton Club, and you'd see the same people at all these places. You'd see Frank and his wife and these different fellows and their wives, all the gamblers, and bootleggers. All they ever did was gamble and bootleg. After all, we were buying it. I mean, I happened to be selling it because I worked in a place, and anybody buying was just as guilty as selling."

The smooth course of Frank Costello's life ran into some heavy seas on December 4, 1925. On that day the lead story in *The New York Times* reported that a forty million dollar a year international liquor ring had been smashed with the arrest of twenty persons in the New York area.

The United States Department of Justice called it the "greatest roundup in the history of prohibition" and said that the kingpin of the alleged ring — which stretched from New York clear to London — was among those nabbed. He was identified as William Vincent Dwyer, well-known sportsman and owner of racetracks.

Arrested with Dwyer were a chief boatswain and four other members of the Coast Guard who were accused of helping the ring smuggle alcohol into the country.

Two others also arrested that day were identified as being the ring's "pay-off men." The pair were Frank and Edward Costello.

The Justice Department warned in the story that this was a continuing investigation and that the arrest of many more ring members in the future could be expected.

Those who had inside knowledge of the bootlegging scene in New York must have been amused by reading the *Times* that chilly December morning. The Government had gotten things backward. Dwyer wasn't the brains and real power behind the ring which had its own ships, armor-plated motorboats, warehouses, armed guards, and distributing force. Frank Costello was.

Whatever the case, Frank Costello found himself before a judge again for the first time since that 1919 unpleasantness. He pleaded "not guilty" along with everyone else. Dwyer, who received the lion's share of attention from the newspapers, was held in forty thousand dollars bail. A twenty thousand dollar figure was put on the Costello brothers. Eddie objected to being described as a "pay-off man" and protested to the court: "I'm in the trucking business." Frank kept quiet. In a matter of hours all three made bail.

As he reflected on the course of events, Costello must have congratulated himself on the wiseness of his low-key style of life. So far as being arrested as a bootlegger was concerned, he knew the Government would have a problem getting a conviction. Prohibition was a highly unpopular law, and the people who made up the juries broke the law themselves everytime they had a drink. They objected to the hypocrisy of it all and usually refused to vote for a conviction.

Being arrested again hurt Costello's reputation about as much as a mink coat hurts a chorus girl's. Bootleggers were a part of the twenties scene and as necessary as milkmen. He continued to be seen in the company of his many legitimate friends, including politicians, city officials, and judges.

The Justice Department kept its word about more arrests and on January 27, 1926, the original total had risen to sixty-one and now included thirteen members of the Coast Guard, a prohibition agent, and a pilot who flew out of Long Island's Curtiss Field. The newspapers were full of stories on how the ring had corrupted the Coastguardsmen with "wine, women, and song," and the Government claimed that the ring even had its own spy network to trail prohibition agents from Washington to New York.

The investigation continued to drag on but instead of picking up steam seemed to be dying. On June 6, a superceding indictment was issued splitting the defendents into two groups: first Dwyer and sixteen others were to be tried; then the Costello brothers and twenty-six others. This made a total of forty-five. Charges had been dropped against sixteen.

Dwyer and his group went on trial in July. It was a dull case that dragged on through most of the month. The prosecution's star witnesses were of the undercover variety, men who had worked for the ring and then gone on the Government's payroll to avenge a grievance. On July 26, the jury acquitted everyone except Dwyer and a man named E. C. Cohron who had a hand in bribing the Coast Guard. Dwyer was sentenced to serve two years in jail and fined ten thousand dollars.

The Costello brothers didn't go on trial until January 3, 1927. Again the Government used the tactic of producing undercover witnesses. At the end of the prosecution's case, the defense made a motion for a directed acquittal on the grounds that a prima facia case hadn't been established. Federal Court Judge Francis Winslow agreed in regard to the charges leveled against Edward Costello, and he was released.

On January 20, the jury filed into the courtroom after deliberating for nearly two days. In the case of Frank Costello and a few of the others, no agreement could be reached. In the case of the rest, an acquittal on all charges had been voted.

The *Times*, in an editorial following the jury determination, took note of the fact that of sixty-one men originally indicted for violation of the prohibition law, just two were convicted. Calling what happened typical in prohibition trials across the nation, the editorial said in part:

". . . Say what you will, men make a distinction between laws affecting their personal habits and those having to do with the rights of others.

Juries are made up of men who do not live apart from their fellows, but understand the common sentiment of the community, and may be expected to frustrate many such trials as the one which lasted for two weeks in the Federal court of this district and ended in a complete fiasco."

Costello was understandably jubilant about the trial's outcome. Even though it was a hung jury, it was extremely doubtful that the Justice Department would attempt to try him again. Except in rare instances, juries just didn't want to convict bootleggers.

Not being convicted meant a great deal to him aside from not having to serve a jail term. In 1925, he had applied for his citizenship papers, and if he had been convicted, his lawyers warned him, the Government then would have had grounds to institute deportation proceedings against him on the basis that he had lied when filling out the papers on which he gave his occupation as real estate broker. The two men who sponsored him when he applied for citizenship — vouching for his character and good repute — were Frank Goss and Harry C. Sausser. Both worked for him and were among the sixty-one arrested.

Following the trial, Costello decided what he needed most was a change of scenery. He decided to take off a couple of months and give everything a chance to cool. He booked passage alone on a steamer and made a sentimental journey back to Lauropoli. Although he referred to the town as a "dump" and would laugh when he told friends that the people wanted to rename the town after him when he handed out lire wholesale, it must have meant a great deal because he told the story of the trip many times to many people.

The East Side gangs had become prosperous during prohibition, with the Italian mobs gaining dominance. They were the chief beneficiaries of the bootleg trade, and much of the credit for this must go to Costello. In the meantime, Joe the Boss Masseria had become the undisputed leader of the Italian gangs, and his word was law.

His chief lieutenants were the energetic Lucky Luciano and the crafty Vito Genovese, a Neapolitan by birth who jealously watched the interests of Joe the Boss. Costello's role was that of an advisor and a bridge between the straight world and the mob. If a politician had to be reached or a judge given a contract, Costello would receive the assignment. He already had the reputation as a contract man, meaning someone who could get others to do special favors. Tammany Hall leader Jimmy Hines was on his payroll. So were the many others anxious to share in the enormous bootlegging profits.

The role of advisor and fixer suited Costello's aims perfectly. He had no ambition to become another Joe the Boss in the secret society. He was busy carving out his own empire. His careful ties with the Mafia gave him the muscle he needed, and his place in the outside world gave him the respectability he craved.

Rudolph McLaughlin, now a retired New York City Police detective-lieutenant, was a young plainclothes cop when he was given the assignment to keep a watch on Costello in 1928.

"In those early years when I knew and worked on him," McLaughlin recalled, "all of his close associates were Jewish or Irish. You'd never see him with Italians. We had no idea he was involved with them."

From Joe the Boss' point of view, Costello's aims were attributes. If Costello was only interested in making money, then that was good for Joe the Boss because he received a share of everything Costello made; and if Costello preferred the world uptown, that was also good because then Joe the Boss didn't have to worry about him becoming too ambitious.

Money and ambition have traditionally been the two greatest causes of violence within the Mafia. An underling who steals or reaches out for power or who threatens the head of the family or one of his lieutenants is playing a dangerous game. Both are looked upon as crimes worthy of the death sentence.

The men of the Mafia are quick to say: "My word is my bond." This has a very real meaning for them and is an important part of the rigid morality of their society. Their business deals or agreements are not made legal by pieces of paper for lawyers to argue about and courts to rule on. A man simply gives his word with the full knowledge that if he breaks his word, a serious, punishable. moral offense will have been committed.

A mob hit man who calls himself "Joey" and claims to have killed thirty-eight men appeared hooded on a television talk program recently to publicize a book entitled *Killer* which deals with his experiences. Asked by the shocked host, David Susskind, to give some of his redeeming features, Joey answered: "My word is my bond."

The only circumstance that would permit you to break your word and commit treachery without losing stature would be when the person you're dealing with is plotting against you. When Joe the Boss pledged his undying loyalty in the restaurant to Umberto Valenti, for instance, he was able to explain it away by saying Valenti was conspiring against him. He had simply beaten him to the punch.

In running the bootleg operation, Costello was scrupulously honest about seeing to it that Joe the Boss was not shortchanged in his share of the spoils. He also was careful never to promise something unless he was certain that he could live up to that promise. This added greatly to his prestige.

In 1928, Costello could see clearly that it was just a matter of time before liquor was again made legal. The American public was becoming more and more horrified by the results of the "noble experiment." Alcohol was flowing more freely than it ever had before, and more people were drinking. The law was unenforceable, and the murder and corruption it caused were chronicled daily in the newspapers and magazines. Governor Al Smith of New York, making a bid to become the Democratic standard bearer in the upcoming Presidential race, headed the voices of reason calling for the repeal of the Volstead Act.

In anticipation of the loss of income from bootlegging once prohibition was voted out, Costello started searching for a new racket. He decided on some form of gambling, but his choice was rather limited in this repect. Arnold Rothstein controlled the bookmaking and Dutch Schultz the policy game. If he had tried to muscle his way in, an all-out gang war would have resulted. After giving the problem some thought, he came up with the answer: slot machines. The one-armed bandits were open territory. With Dandy Phil Kastel as his chief lieutenant, he went about it in his usual meticulous way: (1) he obtained New York City as his exclusive territory from the Mills Novelty Company of Chicago, the manufacturer of the slot machines; (2) he formed the Triangle Mint Company; (3) he promised the Tammany Hall politicians a piece of the action; (4) he promised Joe the Boss a piece of the action; (5) he put high ranking police officers on his payroll; (6) he recruited his own army of collectors, salesmen, servicemen, and even his own police force to track down machines that were stolen.

His biggest stroke of genius was the gimmick he eventually came up with to get around the anti-gambling laws. Each slot machine was fixed so that it would throw out a small packet of candy mints everytime a nickel was dropped in the slot and the handle pulled. If a player came up with three cherries, for instance, then in addition to the mints, the machine would throw out slugs which could be used for replays or redeemed for cash with the storekeeper in whose business the machine was placed. It was a stroke of genius and lucrative enough to eventually rival the profits reaped from bootlegging.

But the mint idea didn't come until about 1930. In 1928, when the slot machines first appeared, it was a straight payoff, just like the machines in Las Vegas today, and Costello had his problems despite the great number of people on his payroll.

"Every machine had a little pink sticker with the name Triangle and a phone number," Lieutenant McLaughlin said. "The idea of the phone numuer was that if a cop came in to take the machine, he was to call the number and one of Costello's agents would come over and settle things. He had maybe twenty agents, and they were all Tammany

Hall hang-arounds — guys who used to work for Jimmy Hines and the others.

"I worked for a captain, a police captain. He was an honest man, and we used to bring in two or three machines a day, and Costello was dying. He came to see us one time and said, 'how come I could pay everybody but I can't pay you guys.' So we told him to see the captain. I don't have to tell you the captain threw him out of the office. But the chief inspector and the assistant chief, everybody down the line was on the pad."

          ❋   ❋   ❋

On November 4, 1928, an extraordinary thing happened that changed the control of the rackets in New York and had its effect around the nation. While in the Park Central hotel, Arnold Rothstein, financier of the underworld and head of a bookmaking empire and burgeoning dope trade, was shot in the groin by a gambler he had welched on. (In later years the hotel would be called the Park Sheraton, and its barbershop would be the scene of the gangland slaying of Albert Anastasia, known as the Lord High Executioner of the Underworld.) Rothstein lingered a short while and died. His murder was never officially solved, although the police believe the trigger was pulled by gambler George McManus who was seeking to collect more than three hundred thousand dollars in I.O.U.'s from Rothstein.

With Rothstein dead, his empire was up for grabs. Lucky Luciano ripped off the narcotics; Louis (Lepke) Buchalter, the union rackets; Costello, the gambling. To handle the bookmaking, Costello installed his close friend Frank Erickson, the bland, pink-cheeked, well-known bookmaker. In no time at all, Erickson was established as the bookmakers' bookmaker, handling the lay-off bets; and with Costello by his side no one was apt to argue. Erickson ran the business, and Costello got a healthy share of the action. This meant that Joe the Boss also received his tribute.

For Costello the year 1929 arrived with its share of promise and trepidation. The promise was twofold: first, the American people showed that they were more concerned with a man's religion than his stand on prohibition and defeated Al Smith, a Catholic, at the polling booths and made Herbert Hoover the thirty-first President of the United States. This guaranteed that the bootlegger's trade would be lucrative for at least four more years; secondly, the successful start of the slot machine and bookmaking enterprises meant valuable new sources of revenue. The trepidation was due to the fact that Salvatore Maranzano, a lean, tall, Sicilian-born Mafia leader with a lust for

power was openly challenging Joe the Boss for control of the organization. Violence had already occurred between the two factions, and
unless a peace plan could be worked out, a full-blown war was inevitable.

In times of war, nothing is stable. Costello knew that. He and Luciano
talked to Joe the Boss about peace and cooperation with the other
gangs. He listened but said nothing. His throne was being threatened,
and next to that nothing mattered. Besides, he believed he held all
the cards. If it came to all out war, he thought he would eliminate
his rival and win.

           ❁   ❁   ❁

If Joe the Boss was adamant on the subject of Maranzano, he listened on other matters. Costello revived the grandiose scheme of
Chicago Mafia leader Johnny Torrio, then in retirement in Italy, to
cut up the United States in slices like an orange, with each faction
getting its share. "Rackets is business," Torrio had preached.

Costello often discussed this visionary concept of slicing up the
nation into racket fiefdoms with his closest mob confederates: Luciano,
Lansky, Adonis, and Schultz. He met receptive ears. With Luciano's
help, he convinced Joe the Boss to add his power and prestige to the
idea. The result was the first crime convention, held, just as if it were
the legionnaires or the Masons getting together, in Atlantic City in the
President Hotel from May 13th to May 16th, 1929.

Members of the Italian mobs weren't the only ones to attend. Costello
believed in cooperation among all the gangs, and whoever had muscle
and power no matter what his ethnic origin, was invited.

Fred J. Cook, in his book *Mafia*, describes the scene:

"According to reports, Enoch J. (Nucky) Johnson, then the unrivaled
political boss of Atlantic City and himself a numbers racketeer, welcomed the brethren. From Chicago came Al Capone, accompanied by
his bodyguard, Frank Cline, and his leading henchman, Frank (The
Enforcer) Nitti and Jake (Greasy Thumb) Guzik. Philadelphia was
represented by Max (Boo Boo) Hoff, Sam Lazar and Charles Schwartz;
New York by Dutch Schultz, Frank Costello, Lucky Luciano and Joe
Adonis. Johnny Torrio, returned from Italy and now in a position of
elder statesman of the rackets, was also there."

In this company, Costello was relatively a lower echelon man. Yet
according to FBI informants, he was the "maitre d' of the convention,"
putting people together, laying out the agenda, influencing the decisions that were reached with his persuasive powers and good sense.
He preached his old themes of peace and cooperation.

Just what decisions were reached is in dispute. Depending upon what law enforcement agency you choose as your source of information the importance of the meeting is either upgraded or downgraded. Some say that the basic decisions which resulted in the establishment of a national crime syndicate were reached. Others say "nonsense," that the reason for the convention was merely to cut up the nation into territories for the gambling rackets. The downgraders also point out that basic decisions couldn't have been made because the top Mafia people weren't there and that even the presence of Al Capone didn't mean much because he was never really important in the Mafia hierarchy.

Everyone, however, agrees on one point: the Atlantic City Convention elevated Frank Costello to a man of real power and stature on a national scale.

War and peace

On April 15, 1931, Joe the Boss lunched with his underboss and most trusted aide, Lucky Luciano. They lunched in Scarpato's Restaurant on Coney Island, a favorite of Joe the Boss. The owner was a good friend, and because no one knew they were there and because it was just lunch with Lucky, whom he regarded as a son, Joe the Boss didn't bring his bodyguards along.

Scarpato's was an excellent restaurant, but on that day the cook's skills soared to match the importance of the luncheon guests. The homemade pasta, the sauces, everything was all that Joe the Boss could ask for. During lunch he talked family business with Luciano. After eating they decided to relax and sipped wine and played cards in the by then deserted restaurant.

After playing for a while, Luciano excused himself to go to the men's room. While he was there, four gunman, believed to be members of the Meyer Lansky and Bugsy Siegel mob, walked into Scarpato's and shot Joe the Boss many times in back of the head. He was taken by surprise and never had the opportunity to go into his famous ducking act.

A report which appeared in the newspapers claimed that at the time of the slaying Joe the Boss was still clutching the ace of diamonds in his left hand. A newspaper photographer even snapped a picture of Joe's bloody hand holding the card as he lay on the floor of the restaurant. From that time on, the legend goes, the ace of diamonds has been known as a hard-luck card among the men of the Mafia.

The legend, however, was manufactured. Irving Leiberman, a veteran reporter for the *New York Post*, covered the murder of Joe the Boss and was at the scene. An imaginative reporter from a rival newspaper, he said, decided to make the story even better. He surveyed things and then picked up the ace of diamonds from the floor and stuck it in Joe's hand. He reported the extra-added ingredient to his newspaper.

Luciano was questioned by police at the restaurant. He knew nothing, he said, because he was in the men's room when it happened. When he heard the shots, he rushed out to find Joe the Boss lying on the floor in a pool of blood. The employees of Scarpato's backed up his story; they all agreed he had been in the men's room. Naturally no one could identify the killers. No one had seen a thing.

The roots of Luciano's betrayal went back to 1928 when Joe the Boss decided to level a bit of discipline against a group of Mafiosi in Brooklyn. He feared they were becoming too independent and demanded homage in the form of a contribution of money. When they refused, he had several of the rebels murdered. They rallied behind their family head, Salvatore Maranzano, and retaliated in kind.

The rebel Mafiosi mostly came from a little town in Sicily, sixty miles west of Palermo, called Castellammare del Golfo, and the violence in 1928 led to what was called the "Castellammarese War."

For a time the war just simmered — a man killed here, an alcohol truck hijacked there. It finally erupted into a full scale battle in 1930, with the forces on both sides shooting each other on sight, lying in ambush for one another, and hitting the mattresses. (This is a term Mafiosi use to describe being under seige when they sleep away from home in bare rooms that contain only mattresses on the floor.)

The lineup on both sides was formidable with many of them — in the minds of the fascinated public — candidates for a mythical Mafia Hall of Fame. On the side of Masseria were Lucky Luciano, Vito Genovese, Frank Costello, Joe Adonis, Carlo Gambino, Albert Anastasia, and Willie Moretti. On the side of Maranzano were Joseph (Joe Bananas) Bonanno, Joseph Profaci, Thomas (Three-Finger Brown) Lucchese, Joseph Magliocco, and Gaetano Gagliano.

At first it seemed certain that Joe the Boss would win, but Maranzano proved to be a very tough nut. He was a superb tactician and the Castellammerese were both disciplined and efficient. Mafia leaders around the country began to take sides. The conservatives saw it as a war to establish rightful authority. The liberals saw it as a war of principle involving the right of individual families to have freedom and independence of action. Al Capone, a traditionalist, sided with Masseria and contributed money to the war chest. Stefano Magaddino, a Castellammarese who ruled in Buffalo, supported Maranzano and sent money and vehicles.

In November of 1930, Joe the Boss narrowly escaped death when gunmen surprised him and his bodyguards as he left a Bronx apartment house. Joe the Boss ducked and ran, and all the gunman got were his two bodyguards (who were killed). In his haste, however, Joe the Boss left his overcoat at the scene.

The Bronx District Attorney was able to identify who the coat belonged to and a manhunt was launched. Joe the Boss, however, couldn't be found. With the heat still on, Frank Costello walked into a Bronx police precinct and told the sergeant on duty that Joe the Boss would give himself up for questioning if he had a guarantee that no one would manhandle him. The district attorney agreed, and the Mafia chief surrendered. He was questioned about the slayings and then released after he swore that he couldn't identify his assailants.

Throughout the Castellammarese War, Costello managed to be a non-combatant without appearing disloyal. He never shot at anyone, and no one ever shot at him. He argued that his real value to the organization depended on the fact that the outside world didn't know he belonged to the Mafia. In addition, his political contacts and money-making enterprises were needed. Joe the Boss, hard pressed for cash because of the war, agreed.

Costello disapproved of the war and had Luciano and Genovese as allies. They argued for peace, but their counsel fell on deaf ears. Following the assassination attempt, Joe the Boss was more determined than ever to bring the Castellammarese to their knees.

It was during this period that Costello built up the slot machine business with Dandy Phil Kastel and the bookmaking operation with Frank Erickson. He even took time out to buy into some legal handbooks at the track where gambling was officially permitted. He became the biggest name in the gambling rackets.

The slot machines proved especially lucrative. About five thousand had been placed around town: in speakeasies, candy stores, luncheonettes, durg stores, and other locations. In stores that attracted school children, the machines came equipped with wooden stairs so kids not tall enough to reach the handle could play just like the grown-ups.

It was a very lovely racket. Even if you use the low figure of ten dollars per day for the average gross of each machine, it meant that the combined daily gross for all the machines was fifty thousand dollars, and that came to better than eighteen million dollars a year. Most estimates double that figure. Not that it was all profit. There were very, very heavy expenses. Half the police department and all of Tammany Hall was on the payroll.

Lieutenant McLaughlin, who spent a good deal of his career tailing Costello, says that during the slot machine days he would walk five to seven miles a day just keeping up with Costello and Big Jim O'Connell. Costello was a walker and would walk all over town tending to his businesses. Big Jim, a huge, fleshy man about six-foot-two and weighing more than two hundred fifty pounds, had been the skipper of one of Costello's speedboats. McLaughlin thought he was Costello's bodyguard, but he really wasn't. His role was that of companion and buffer. To see Costello, you had to go through Big Jim.

By 1931, it became obvious that Joe the Boss was going to lose the Castellammarese War. The power had shifted. Joe the Boss had lost about fifty men in casualties since the war started, and there had been defections in the ranks.

Luciano and Genovese continued to urge him to make peace by reaching some sort of compromise with Maranzano. When Joe the Boss still refused, they began to plot against him. First they protected their flanks and took Costello and the other lieutenants in their confidence. They all agreed that Joe the Boss had to go.

Then they met secretly with Maranzano and obtained guarantees that there wouldn't be any purges once Joe the Boss was gone. Maranzano was reasonable. He said that he too wanted peace and guaranteed everyone's safety. Joe the Boss' death warrant was signed with a handshake.

After Joe the Boss had been buried with the proper respect, Maranzano called all the local Mafiosi to a meeting. He had a scholarly turn of mind, was reputed to be able to speak twelve languages, and was a serious student of the life and the campaigns of Julius Caesar. Joe Valachi, the Mafia informer, told a Senate subcommittee many years later: "Gee, he looked just like a banker. You'd never guess in a million years he was a racketeer." In Gay Talese's book, *Honor Thy Father*, the meeting Maranzano called is described as follows:

" . . . Maranzano presided at a meeting attended by 500 people in a hired hall in the Bronx and explained that the days of shooting were over and that a period of harmony was about to begin. He then presented them with his plan of reorganization, one loosely based on Caesar's military command — the individual gangs each would be commanded by a *capo,* or boss, under whom would be a *sottocapo,* underboss, and beneath the underboss would be *caporregimi,* lieutenants, who would supervise the squads of soldiers. Each unit would be known as a family and would operate within prescribed territorial areas. Over all the family bosses would be a *capo di tutti capi,* a boss of all bosses, and it would be this title that Maranzano bequeathed to himself."

Luciano, Genovese, and Costello immediately recognized that Maranzano was seeking to install himself as dictator of the Mafia. They concluded that with a "boss of all bosses" no one would be safe, least of all themselves, because their opposition to that kind of an organization was well known. Cautiously they began doing missionary work, sounding out other leaders to see how they felt. If it came to war again, they needed allies against the all-powerful Maranzano. Capone was consulted in Chicago; the leaders of many of the other families were sounded out. The heads of the Jewish gangs were told that Maranzano would seek to crush them once he had complete power. Even leaders of Maranzano's own group, men like Profaci, and Bonanno, secretly agreed that the boss was going power mad. A net of invisible silk was slowly being drawn.

The wily Maranzano sensed what was going on and decided the organization needed to be purged. He showed Joe Valachi, one of his most trusted soldiers, a list containing about sixty names of those slated for death and said: "We have to go to the mattress again. We have to get rid of these people."

Those on the list, so far as Valachi was able to recall when he testified, included Luciano, Genovese, Costello, Adonis, Capone, Vincent Mangano, and Dutch Schultz.

Meanwhile, Luciano and Genovese were preparing their own purge list which was headed by Maranzano. It also included all the Mustache Petes, the old-style Mafiosi across the nation who didn't fit in with the modern-world concept of the plotters. They were the expendables who could be counted on to hinder progress. The list was long and contained about forty names.

Luciano and Genovese arranged a meeting with Maranzano to discuss their differences. He agreed but insisted on protocol: if they wished a meeting, it must be held in his offices at 230 Park Avenue. They agreed and the meeting was set for September 10, at two o'clock.

Maranzano contracted for Vincent (Mad Dog) Coll, a notorious and deadly killer, to arrive at his office a little before the scheduled meeting. His purge was to begin. Luciano and Genovese made their own arrangement — they again reached out for Lansky and Siegel who provided four gunmen.

Perhaps thirty minutes before the appointed hour, four Jewish gangsters, led by an Italian to point out Maranzano, walked into the outer office and identified themselves as detectives. Maranzano invited them into his private office to straighten out any problems and then realized he had made a fatal error. He lunged for a gun kept in his desk, seeking to defend himself against his assassins. His move to defend himself, however, failed. He was shot four times and, like his hero Caesar, stabbed repeatedly in the abdoman. The four killers then fled, one of them, Sam (Red) Levine, pausing to warn Coll — about to walk into the offices to keep his appointment for murder — to "beat it, the cops are coming." Coll heeded the warning, prompted by professional courtesy, and also fled.

The others on the Luciano-Genovese purge list were executed in the next twenty-four hours. Across the nation an estimated forty Mustache Petes were slaughtered in what has become known as the Night of the Sicilian Vespers. It was all planned and executed by the young Luciano, not yet thirty-four, who showed a precocious talent for organization and a ruthlessness worthy of Machiavelli.

❖   ❖   ❖

Luciano, or Charley Lucky as he was called by everyone in the Mafia, was born November 24, 1897 in Lercara Friddi, Sicily. His baptisimal name was Salvatore Lucania, the middle child of five children born to his parents. The entire Lucania family emigrated to the United States in 1906, settling in a mixed neighborhood on East Tenth Street. His father, a carpenter, was well respected as a decent, hardworking man. While still in grammar school, Luciano changed his first name to Charles. He quit school in the fifth grade at the age of fourteen; then got a job in a hat factory at five dollars a week. One of the apocryphal stories attached to him is that he won $244 in a floating crap game at the time and promptly quit his job, saying: "I never was a crumb, and if I have to be a crumb I'd rather be dead."

In his later teens and early twenties, he worked for an assortment of hoods on the Lower East Side and in Little Italy. It was at this time that he began using the last name of Luciano. He also became friendly with Vito Genovese, and the pair became inseparable. Genovese was just three days older than Luciano, and they celebrated their birthdays together for years.

Luciano was arrested in 1916 and charged with possession and selling of two ounces of heroin. He pleaded "guilty" but managed to squirm out of a stiff sentence by offering to supply the Government with information about other drug dealers. The sentence he received was just a light pat, six-months. A probation report at the time noted that he had acquired "a definitely criminalistic pattern of conduct."

He was arrested again in 1921 for possession of a gun; in 1926 for narcotics; in 1927 for gambling and violation of the prohibition law; in 1928 for assult and robbery; in 1929 for grand larceny; in 1930 for running an illegal gambling game. All these charges were dismissed.

A gangland story says that he earned the name "Lucky" when he was taken for a ride out to Staten Island by a rival gang in 1929. He was tortured for hours, nearly fatally beaten, and then abandoned to die on a beach. Miraculously he survived, but he carried vivid scars on his face and a drooping right eye as a result of that encounter.

Since it is highly unusual for mobsters to be so clumsy and to allow a ride victim to live to tell the tale, another theory contends that Lucky was grabbed by some narcotics cops seeking to make him become an informer again. This time he refused, stoically accepted their persuasive methods, and was then dumped.

Frank Costello added still another twist to the story of how Luciano came to be called Lucky. Luciano just gave himself the name Lucky, Costello confided to a friend, and pushed it and pushed it until everyone began to accept it. He said Luciano even made up the stories about his fabulous winnings at dice and cards because he wanted to be known as a lucky guy. "He felt that people are attracted to a guy when he's lucky. Everyone wants to be with a winner."

Luciano and Genovese began working for Joe the Boss in the early twenties. By the end of the decade, they were number one and number two in Joe the Boss' gang and powers in their own right.

As a young hood, Luciano was wild and unpredictable, but as he became older and more experienced he calmed down and showed that he had both talent and shrewdness. Costello felt he had a lot to do with the seasoning of Luciano. They became quite close in the early thirties, and Luciano moved into a sumptious suite at the Waldorf-Astoria because he knew it was Costello's hangout.

He was slim, middle-sized with a round face, a full head of dark hair, and dark, brooding eyes. On his right arm he had a tattoo that said "Lucky." He looked like a movie gangster and many of the early bad-guy films always had a lead that looked like him. Whether it was art imitating life or life imitating art is anyone's guess. He wore silk shirts and underwear and custom-made suits, and when he traveled, a sleek, fast car equipped with bullet-proof glass was always at his disposal.

Following the successful elimination of Maranzano and the Mustache Petes, Luciano clearly became the most powerful man in the Mafia. Despite the temptations of the situation, he moved with extreme caution so as not to make any of his predecessors' mistakes. With Costello and Genovese as advisors, he eliminated the title "boss of bosses" and established the family system and national commission as we know it today.

There were twenty-four separate Mafia families in the nation, and each one selected a capo or boss. The capo of each group — whether he represented five hundred Mafiosi in New York City or a dozen in Tucson, Arizona — was to have the same rights and power. Every capo was to serve on the national commission which would consist of nine members serving on a rotating basis. The commission was given the authority to adjudicate territorial disputes between families, punish capos who stepped out of line, and generally keep the peace. A capo guilty of a serious breach of the rules was not to be killed without the commission's approval.

In New York City, with its great population and great potential for profits, five families were established. Luciano became the head of Joe the Boss' old family. The other dons selected were Joseph Bonanno, Joseph Profaci, Vincent Mangano, and Gaetano Gagliano. While Luciano was just one don among twenty-four throughout the country, the reality of the situation made him much more powerful. His prestige was such that he became a "first among equals."

The problem of whether to open the organization to non-Italian gangsters was also settled. The overwhelming majority of the dons felt that the Mafia would lose some of its mystique and cohesiveness if other nationalities were allowed to join. Luciano, mindful of his great debt to Lansky and some of the others, recommended that the organization cooperate closely with the other ethnic groups. Everyone agreed.

✿   ✿   ✿

With peace restored, the men of the Mafia again devoted all their energies to the business of making money, but the lush, free-wheeling days of the twenties were over. The stock market crashed in 1929 and the nation plunged into a deep depression. Franklin Delano Roosevelt was a cinch to be the next President, and Prohibition would soon be a thing of the past. (It officially died in December of 1933 when the Twenty-first Amendment was passed, making it legal to drink again.) A wave of reform swept New York, bringing on the Seabury Investigation in which much of the fabric covering the thievery and corruption in the city was ripped to shreds. Mayor Jimmy Walker, the city's dapper "Beau James," was himself implicated in the mess and, after a stint on the witness stand, resigned and fled to Europe.

Then, in 1933, an unlikely looking knight in shining armor rode the white horse of reform into New York's City Hall. He was Fiorello LaGuardia, a five-foot-two, comical-looking, fat man with a high-pitched, squeaky voice that made him sound as if he had just been goosed. At midnight, on December 31, 1933, he was sworn in as mayor. A few minutes later he picked up the phone and ordered the arrest of Lucky Luciano on whatever charge the police department could dream up.

LaGuardia went after the gamblers with a vengeance, saying over the radio: "Let's drive the bums out of town." He was talking about Erickson and Costello. Police were told to harass them in every way possible.

Lieutenant Rudolph McLaughlin remembers receiving orders to flush them out of their Waldorf-Astoria hangout. He began by politely asking them not to come into the hotel. He didn't have a legal reason, but orders were orders, and he did what he was told.

"First I asked them nicely," McLaughlin said. "It worked with Erickson because after that first request he stayed away. Costello, though, was another story. He continued to show up every day. I'd say to him, 'look, you know my orders. You've got to stop coming here.' He'd just look at me and say calmly, 'I won't be here tomorrow.' This went on for quite a while. Every day he'd say that he wouldn't be there tomorrow, and I'd check and he'd be there. Finally I lost my patience and said, 'Look you guinea bastard, next time I'm goina punch you in the mouth. I told you to stay out of here.' He didn't blink an eye. After all, I was just a kid then, and he was a big shot. He just looked at me the same way and said he wouldn't be there tomorrow. He never did stop coming."

LaGuardia was doing a lot more than just causing a young cop to speak to Costello in a disrespectful manner; he was ruining the slot machine business. He ordered the police to pick up the slots in wholesale lots, and then, while wearing a ten-gallon hat, joyously went about smashing them personally with a fireman's axe while photographers clicked away.

During the Walker administration, protests by citizens dismayed at the presence of slot machines near schools had forced some action, and a few machines were seized. One of Costello's lawyers promptly went into court and convinced Supreme Court Justice Selah B. Strong that the machines were merely for the purpose of vending mints. He issued an injunction forbidding the police from seizing the machines. This wasn't the first time Justice Strong did the mob a favor. In 1920, incredible as it sounds, he signed a permit making it legal for Joe the Boss to carry a gun.

LaGuardia simply ignored the injunction and proceeded to order the slot machines to be seized anyway. Costello was very upset at the thought of the mayor breaking the law. To his dying day he never forgave the "Little Flower," as he was called by the newspapers, for breaking the rules of the game.

Not that LaGuardia was quite as holy as his many admirers made him out to be. During the entire twelve years he was in office, from 1933 to 1945, a Costello-owned crap game was in operation daily in LaGuardia's own political club, the Horace Harding Republican Club on Lexington Avenue, in Harlem. The game was never touched because it was under the protection of Harlem Congressman Vito Marcantonio, LaGuardia's political protege. Marcantonio was owned lock, stock, and barrel by Mafia underboss Thomas Lucchese.

Here is what a former police inspector, now retired, had to say about the situation: "Every cop in town knew about the crap games that went on there, and they also knew enough to stay away. That was Marcantonio territory."

❊   ❊   ❊

With his slot machine business in shambles and LaGuardia causing him all sorts of problems in other areas, Costello decided to start living the life of a gentlemen of means. He had all the money he needed and a great deal of patience. New York would open up again. It always had, and it always would.

He joined the swank Lakeville Country Club in Great Neck, Long Island. Members of the club included highly successful businessmen, city officials, judges, politicians, and a few celebrities. Comedian Eddie Cantor was a member.

Among his constant golfing companions were Frank Kelly, the Democratic leader of Brooklyn; George Morton Levy, then a well-known trial lawyer and now head of Roosevelt Raceway; and Supreme Court Justice Edward Reigelman. Frank Erickson would also join him for a round on the links quite often.

Costello cheerfully told members he became friendly with that he was a retired bootlegger. No one thought the less of him for it. On the contrary, everyone was fascinated with his stories of how he managed to smuggle the liquor in.

He didn't shoot golf very well at first, chalking up scores of 115 or 120 for an eighteen-hole round, but after four or five years of determined effort on his part he brought his score down to the respectable nineties.

"He was easily the most popular man in the club," an old member recalled. "He was meticulously honest in golf. He always bet on the game he would play, but no one ever worried about Costello improving his lie or moving the ball or forgetting a stroke on his score. So far as his golf ethics were concerned, he was as honest as a minister's son is supposed to be.

"In the afternoon he would play klobiosch (A Hungarian card game which roughly is a combination of bridge, pinochle, and gin rummy. Card players consider it one of the most intricate and difficult games to play well.) and bet anywhere from one hundred dollars to five hundred dollars a game. He was a pretty good klobiosch player. Other times he would go to the track. The wives of all the members just loved to go with him because when they went along they would always win. They used to fight among themselves over whose turn it was to go to the track with Costello.

"Another thing about him that everyone liked was that when he said something it would be done. His word was his bond. He was a quiet, reserved fellow. He wasn't a blabbermouth and always conducted himself like a gentleman. One time curiousity got the better of me, and I asked him, 'What the hell are you doing around here all the time? Don't you work?' He answered, 'I don't have to work. I'm retired.' Another time I hustled him for a contribution to a charity I was collecting for. He just reached into his pants pocket and pulled out five hundred dollars in cash. Just like that.

"He wasn't very well educated. You could tell that quick enough by the way he talked, but he had an opinion on everything and a lot of pride. From his point of view, you could tell that he thought he would have made a good president, a governor, a mayor, you name it. I remember one time he became involved in a discussion of courtroom tactics with the lawyer George Morton Levy. He wanted to know whether Levy thought someone accused of a crime is better off going on the stand or not. Levy offered the opinion that someone accused of a crime really doesn't stand much of a chance of winning unless he takes the stand. Costello disagreed vehemently, saying something to the effect that if someone with a bad reputation takes the stand, he doesn't stand a chance."

No one at the Lakeville Country Club had any idea that their most popular member was in the rackets, according to the old club member.

"The first hint of it," he said, "was in 1943 when his name appeared in headlines in all the papers. It had to do with the Aurellio case, and the stories said that he was a big power in Tammany Hall and was able to name judges to the bench. I asked him about it, and his answer was, 'Isn't that ridiculous.' "

✿ ✿ ✿

In 1933, Costello began to have trouble with his throat. He was an extremely heavy smoker and went through two to three packs of English Oval cigarettes a day. He began to suffer from chronic sore throats and noticed that the character of his voice had begun to change. It had developed a huskey quality that never seemed to go away. After ignoring the symptoms for a time, he finally decided to visit a throat specialist.

The throat specialist, according to prison health records, diagnosed his problem as a malignancy and treated it with radiation. As a result, his left vocal cord was paralyzed, leaving him for the rest of his life with a raspy voice that he couldn't get much above a loud whisper. Nevertheless, he continued to smoke forty to sixty English Ovals every day.

In regard to his voice, the distinctive sound of which became famous during the televised 1951 Kefauver Committee hearings, Costello told writer Peter Maas that its roughness was not caused by cancer. His explanation was that polyps had formed on his vocal cords and that they were scorched when a doctor burned them off.

"I went with the wrong doctor," he told Maas.

Why there should be a discrepancy between his explanation and what the medical records show is unknown. Perhaps Costello had his original medical records altered to back up the story he gave of being sick when he walked out of the Kefauver Committee hearing room.

While Costello was playing golf with businessmen, judges, lawyers, and cronies, a series of incidents occurred in the underworld that changed the lineup of mob leadership. It all began in 1935 when Dutch Schultz made vocal death threats against Special Prosecutor Thomas E. Dewey who was vigorously hounding him.

Schultz proclaimed loudly to friends that "Dewey's gotta go," or "We gotta knock off Dewey."

The Dutchman was, at that time, the policy king of Harlem; the proprietor of a twenty million dollar a year racket that was the envy of everyone. Virtually the entire black community played the numbers every day. It was a nickel and dime game based on a complicated system involving the parimutuels at the track. It worked this way: a player placed a wager on three numbers of his choice from zero to nine. The winning number was arrived at by taking the last numbers of the total parimutuel handle at the track. Although the odds against hitting the right number were one thousand to one, the payoff was only five hundred to one. It was a goldmine for Schultz and to this day policy is still the most popular form of gambling in the black ghettos.

Schultz's threats stirred up a storm as noted in *Kill the Dutchman!*, the book on the mobster written by *New York Post* Executive Editor Paul Sann.

"Apart from his legal difficulties with the Federal Government," Sann wrote, "the Dutchman was at that moment out of favor with the more formidable shooting mobs. In his time of travail, he had turned into something of a wild man, sending shivers down the collective back of the underworld by openly announcing he was going to kill Thomas E. Dewey, recently named by the Democratic Governor, Herbert H.

Lehman, to supersede the policy mob's own handpicked District Attorney, William Copeland Dodge, and to do something about the city's
rampant crime."

Schultz was a crazy, unpredictable Neanderthal-type, and the mob
leaders didn't take his threats lightly. If Dewey was assassinated,
they knew that it would bring down on their heads every man the
Federal, state, and city law enforcement agencies could muster. Killing
Dewey would be a disaster for everyone.

With this in mind, plus the obvious fact that when Schultz was
gone his lucrative racket would be up for grabs, Luciano met with
the other top gang leaders in the city, and a contract was put out for
the Dutchman's hide. The contract was fulfilled on October 23, 1935
when two gunmen walked into the Palace Chop House and Tavern
(just across the Hudson in Newark, New Jersey) and fatally wounded
Schultz and his two bodyguards. The Dutchman lingered long enough
to babble incoherently — with a police stenographer at his hospital
bedside — a stream of subconscious thoughts dealing with the threads
of his violent life. He then died.

A second incident of importance occurred in 1936 when Special
Prosecutor Dewey arrested Luciano on compulsory prostitution charges
and then held a press conference in which he called him "the most
dangerous and important racketeer in New York, if not in the country." In those days prosecutors didn't worry too much about prejudicing
the community from which the jury was to be drawn.

Luciano was defended by George Morton Levy who stepped into the
case — on the recommendation of Costello — at the last minute when
ill health forced Luciano's original trial lawyer to withdraw. Moe Polakoff, who had been Luciano's lawyer for several years, didn't try the
case because it was decided that the notorious mobster would stand a
better chance of acquittal if he were defended by someone who didn't
have such a Jewish-sounding name. The anti-Semitic theory that gangsters were being saved by smart Jew-boy lawyers was a popular thirties
theme.

The trial of Luciano was one of the spectacles of its time and the
vehicle which Dewey used to parlay his image of the "racket buster"
into the Governor's chair of the State of New York and very nearly
the Presidency of the United States.

Levy and Polakoff to this day feel that — while Luciano may have
been guilty of many things, including murder and dealing in heroin —
the trial was a travesty of justice. Dewey, they've told friends, was
guilty of subordination of witnesses, inflaming public opinion against
Luciano, and rigging the trial in such a way that the defendant didn't
stand a chance.

When Dewey's trial was discussed with Manhattan District Attorney Frank Hogan recently, once one of Dewey's top aides, he was asked what he thought about the trial.

"I sort of doubt that Luciano could be convicted today," he admitted.

Dewey's star witnesses included a string of broken-down whores who were drug addicts. They were held as material witnesses for quite a while, and by the time the trial rolled around, they would have sworn to anything for a fix. They went by the nicknames of Cokey Flo, Gashouse Lil, and Jenny the Factory. On the witness stand they testified that Luciano had forced them into prostitution and collected money from them.

Luciano, at the time they implicated him, was one of the biggest names in the rackets and a millionaire. One's credulity must be strained to believe that at that stage of his life he would have been involved with the likes of the prosecution's witnesses. The jury, nevertheless, bought Dewey's case, and Luciano received the unheard of sentence (for the charge on which he was tried) of thirty to fifty years.

The next incident occurred after Luciano's conviction when Dewey announced that Vito Genovese was his next target, saying: "Genovese is an associate of Lucky Luciano. He is getting ready to take over all the rackets."

In the case of Genovese, an unemotional killer, Dewey had assembled a case of substance. He had a mob informer who fingered Genovese as the one who had ordered the rubout of Ferdinand (the Shadow) Boccia in order to keep all the profits of a gambling score they had made together. Genovese, who was as cunning a Mafia leader as ever lived, observed what Dewey was able to do with the compulsory prostitution charges against Luciano and promptly fled the country, returning to the land of his birth. Years later he bragged to Valachi that when he fled he carried a suitcase with him containing $750,000 in cash.

The flight of Genovese in 1937 created a power vacuum in what had been regarded as the most powerful of New York's five families. Luciano surveyed the situation from his prison cell and ordered Frank Costello to take over as acting boss. He made it clear that he would still continue to have a hand in the decisions, but that until he got out, Costello would be his representative.

In this manner and in this way Frank Costello, who believed almost all things could be worked out peacefully and had dreams of respectability, became the most powerful figure in the Mafia. The capo of the Luciano family.

New Orleans

"Who gave Louisiana to Frank Costello?"

Crazy Joe Gallo (From a taped conversation.)

In 1935, Frank Costello had about one million dollars worth of slot machines gathering dust in storage. LaGuardia's crusade had forced the slots out of the city, and those that weren't confiscated had been shipped to New Jersey warehouses to save them from the axe.

For the slot machine king, it was a little like owning a gold mine and then being forbidden to dig. Yet there was little Costello could do as long as LaGuardia was mayor except hope and wait for a miracle. The Little Flower just wouldn't listen to reason.

The miracle arrived in the form of flamboyant Southern demagogue who extended the traditional hospitality of his region by saying, in effect: "Y'all come on down."

* * *

Huey Pierce Long, one of the most colorful and dangerous men ever to appear on the American political scene, extended the invitation. The Kingfish, as he was called by the faithful, was the virtual dictator of the State of Louisiana. He controlled it to a degree which had never been seen in America before. His word was law.

The Kingfish was elected governor in 1928. He then decided to extend his powers beyond his state and, before completing his term as governor had himself elected to the United States Senate. When he

97

invited Costello and his slot machines to New Orleans, he continued to rule Louisiana through handpicked stooges who filled every state office from the governor's chair on down.

Long rode to power posing as a populist who proclaimed that his mission in life was to distribute America's wealth more equitably. His favorite target was the Wall Street plutocrats whom he accused of living off the fat of the land. It was all something he had read in a book somewhere, and the heart of his proposals was to limit income to one million dollars a year. He was shrewd, had a talent for political mischief, and was the owner of a tireless voice box that mesmerized the unsophisticated. While he was Governor, a group of investors built a badly-needed toll bridge across Lake Ponchatrain. Long promptly had a free bridge built right alongside. The simple folk of the bayous loved him for it.

Huey Long possessed a sense of humor, homespun in character, that often prompted him to irresponsible actions. When he was drinking — which was often — he lost all control and was capable of most anything. During the early thirties while attending a party at an exclusive country club in Sands Point, Long Island, he wandered into the men's room to find the urinal being used by someone else. Long took careful aim between the other fellow's legs and let fly. He missed. The man on the receiving end of his stream beat him bloody.

Long's ambition was to become America's first dictator. He planned to take over the nation the same way he had taken over Louisiana — by gaining control of the key political machinery and police — and would harangue intimates for hours with the details of his plans. He wasn't kidding.

There are several stories of why he invited Costello to New Orleans.

1. Besides being a boozer, Long was also an insatiable womanizer. During his senate years in Washington, he often would come to New York for fun and games. He became involved with a prostitute who was tied in with mobsters, and she arranged for a few candid photographs to be snapped while they were in bed. Blackmail followed. Long then went to Costello who was able to have the photos destroyed. A grateful Long then invited him to install his slot machines in New Orleans.

2. Many years after the fact, New Orleans politician Peter Hand gave a different story when, before the New Orleans Metropolitan Crime Commission, he voluntarily told all he knew about the Frank Costello — Dandy Phil Kastel slot machine racket. He said he got his version right from Kastel himself.

"They originally came down to Louisiana from New York through Huey Long," Hand told the commission. "One time Huey went up to

New York, and poor Huey was a coward, and he went into the powder room of one of those clubs, I think it was Long Island somewhere, and somebody punched him in the mouth, and Costello, that is one of Costello's friends, saved him from getting a beating, and he became very, very friendly with Costello, more so than Kastel . . . anyway they made a deal with Huey to run some slot machines here . . . "

3. Long, always on the lookout for new sources of graft, decided slot machines would be lucrative. In his characteristic fashion, he sought out the biggest and best slot machine operator in the country and that, of course, led him to Costello.

4. In 1951, Costello testified before the Kefauver Committee that Long invited the slot machines in because he thought it would be a good way to raise money for charity. He said that he met with Long in a hotel in midtown New York and agreed to pay forty thousand dollars a year to charity for being allowed to run slot machines in New Orleans. Long, Costello insisted, promised also to have a law passed in the state legislature making slot machines legal.

❊   ❊   ❊

In the spring of 1935, about one thousand slots were installed throughout the New Orleans business district. From the very beginning, it was Dandy Phil's operation, with Costello making the key decisions from New York. Kastel moved to New Orleans and took with him Frank's brothers-in-law, the Geigerman boys, Dudley, William, Harold, and Jerome. The Geigermans were the collectors, and every nickel that was dropped in the slots went through their hands.

The slots, according to Peter Hand, were a smash hit in New Orleans:

"It knocked a hole in all the other kinds of gambling because the people went wild over the slot machines," he said. "Put a nickel in, and the nickels come out; put a quarter in, and the quarters come out. We haven't seen that in forty years around here."

The Costello-Kastel syndicate formed the Pelican Novelty Company as an umbrella for the slot machine racket. It was incorporated under a charter which earmarked part of its profits for charity, enabling the company to receive special dispensations under Louisiana law. Kastel headed the corporation and Jake Lansky, Meyer Lansky's brother, was one of the officers. Costello's name was nowhere to be seen. His share of the take was funneled through Jake.

Under the all-embracing protection of the Kingfish, the slot machines were able to operate with a minimum of payoffs to the locals. Each month, according to Hand, twenty thousand dollars was left for Long in a tin box in New Orleans' Roosevelt Hotel. The Roosevelt was operated by Seymour Weiss, a transplanted New York bootlegger who had ties to Costello dating from the twenties. He was Long's bagman in New Orleans and, naturally, also got a piece of the action. During that first year of business, the slot machines reaped a profit, after all expenses, of eight hundred thousand dollars. Of this amount six hundred dollars was distributed to charity.

On September 8, 1935, though things suddenly became more complicated for the operation, the Kingfish was walking through the corriders of the Louisiana House of Representatives in Baton Rouge when Dr. Carl Austin Weiss, a brooding, intense, young physician who was a brilliant throat specialist in Louisiana's capital city, decided he had to do something about Long's dictatorial ambitions. He managed to slip by the Kingfish's bodyguards and was able to shoot Long once in the stomach before he was overpowered and thrown to the marble floor of the then new building. A total of sixty-one bullets were pumped into Weiss' body by the bodyguards, many of them members of the state police. On September 10, Long died from the effects of the single, small caliber bullet. One of the last things he said was: "God, don't let me die. I have so much to do." He was forty-two.

With the Kingfish dead, it was a whole new ball game for the Pelican Novelty Company. A new group of officials had to be paid off. Huey Long's political heirs and everyone else who had the power to effect the operation had to be put on the payroll. Kastel, under Costello's direction, began by calling in three of the most powerful local politicians, Freddie Rickerfor, Tom Hill, and Peter Hand. Rickerfor, who had the most muscle, was given twenty per cent of the operation and Hill and Hand ten per cent each. In return, they were responsible for seeing to it that a crusading district attorney or honest police chief didn't upset things.

Hand made the deal with Kastel for himself and Hill. This is his story of the negotiations: "Now here's what Kastel told me when I made the deal with him for me and Hill in the Roosevelt. I went down to see him, and foolish me like I was, he wanted to give me twenty per cent between us, I told him we wanted forty per cent. I didn't know the strength of the machine to tell you the truth. I thought I was talking to a baby but I found out I was talking to a very smart fellow. He told me, he said, 'You can forget about it because if you think I'm going to work for you and Tom Hill, just leave the room. That's your deal and that's that. I got to take care of the police, city hall, and everybody . . . ' "

Hand agreed to the terms and said that Kastel handled the payoffs to the city officials personally. The mayor's commissioners, he said, got five hundred dollars a month; the superintendent of police one thousand. Hand's ten per cent of the net earned him thirty-five

hundred dollars every month. If he was given a fair shake, this meant
that the Costello-Kastel-Lansky combine earned twenty-one thousand
dollars a month from the sixty per cent they retained.

The combine also took care of Carlos Marcello, the local Mafia
chief who controlled the Algiers section of the city, located on the
West bank of the Mississippi. Marcello was supplied two hundred
fifty free slots to distribute in his area. He kept two-thirds of the take
and turned in one-third. In return, Marcello kept the other racketeers
in line.

❊   ❊   ❊

The New Orleans officials went on the pad with a minimum of
difficulty. It was never a question of would they or wouldn't they. It
was always a question of how much. The old principle that a buck
opens all doors worked in the "Cicero of the South," as the city has
often been called. The soil of New Orleans had been conditioned to
corruption and flagrant, flamboyant, wide-open illegal activity throughout its history. In the late 1860s, Governor Warmouth, a Northerner
who had been sent South by the Federal Government, told a reporter
from the Chicago Tribune who had asked about corruption that certainly he was corrupt, that everybody was corrupt down there. Significantly, in the 1890s New Orleans was one of the first cities to
develop its own branch of the Unione Siciliano. Wide-open gambling
and prostitution was as much a part of its heritage as the Battle of
New Orleans and creole cooking.

The first slots the Costello-Kastel syndicate installed were called
"chiefs." They made no pretense of being anything other than a gambling device. The operation continued smoothly, even after Long's
assassination, until the same trouble as they had had in New York
cropped up. Citizen complaints became so heavy that the police were
forced to act. Slots were seized. The entire operation, despite the
payoffs, was thrown into jeopardy.

Costello found the solution to the problem by borrowing from the
past. The Louisiana Mint Company was formed, and the slots were
converted to throw out mint candy. Then a test case was hurried
through the courts so that the Louisiana Supreme Court could rule
whether the slots were candy vending machines or gambling devices.
A favorable decision was assured by buying four Louisiana Supreme
Court Judges, and the slots became legal for a time.

The slots continued to prosper in New Orleans well into the forties.
In 1944, Costello declared on his income tax that he had earned
$71,346.46 from the operation. In 1945, he listed his earnings as

$62,087.64. This, of course, was only what he was willing to tell the Government. The Government, on the other hand, in a future income tax trial estimated his take at more — much more.

Dandy Phil, meanwhile, extended the operation until there were sixteen hundred slot machines on the streets. Subsidiary corporations, the Crescent Music Corporation and the One-Stop Coin Machine Company, were formed for the operation of juke boxes and vending machines. Mrs. Loretta Costello was a partner in the juke boxes, and in 1944 her share of the profits was $15,864.36. Carlos Marcello was a partner in the vending machines.

Dandy Phil ran the New Orleans operation, but Frank Costello was the boss. They conferred almost daily by telephone. Costello, according to wire taps, set the price to be paid for new slot machines, solved the problems that arose, planned the strategy, and kept a careful watch on the volume of business. Several times a year he would fly down and confer with everyone connected with the organization in the manner of a chairman of the board tightening up the corporate ship.

"Frank was fond of telling the story of what he said was the only act of violence in his life," a friend recalled. "One of their key people in New Orleans was discovered stealing money, and Kastel checked with Frank to ask him what they should do about it. Frank told him to do nothing because he was coming down soon and said he'd handle it himself. When he arrived, a meeting was arranged so he could address the entire organization. They had to hire a hall because a lot of people worked for them, and Frank stood in back of an old wooden podium like they have in schools in assemblies, and this particular fellow had been singled out. I'm a little vague on what excuses was used to have him come up to the podium. But some excuse was used, and Frank had a monkey wrench underneath the podium and took it out and hit him over the head with it in front of everyone. Then he explained to his audience that the man was stealing money and said that this was meant for a lesson for anyone else who was thinking of doing the same thing.

"The way Frank looked at the violence was that it was business rather than physical because it was a way of preventing theft and future harm from all the other guys in the room. He used to say that this was the only act of violence he ever committed in his entire life, and he didn't like it but felt it was necessary."

✻   ✻   ✻

Dandy Phil Kastel was born on Henry Street, the heart of New York's Lower East Side, in 1886. He grew up with many of the East

Side gangsters of his generation, but he didn't have a stomach for violence and was on the periphery of the mob rather than a part of it. He was the classic con man: he made a good front and had a conniving mind. He was quiet, soft spoken, suave, debonaire, and wore expensive clothes that he chose with taste and care. He looked like he had just concluded a deal to buy the Bank of England. During the twenties, especially, he was a sight to see along Broadway, a little man dressed to the hilt with a gold mounted walking stick and pearl gray spats.

Despite his front, Dandy Phil had a taste for the high life. He liked gaudy cabarets, the really expensive restaurants, chorus girls, and the racetrack. He was constantly in the company of touts and would compulsively bet large sums of money on a tip from even a janitor.

During World War I, he ran a nightclub in Montreal. Then he returned to New York where he ran an extortion racket which resulted in his first arrest. The charges were dismissed. He then went to work for Arnold Rothstein and ran a series of bucket shops (storefront and telephone operations that sold phony securities). His specialty was swindling chorus girls, and in 1922, a Miss Betty Brown accused him of swindling her out of eleven thousand dollars. Again the charges were dismissed.

His method of operation was rather crude but effective in those free and easy times. As a stockbroker he would purchase stock for a customer, send confirmation for the purchase, say he was holding the stock certificates for safekeeping, and then sell the stocks and pocket the money. He was held as the man chiefly responsible for causing Dillon and Company, a brokerage house, to go into bankruptcy with an estimated loss to its customers of more than six hundred thousand dollars. He was arrested on mail fraud charges in connection with the bankruptcy and convicted and sentenced — after three trials — to serve three years in jail. He was released just in time to go to work for Costello, and he played an important part in the New York phase of the slot machine racket.

Dandy Phil's talents were given the opportunity to flower in New Orleans. He was a gifted organizer and corrupter, and much of the credit for the success of the New Orleans operation belongs to him. He was well liked and accepted by the people there, and while his marriage to a New Orleans prostitute named Margie Dennis lifted a few eyebrows, he continued to be accepted in polite company.

"Phil Kastel was a very quiet and, I will say, a refined man," said a retired New Orleans Criminal Court Judge who knew him well. He wasn't flamboyant. He was a neat man. He wasn't a handsome man because he had a flat face, dark complexion, and a cast in one eye, but he was a highly intelligent man. He was a good business man. From what I knew of him, if he had gone into legitimate business, the restaurant business, he could have had one of the finest restaurants in the United States. You just had to see how he ran the Beverly Club to know that.

"He was liked, generally liked. He wasn't pushy or anything like that. None of those fellows, the Geigermans, were pushy. They were all liked. They were all quiet. Let's face it, they came down here to make friends, and they made them."

*   *   *

One of the friends the Costello-Kastel syndicate made in New Orleans was the rich and politically influential William Helis, a self-made millionaire businessman who was dubbed the "Golden Greek." Helis had a pipeline directly to the White House through his "dear" friend Major General Harry Vaughn, one of President Harry Truman's chief aides. During the Truman Administration, Vaughn got in trouble over charges of "influence peddling."

In order to understand the chain of events that tied Vaughn to Costello and Kastel, it is necessary to go back to New York in 1933, just after prohibition had ended. At that time a former bootlegger named Irving Haim formed Alliance Distributors, a liquor wholesale house. Haim obtained the exclusive right to distribute House of Lords and Kings Ransom scotch whiskey, manufactured by the eminently respectable Whitley Company, an old English firm.

Haim's agent for the sale of these popular brands was none other than Dandy Phil Kastel who earned a commission or override on each case imported into the United States. His commissions averaged thirty-five thousand dollars a month. Since wherever Dandy Phil was, Frank Costello was sure to be close behind, there is little doubt that Costello also had a piece of Alliance. In fact, during the mid-thirties, Costello was frequently seen in Alliance's midtown New York offices and, on occasion, represented himself as general sales manager for the firm when he filled out insurance questionnaires and bank reference forms.

Costello was introduced to William Helis by New Orleans Mayor Robert S. Maestri. They became good friends. So good, in fact, that Helis guaranteed a $325,000 note as a downpayment for the purchase of the Whitley Company by Alliance. The note was also signed by Haim with Costello and Kastel endorsing it.

The deal was close to consummation when word leaked out that the man really behind the purchase of the old distillery was the ex-bootlegger Frank Costello. Several Whitley stockholders raised a furor, and it was publicly announced that the sale had been cancelled. Whether it really was or not is open to question.

General Vaughn was dragged into the complicated picture during a 1949 Senate subcommittee hearing when Wisconsin Senator Joe McCarthy charged that the General had used his White House influence to obtain an extra supply of grain — during a time when grain was in short supply — for the Whitley Company. McCarthy said that he had learned that Whitley was really owned by Helis, Costello, and Haim.

All three denied the allegation.

❈ ❈ ❈

The Internal Revenue Service went after Costello for the first time in 1939 when he and Dandy Phil were arrested and charged with a criminal attempt to evade income taxes. The indictment charged that the slot machine kings made a profit of $2,392,575 in nickels and quarters from 1935 to 1937, and that they had shortchanged the Government of $529,465 in income taxes.

They went on trial in United States District Court in New Orleans in May of 1940. But the Government had a weak case, and the jury returned a verdict of "not guilty."

❈ ❈ ❈

Things then ran smoothly for the next couple of years. There were periodic crackdowns on the slot machines but that just meant some official or politician wanted to be put on the payroll. A little grease and everything returned to normal. The nickels and quarters continued to roll in.

The inevitable happened when the spirit of reform came to New Orleans with the election of Mayor Delesseps S. Morrison in 1946. One of his campaign promises was to cleanup the city and drive the racketeers out. When he captured the Mayor's office he proceeded to do just that. The police were ordered to seize the slot machines, and Dandy Phil had to stick them in a warehouse. The syndicate fought Morrison in the courts, but the old Louisiana Supreme Court ruling was overturned, and they lost. The candy mint dispensers were decleared unmistakable gambling devices.

For the cynical, the reform movement of Mayor Morrison is not without its satisfactions. When he was elected, the good-citizen element in New Orleans enthusiatically proclaimed the dawn of a new era in the city that had become one of the symbols for political corruption in the United States. They really thought that city hall was at last being run by an honest, incorruptible man.

"I was one of those who believed in Shep Morrison's integrity," confessed Aaron Kohn, a former member of the FBI, who then headed and now continues to head the Metropolitan Crime Commission. "I found out I was mistaken. He kicked out one group of racketeers to bring in his own group."

(The commission, which has no tie with government, is wholly supported by New Orleans businessmen who are limited to a two hundred fifty dollar contribution. It acts as a watchdog and deserves the major credit for changing New Orleans into a city where corruption is now minimal.)

The end of the slot machine racket, however, did not mean the end of the Costello-Kastel New Orleans operation. When New Orleans Parish was closed to them, they cast their eyes on adjoining Jefferson Parish where Morrison was powerless. Jefferson Parish was ruled politically by Sheriff Frank (King) Clancy who allowed a number of selected gambling houses to conduct business. It was strictly a local operation, and no one seemed to care that King Clancy was making a buck allowing a few casinos to function.

Costello and Kastel scouted the parish and decided to open a class nightclub-gambling casino that would feature top Broadway entertainment, really good food, and a plush gambling room. They even decided upon the name and location. It was to be called the Beverly Club and was to be situated just over the New Orleans Parish line so that it could be reached with a minimum of inconvenience. In anticipation of obtaining permission to operate, they purchased the old Suburban Gardens nightclub from New Orleans' top bookmaker, Joe Brown, for fifty-seven thousand dollars.

Freddie Rickerfor, who had helped in the slot machine racket and was the collector of campaign funds for state-wide candidates, was called into the deal as the "fixer." He was offered twenty-five per cent of the Beverly if he could make satisfactory arrangements with King Clancy.

"Clancy was already a rich man and had a good thing going when he was approached by Rickerfor," explained Aaron Kohn who has thoroughly investigated how the Beverly came into existance. "He was now confronted with a serious, amoral question: do I let these outside racketeers come in with the danger of a future nationwide spotlight on our activities and thereby risk the geese laying my golden eggs?"

"Hell, no," was Clancy's answer to Rickerfor.

Rickerfor knew where to apply the screws. He traveled to Baton Rouge and conferred with Governor Jimmy Davis. The governor agreed

to use his persuasive powers for a sizable, monthly stipend. He then
sent a message to Sheriff Clancy which supposedly said, "If the Beverly
doesn't open, I'll close everything down."

Clancy bowed to the Governor's persuasive rhetoric.

The Beverly was owned by Costello, Meyer Lansky, Kastel, and
Rickerfor. Kastel was the club's president, and Costello was on the
books for seventeen thousand dollars a year as a talent recruiter. (That,
of course, was just for the income tax people.) Local Mafia chief Carlos
Marcello was later sold seventeen per cent for forty-five thousand
dollars to insure his good will.

It developed into one of the most lavish nightclubs and gambling
casinos in the nation and presented headline talent like Sophie Tucker,
comedian Joe E. Lewis, and singer Tony Martin. It featured exquisite
cuisine, top name bands to dance to during dinner, beautiful silverware and the finest china, huge crystal chandeliers, and a plush gambling room that attracted the best people. Within a short time it was
the place to go for everyone who lived in or visited New Orleans.
Everyone agreed that it was a helluva operation, and Dandy Phil ran
it with lavish and loving care. If you weren't dressed properly, you
weren't welcome.

During the first three months of business, the partners were reputed
to have split up $250,000 in profits. It continued to be a big money
maker until 1951 when heat generated by the Kefauver Committee
caused the politicians on the pad to force Kastel to close its doors.
After being shuttered for many years, the Beverly is operating again,
catering to a very different crowd. A group of New Orleans businessmen have converted it into a supper playhouse where roadshow Broadway plays are performed while the audience burps its way through the
effects of the dinner.

*   *   *

Frank Costello's last involvement in New Orleans occurred in 1955
when his brother-in-law William (Bonny) Geigerman became involved
with the notorious Frankie Carbo, boxing's czar of crime. Carbo, a
boxing promoter with a long arrest record that included a murder
rap, had been thrown out of New York State because all his fight
promotions were suspected of being fixed. He then attempted to establish Louisiana Boxing Enterprises, Incorporated, the idea being
that it would handle boxing promotion for the southern half of the
United States.

The deal was too big for Bonny to handle because getting Carbo
permission to operate in Louisiana would take heavy political muscle,

and he just didn't have it. He brought Frank into the deal. Sometime between July 6 and July 9 of that year, Costello, Carbo, Marcello, and a number of associates of Earl Long, Huey Long's nephew, met in the New Orleans' Roosevelt Hotel to iron out details.

According to information released by the Metropolitan Crime Commission, $750,000 was pledged to Long's upcoming gubernatorial race with the understanding that Carbo would have clear sailing in Louisiana if Long were elected. Due to the publicity thrown on the upcoming deal, it died stillborn.

❋   ❋   ❋

The Costello-Kastel New Orlean's story ended on a sad note. On August 16, of 1962, Dandy Phil Kastel, in failing health and fearful that he was going blind in his one remaining good eye, was found dead in his apartment in the Roosevelt Hotel by his nurse. He had a gunshot would in his head, and a gun lay besides his body. The coroner ruled that his death was an apparent suicide.

Uncle Frank

"It doesn't matter whether it is a banker, a businessman, or a gang-ster, his pocketbook is always attractive."

Mayor William O'Dwyer

Frank Costello, operating secretly behind the scenes, was a political powerhouse in New York City in the forties. He named political appointees to jobs, placed judges on the bench, and even put a mayor in City Hall. An old-line Tammany Hall politician tells in his own words how these incredible events occurred.

❊   ❊   ❊

"In the 1940s, I was politically involved on a city-wide level with the high echelon of Tammany Hall. Prior to that I was with the lower echelon people in a certain community but politically inclined. I first saw the light of the political situation in the forties when I received my first political job. Prior to that I was on my own so far as the community was concerned. I was political but never affiliated with a payroll job.

"I was recommended for a position that gave me my first insight into the political situation when I was recommended for a job with the Board of Elections. And the position I held, although it was a minor position, it was a position of influence because I was associated with the Democratic leaders and the Republican leaders. In those days it was a two-party system. Of course, a little later on, maybe a year or two later, it became a three-party system with the American

109

Labor Party. Now in my position in the Board of Elections I met all types of politicians, leaders, non-leaders, judges, assistant district attorneys, assistant corporation counsels, congressmen, senators, district attorneys, assemblymen, powerful party leaders, and powerful elected officials. And regardless of what anyone says, they were all politicians. That includes the judges because in those days you couldn't become a judge without becoming a politician.

"That was the lineup, and I met them all, and I was naive. But it didn't take me long to find out the score. I found out that certain district leaders were powerful in certain areas. In other areas you had nonentities. And a nonentity, regardless of who they were, a law background or a business background, they were nonentities unless they had certain clout. And the clout was the underworld.

"It was very simple for me to find out who had clout and who didn't have clout. In this business there are no secrets. There is a Green book, and when someone dies or retires or there is a change in administration, there are vacancies; and that little Green book would always tell you where a vacancy is, and somebody had to replace that vacancy, so you would always notice that in the book. And before it even became public you'd hear on the grapevine, 'Hey Joe Blow from Kelly's club is getting that job, or so and so is getting the clerk's job with the judge.

"Now I noticed that certain leaders always seemed to put their people into the jobs while other leaders were always out in left field. The ones with the clout were the ones aligned with the underworld.

"You ask who was the underworld and how did they get the clout. In the forties the underworld were the graduates from the bootlegging days, the roaring twenties. They were the racket people, and they had their finger in the pot. I mean, what's the use of kidding. They had the numbers game. They had the bookmaking game. They had all the rackets and all the money. You had Frank Erickson in bookmaking. You had Joe Adonis, Joey A, in Brooklyn. You had Bugsy Siegel and Meyer Lansky. You had the Herbert brothers, Eddie Herbert and Charley Herbert, who used to run the market unions. You had Joe Lanza, Socks Lanza, at the Fulton Fish Market.

"As I went along I would see different leaders had certain groups. In those days you had Charley Perry; he came from the Perry family. You had Christy Sullivan; he was a congressman and then became the leader of Tammany Hall. You had Eddie Hine; you had Albert Marinelli; you had Jimmy Kelly. You had the Harlem leaders who were white leaders in those days. Hardly any black leaders — they came later. You had Mancuso, former Judge Francis X. Mancuso, a* leader in East Harlem. You had the West Side leaders, and you had the East Side leaders. And there were combinations of leaders, and each one had their different groups.

"Now who was it who put the whole power play of all these combinations together? A fellow named Costello, that's who. When he needed something, he wouldn't go to the leaders. He'd go to the mobsters who controlled the leaders. And they would say, 'Look, we're interested in Joe Blow or Mr. X or Mr. Black, and we need your help on election day; and see it our way because throughout the year you're looking for certain donations, contributions to club affairs, to journals, you know, we support your clubhouses, we put your people on the payroll.

"In those days the mobsters had lots of payrolls. They put people in the chicken market, in newspaper circulation departments, into Con Edison. You name it, and they had their fingers in the pie. They put them into crap games, so much a night. Even if the fellow wasn't there, he got paid because of the okay of the crap games and the payoffs and things. These are the things I learned as I went along, and it was quite interesting, and Costello was spokesman for the combinations. He was their boss. He was boss of most of the leaders. This is in the forties, and I understand this was the way it was in the thirties, and if anyone wanted to go places politically he had to get the okay of his leader. He got the okay if he agreed to be friendly with certain people, meaning the mobsters. The leaders who were friendly with the mob guys got the patronage. The ones who didn't want any part of the mob, they were leaders in name only, and they got nothing.

"The leaders didn't go along because they were afraid or anything like that. Well, maybe some were. But from what I gathered when I was there, it wasn't so much the fear of violence as the lust for money, if you know what I'm talking about. These people from the rackets were the demanding ones. And it was like the coffee commercial, this is the Demanding One, whatever he wants he gets; and those mobsters, whatever they wanted they got. It came to election day, they sent an envelope down. The leaders would then send the captains out with envelopes. And if the voters needed coal or rice or a job or money to pay the rent or money to put somebody through school, the leaders had it from the mob. The leaders also had money for their fun and pleasure. This is what I observed through the years, and that's the main reason there were political leaders with strength. The others, they were always in the minority. And then, after a while, even if the minority wanted to join, they couldn't because what's the use of kidding ourselves — they couldn't be trusted.

"That's how Costello was able to have his finger in certain areas, all except in the Board of Education, all except in the Police Department and the Fire Department. But he had some Italians with the lower echelon in the Police Department, and he was able to make certain moves there. He had a policeman he wanted to make a detective, he made recommendations through certain sources, and he got a certain policeman to become a detective; others he got assigned to certain areas. These detectives would then be politically motivated and overlook a lot of things, except maybe murder. And then in some instances you had the district attorneys and the assistant district attorneys who would help out when you needed them.

"Then while I was around the Board of Elections, the chief clerk died. So we protected that spot because it was a vital spot; that was the making of leaders with petitions and everything. Even if you had a good petition come along, you could throw it out. You'd just say there were insufficient signatures or have a flunkey tear out some pages. This way you had protection from political insurgents.

"Abe Rosenthal, who was a leader on the Lower East Side on Second Avenue, got the chief clerk's job. And how did Abe get the leadership? I'll tell you because, as I said before, I was close to the situation. There was a congressman who was the leader on Second Avenue, and he died suddenly. He was a hard working guy, a nice guy and a straight-laced guy. So he died, and there's a vacancy for the leadership. Now four guys on Second Avenue wanted it, and they were all ready to do battle — a fellow by the name of Arthur Snider, he later became a leader; a fellow by the name of Arthur Klein, later a congressman, but at the time he was a lawyer working for the Securities Exchange Commission; Abe Rosenthal, he had really solid connections; then there was a fourth guy who was a nothing. He just wanted to make a lot of noise.

"Well, there was a conflict there. Each one had his backers. So it finally came to a standstill. And what did they do? They went into the hallway at the Board of Elections and put four numbers into a hat and shook the hat. Whoever became number one would become the leader; number two would become the congressman; number three would be the chief clerk; number four would be left holding his cock. Well, to make a long story short, it didn't work out that way. Abe Rosenthal got the low number and became the leader. Then he says I want to be the chief clerk. The other spot went to Arthur Klein, and he became the congressman. The other guys got nothing.

❊   ❊   ❊

"Now one of the powerhouse leaders who dealt directly with Costello at the time was Dr. Paul Sarubbi. He was Costello's doctor — A helluva *doctor and a helluva guy; a good surgeon who worked with the racket guys and he was a powerhouse.*

"Then with Costello you had Michael Kennedy who was a congressman and who owed the East Side leaders an obligation because they put him over; and you had Bert Stand who was secretary of Tammany Hall, and he had a brother Murry Stand who was the city clerk. And there was Clarence Neal who came out of Harlem. They were friendly to Costello and all the combinations of leaders and mobsters. That was the reason Bert Stand was able to remain as secretary when there were five, six changes of leadership. Then, I want you to know, that a fellow by the name of Vito Marcantonio, who was a congressman, was part of the East Harlem combination with Tommy Lucchese (Three-Finger-Brown). So you had the Marcantonio combination that had City Hall, and they had the Hall because Marcantonio had Fiorello LaGuardia, and I don't care what anybody says about LaGuardia, you might say that he was the greatest of everything; he was tied in with Marcantonio who was tied in with the East Harlem combination. Then you had the Costello combination with the Stand brothers, Kennedy, Neal, and Dr. Sarubbi, and that's how the whole thing worked."

❊   ❊   ❊

"Now the first time I met Costello we were in a restaurant, about forty or fifty people in a restaurant at the same time. It was a public assembly, and the reason I remember that first meeting is because he and I smoked the same kind of cigarettes, English Ovals. I remember he offered me a cigarette and I said, 'You know something, I smoke the same thing.' I was a nonentity, but he remembered me after that, and when I would meet him he would always offer me an English Oval.

"I found him to be a charming, quiet spoken man. A real gentleman. That's the truth. He was a prince of a fellow. All those young fellows who needed help — let's say they were in the music business or maybe the cigarette machine business — whenever these little people came to him for help, they'd say, 'Uncle Frank, will you try to help us? We want to put some cigarette machines in this place, but the competition is too rough; or we went into this restaurant, and they want one thousand dollars up front;' or 'Uncle Frank, I got a linen route, and I went into this restaurant, and they want big money up front. This is my area but they won't let me service them unless I come up with one thousand dollars. I don't have that kind of money.' Things like that all the time. And he would make a couple of calls and say that he had a nephew who was very much interested, and the people he talked to — they would listen.

"He was like a godfather. You call him the godfather. To them he was the uncle. And he did a lot of good things for a lot of these people.

"From my reports from people I knew who were very closely associated with him, they all spoke highly of him. He never killed anybody or abused anybody or assaulted someone. He was a gentleman that spoke in a mild tone, kept his peace, didn't like violence. His word was one million per cent. When he said something he always backed it up. Congressman Arthur Klein said he was the nicest guy in the world. As a matter of fact, Klein recommended one of Meyer Lansky's sons to West Point. Sponsored him. Actually got him the appointment because he was qualified."

❊   ❊   ❊

"Of course things were tough when LaGuardia was mayor, but when O'Dwyer got in, Costello had an open door. There's no question about that. So far as the story that he got O'Dwyer the nomination, all I know is that O'Dwyer was having difficulty getting the nomination, certain leaders were against him. He went to see Costello because he knew where to get friendship. He needed the support; he wanted to be the mayor of this town."

❊   ❊   ❊

Frank Costello, of course, was hardly the first racketeer to bribe a politician in New York City. William Marcy Tweed, who ruled Tammany from 1860 to 1870, was the boss of an army of thieves and is credited with bilking the city out of thirty million dollars before he wound up in jail.

One of Boss Tweed's successors, Richard Croker, further damaged the image of the political arm of the Democratic Party in New York City by his ostentatious display of prosperity, mysteriously acquired despite the fact that he didn't even hold a job. Croker owned a racing stable, a luxurious resort hotel, and generally lived like a king. His answer to an investigator who asked him if his political career was the source of his wealth was the classic: "Sure. I'm working for my pocket all the time, same as you."

Tammany Hall came into being with the birth of the United States. When George Washington was President, an organization was founded that called itself the Society of Tammany. The organization flourished, was later called Tammany Hall, and became synonymous with the Democratic Party in New York City. From its inception, Tammany was regarded as the political organization of the common man and became all powerful as the "poor and huddled masses" poured into the city.

As political writer Warren Moscow pointed out in *The Last of the Big-Time Bosses*, his penetrating book on Carmine DeSapio:

"The boss system took the immigrant fresh off the boat and made him an American citizen. It found him a place to live, kissed his babies, entertained his whole family on the district club's annual boat ride, picnic, or clambake, which was the event of the year in a lower-class society of limited pleasures. It fixed traffic tickets and jury notices for the shopkeeper, winked at the building and sanitary-code violations of the landlord or sweatshop operator, reduced tax assessments for the big property owners. The boss system made money for the boss and for the party organization, but it also made life more bearable for a lot of little people who had no access otherwise to government, who knew of its operations only through contacts with the machine. Tammany and its counterparts were whipping boys for the editorial writers in their ivory towers, but they were friends to the man in the street."

This writer can remember clearly when he was growing up in the Bronx, how his cab-driver father would have the luxury of taking a whole day off on election day. Joseph Katz would bathe, shave carefully, put on a fresh shirt and tie, light a ten-cent cigar, and go and vote several times. At each place, a man wearing a derby would solemnly shake hands with him outside the voting booth. The handshake was worth anywhere from two to five dollars. Election day meant a big pay day for Joseph Katz.

❋   ❋   ❋

At the time Costello was growing up in East Harlem, Tammany was ruled by Charles F. Murphy who followed the time-honored Tammany tradition of providing protection for gamblers and other entrepreneurs of vice in return for cash and muscular "poll watchers" on election day. It was a loose arrangement and had not anywhere near the scope and organization that Costello added to the scheme.

Costello learned the political realities of life on the streets of East Harlem. He saw how political power could take an Irishman right off the boat and put him in a police uniform or in a job for one of the utility companies. He saw how cops could enforce or ignore the gambling and vice laws depending upon whether they and the local politicians had been taken care of. He also saw that being arrested wasn't a really serious matter if you went in front of the right judge. Graft was a part of life. That's the way things were run and always would be run. Tammany controlled much of the flow of graft and dealt out many of its favors through its district political clubs.

It is probable that Costello's first two arrests ended in dismissals because of the influence of some East Harlem Tammany politician. The magistrates who sat in the lower criminal courts had always been creatures of the Democratic political machine in the city, more so than the higher courts. This was especially true when Costello was a young man.

*   *   *

The free and easy money of the bootlegger ushered in an era of enlarged cooperation between the politician and the racketeer. An unenforceable law attracts graft the same way a magnet attracts metal. Joe the Boss, Louis (Lepke) Buchalter, Big Bill Dwyer, Dutch Schultz, Owney Madden, Frank Erickson, Meyer Lansky, and Joe Adonis, to name a few, all had their political rabbis or protectors — so did Frank Costello and Lucky Luciano.

The most powerful political rabbi of the mid twenties and thirties was Jimmy Hines, a square-built, gutsy Irishman with a perpetual twinkle in his eye who was a Tammany leader from the West Side. Through a series of alliances with other district leaders, he was able to become a powerhouse, and the graft he collected trickled down the system. Schultz and Costello were two of his more famous clients.

As a result of his bootlegging activities, Costello gradually built up relationships with a number of Tammany district leaders. He needed them because of their influence with the magistrates in the lower criminal courts (the easiest place to kill an arrest by a dumb cop who didn't know the score) and high echelon members of the police department — and they needed him for his pocketbook.

Costello was extremely acceptable to the politicians because he neither looked nor acted like a hood. Most of the Italian mobsters; on the other hand, appeared menacing to outsiders, were suspicious of anyone who wasn't Italian, sought only the company of each other, and were a source of embarrassment to the politicians who lived by the facade of their respectability. Costello was the first member of the Italian mobs to come uptown and mix with relatively polite society. In later years he convinced Luciano to come uptown.

"Costello and Luciano were the only two Italian racket guys you'd see midtown," Toots Shor said.

*   *   *

At first, Luciano had his own ideas of how to gain political friends. In 1931, he decided the Italians needed some representation in Tammany Hall and sent a few gunmen to call at the office of City Clerk Harry Perry which was close to City Hall. The gunmen showed Perry their hardware and then suggested he give up his downtown district leadership. He didn't argue. Perry promptly resigned and his spot was quickly filled by Albert Marinelli.

Costello was upset by this display of old-fashioned hoodlum power. He explained to Luciano that an incident of that nature caused more harm than good. The story of Perry's resignation had made the other district leaders distrustful of all Italians. It was getting more difficult to deal with them. Luciano promised to never do it again.

*   *   *

The 1932 Democratic Convention in Chicago was one of the highlights of Costello's life up to that point. This was the convention where Franklin Delano Roosevelt was nominated to be the Democratic standard-bearer. Costello, who was a great admirer of Roosevelt, attended the convention and shared a room at the Drake Hotel with Jimmy Hines. Luciano also attended with Marinelli, and they shared an adjoining room. Through Hines and another politician, Costello was given a brief audience with FDR. He was introduced as a well-known New York City businessman and a substantial campaign contributor.

The Seabury investigation revelations of wholesale municipal corruption, followed by the election of Republican Fiorello LaGuardia, had the effect of driving the Tammany leaders deeper into the arms of the racketeers. The Democrats were suddenly deprived of much of their political patronage and faced starvation. With LaGuardia in City Hall, jobs that would normally have gone to Tammany went to lean Republicans.

In the American political system, a political party exists not only to rule but also for what it can do for its members. In most areas of the nation the political pendulum swings back and forth, and the Republicans and Democrats take turns at the spoils. In New York City, however, the two-party spoil system had broken down, and the Democrats had dominated completely for many years. Voters elected Democrats no matter who was running. Democratic politicians had grown up thinking things would always be this way.

For Tammany the cruel facts of life were that LaGuardia now had the power to appoint the magistrates to the lower criminal courts. This meant that as the ten-year terms of the Democratic-appointed judiciary expired, a man who had no obligation to Tammany would take his place. As time passed, this would serve to deprive Tammany of much of the protection they offered mobsters. So even though the Tammany leaders had less to offer, their willingness to accept graft increased.

The election of LaGuardia didn't mean, however, that New York suddenly had turned into a Republican town. The little Mayor had to govern with the good will and cooperation of the Democrats who

filled the ranks of the City Council and other areas of elected government. So while he was able to greatly reduce Tammany patronage, he
couldn't shut it off altogether. In addition, Tammany still had the
judgeships of the Supreme, City, Municipal, and Surrogate Courts
because they were chosen by the voters; but generally speaking, things
were tough, and as politicians out of power everywhere do, the men
of Tammany sat around and plotted how to get back into power.
They didn't for twelve long years. In the meantime, however, they
wheeled and dealed as best they could, looked for chinks in LaGuardia's armor, and attempted to bypass City Hall whenever they could.

                    ✾   ✾   ✾

Political friendships and accomodations are not made quickly. It
takes years to build up relationships and establish a power base. This
was true in the case of Costello. His activities in the political field were
given a major boost when Luciano was convicted and sent to jail. He
fell heir to Lucky's formidable circle of political friends. This, coupled
with the fact that he was now head of the family, gave him massive
power in two worlds. While keeping these two worlds apart from one
another, he skillfully orchestrated the actions of each. Costello was
generally regarded by the public merely as a former bootlegger and a
gambler. As late as 1941, the *New York Times* referred to him as a
"sportsman" in a story.

To know Costello's circle of political friends, one only had to follow
him around for a day. By 1936 he long since had shaken the dust of
Bayside Queens from his always freshly-shined shoes and lived in the
thirty-two-story Majestic apartment building on Central Park West.
He also had acquired a red-brick Colonial house surrounded by two
acres of land in the upper-crust area of Sands Point, Long Island.

On weekdays many of the Tammany leaders would arrive for breakfast at his Manhattan apartment, adjusting their habits to Costello's
preference for starting the day early. Men like Bert and Murray Stand,
Clarence Neal, former Judge Francis Mancuso, Judge Anthony P. Savarese, gambler Irving Sherman, Dr. Paul Sarubbi, and others were
frequent guests. The politicians and favor seekers would also gather
at the Waldorf-Astoria, where Costello held court every morning, or
catch him at the Madison Hotel where he usually lunched.

"Sometimes you'd see two tables of men waiting patiently to see
him at the Madison," recalled a lawyer who observed the scene many
times. "Costello would be sitting at a third table, and when the person
he was talking to was through, someone from one of the other tables
would take his place."

In the late afternoon the Copacabana lounge, a nightclub, would be the meeting place as Costello and his friends sipped drinks and talked in whispers.

The Democrats weren't the only politicians Costello had connections with. Republican leader David Costuma, a Board of Elections commissioner, was a Costello friend. So was his brother Louis F. Costuma, the first deputy police commissioner under Police Commissioner Lewis J. Valentine. In 1929, Louis Costuma had been a deputy inspector, the highest office held by a Jew in the police department at that time. As Valentine's first deputy, he became the acting police commissioner when Valentine was out of town or on vacation. Upon his retirement from the force, Governor Dewey appointed him a commissioner on the Parole Board.

❊.   ❊   ❊

An insight into Costello's soft-sell method of political operation was given by Assemblyman Patrick H. Sullivan, a Tammany leader who didn't play ball with the racketeers. Costello invited Sullivan up to his apartment for a friendly chat. When he arrived he was amazed to see Socks Lanza acting as Costello's receptionist. Christy Sullivan, no relation to Pat Sullivan, had recently resigned as head of Tammany Hall, and Pat figured Costello was seeking to put together enough votes to put his man, former Congressman Jimmy Fay, in the spot. He also knew that Costello knew he was facing a primary fight for the assembly.

After a few minutes of talk in which the amenities were observed, Costello got to the point. "I have a candidate to take Christie Sullivan's place, and I would like to know if you would go for him?" he asked. "He is Jimmy Fay. Are you interested?"

"That's impossible," Sullivan answered. He then went on to explain his objections. Fay was backed by Clarence Neal, and anyone backed by Neal couldn't get his vote.

It was a direct challenge to Costello because Neal was his man, and everybody knew it. What Sullivan was saying was that anyone backed by Costello was unacceptable.

"Well, how about this proposition," countered Costello without a change of his amiable manner and expression. "Leave your vote with me, and I'll deliver it the right way. If you do that, you'll never have to worry about primary fights. I'll give you all the manpower you need. You'll never have to worry about financing your leadership and clubroom."

"You don't come from my district," Sullivan replied angrily, "You have no right to ask for my vote."

Costello acted as if he hadn't noticed the belligerent tone of Sullivan's voice. Still pleasant and calm, he answered: "I'm sorry you can't play it my way. If you should happen to change your mind, call me up."

Sullivan never did change his mind. Costello, meanwhile, went about the business of seeking to beat the hard-headed Irishman in his own district with a candidate he personally selected. It took three years for the feat to be accomplished.

✿   ✿   ✿

The head of Tammany Hall is chosen by an executive committee made up of district leaders. Each leader has a vote or a part of a vote depending upon the size of his district. Tiny districts are entitled to only one-third of a vote.

By 1942, Costello controlled six executive committee votes and was in a position to make a bid to put his own man in as head of Tammany. He threw his support behind Fay, but there was a great deal of opposition to the former Congressman, and he couldn't put him over.

About this time Congressman Michael Kennedy, who was a district leader on the West Side and controlled one-third of a vote, happened to go to the fights at Madison Square Garden. By chance he sat next to bookmaker Frank Erickson, and a friendly political discussion ensued. After sounding Kennedy out, Erickson suggested that he meet Frank Costello and promised to arrange things. Erickson was as good as his word and in no time at all was at the Costello apartment. Kennedy wanted the job as head of Tammany Hall and let Costello know he wouldn't be ungrateful if he threw his support his way.

"I'm committed to Fay," Costello answered, "but if anything happens, and he withdraws, I'll throw my support to you."

The Fay candidacy became hopeless, and he withdrew. Costello then kept his promise, and Kennedy became boss of Tammany. His easy win caused Bert Stand to later quip to political writer Warren Moscow: "Kennedy went from one-third of a vote to six and one-third on one quick handshake."

Putting Michael Kennedy in as the head of Tammany elevated Frank Costello into the most important Democratic power in the city. In New York, under normal conditions, this meant that he would be the second most politically powerful man in the city, but these weren't normal conditions. Fiorello LaGuardia still ruled City Hall.

Costello enjoyed the role of power broker. It satisfied his monumental ego which he kept in check and rarely showed. Nevertheless, the fact that he could attain a position of power and respect in the world outside the rackets reinforced his belief that if he had been born under different circumstances there was no limit to how far he could have gone.

Kennedy was the puppet and Costello the puppeteer. Every judge the Democrats put on the bench, every assistant district attorney job that came their way through patronage, every sensitive post that Tammany was able to fill, and every policy position arrived at by Tammany's executive committee now had to meet his approval.

It was under this situation that the real talent of Frank Costello emerged. He was a model of restraint. In acquiring power he learned to understand power: its uses, its limitations. He didn't abuse power. He never sought to shove some bumbling, unacceptable idiot down everyone's throat. He was always willing to compromise and reach a consensus of opinion. But when he did give his backing to someone he backed them all the way. In an arena where the doublecross was normal conduct, Frank Costello's word on something was absolute. This was a novelty among the Tammany politicians and they respected him for it.

✾   ✾   ✾

In 1942, Bill O'Dwyer was a brigidier general in the United States Air Force at Wright Field, Ohio, responsible for production and labor contracts relating to Air Force supplies. America was in the midst of World War II, but the astute and personable "Bill-O," as his close friends called him, already had his mind on 1945, when the next mayoralty race would take place in New York City. LaGuardia was in his third term and almost certain not to run again. O'Dwyer wanted to be the next Mayor of New York.

He had run against LaGuardia in 1941 and lost. Yet he still had impeccable credentials as a crime fighter. As the Brooklyn District Attorney, he had successfully smashed the infamous gang of killers known as Murder, Inc., an underworld organization headed by Lepke Buchalter and Albert Anastasia. Murder, Inc. was in the business of murder and extortion for profit, and police say that between 120 and 130 persons were executed throughout the country by the organization.

Despite O'Dwyer's reputation as a vigorous foe of crime, he lost some of his glitter when LaGuardia won the 1941 election, and opposition to his current ambition arose within the Democratic organization. He faced a tough primary fight at best. So Bill-O did what all politicians do under similar circumstances — he sought political help.

Through his longtime stooge and bagman, Jim Moran, O'Dwyer made arrangements for a meeting with the man who could sew up the nomination for him in 1945. Moran was close to Irving Sherman, a shadowy gambler and businessman who was Costello's political

messenger boy. Sherman was once described by FBI chief J. Edgar
Hoover as one of the nation's "top underworld figures" and in the
past he was known to be a close associate of Bugsy Siegel. O'Dwyer
could have arranged it all directly with Sherman, because they were
friends, but things don't work that way in politics. Middlemen are
needed to test the waters, and if all appears safe and comfortable,
then the principles meet.

So in 1942, United States Air Force Brigadier General William
O'Dwyer paid a visit to Frank Costello's Central Park West apartment. Present at the little get together were Tammany Hall boss Michael
Kennedy, Tammany Hall secretary Bert Stand, Judge Anthony Saverese, Irving Sherman, and Jimmy Moran. Costello and O'Dwyer greeted
each other cordially and then talked alone for about thirty minutes.

Whatever political deal was made is unknown. O'Dwyer maintained
before the Kefauver Committee that he met with Costello to try and
straighten out problems he was having with Air Force business at
Wright Field. He said someone told him that Costello might be able
to help. No one believed the story, but O'Dwyer stuck to it tenaciously,
and that was that.

Following the O'Dwyer-Costello meeting, opposition to Bill-O's
mayoralty aspirations mysteriously vanished, and the Democratic
party got behind him. He was an easy winner in the 1945 election.

*   *   *

In 1943, a political scandal broke which revealed to everyone, except the politicians who dealt with him, the political clout Costello
wielded in Tammany. A tap on Costello's phone produced cold, un-
shakeable evidence that he was responsible for Magistrate Thomas
A. Aurelio being made the bipartisan choice for Supreme Court Justice in New York State. Although Aurelio still had to win an election,
the bipartisan support made his victory a certainty.

A furor was raised following the printing in all the newspapers of
the phone conversation between Costello and Aurelio. The effect was
to force Costello to severly curtail his political activities until things
calmed down. He had become an embarrassment, and from that point
on, his every move had to be covered with the utmost subterfuge. He
continued to wield political power, however, and was able to help
name the next four Tammany Hall bosses that succeeded Kennedy:
Edward V. Loughlin, Frank Sampson, Hugo Rogers, and Carmine
DeSapio. The first three named were totally under Costello's thumb.
DeSapio, who played ball with Costello to get into power and then
split from him, was instrumental in reforming Tammany and breaking

with the racketeers. Ironically, he gained the most sinister reputation
of all.

DeSapio was an intelligent and relatively honest Tammany boss,
probably more honest than the city deserves. In later years, after his
power had been broken, DeSapio was indicted and convicted for his
part in a scandal involving Mayor John Lindsay's protege, Water Supply
Commissioner James Marcus. DeSapio was sentenced to two years in
jail.

❋   ❋   ❋

Costello became the big political issue in the 1949 mayoralty campaign when O'Dwyer ran for reelection. His Republican opponent,
Newbold Morris, accused O'Dwyer of being the front man for Costello. Costello, who maintained he was now out of politics, issued a
public statement saying that Morris had asked him to help him get
the Italian vote and had solicited financial support. Morris denied all.

O'Dwyer won easily and, in a prearranged deal with President
Truman, resigned his office in 1950 to become Ambassador to Mexico.
His successor, Vincent Impellitteri, was a wholly-owned creature of
Vito Marcantonio and Mafia underboss Tommy (Three-Finger-Brown)
Lucchese. Following Impellitteri's election, a strange trio would lunch
together once a week in one of Little Italy's excellent restaurants. The
luncheon companions were Impellitteri, Three-Finger-Brown, and
Police Commissioner Thomas Murphy.

❋   ❋   ❋

What did Costello get out of politics? Was he simply being the fixer
for the Mafia and the other elements of organized crime? Of course,
he was an agent for the Mafia, but there were other reasons for his
heavy involvement in political affairs. He enjoyed the behind-the-
scenes role he played and the give-and-take of politics. He enjoyed
the delicious feel of power. He also sincerely believed that Italians
were entitled to a greater share of the political spoils, and many of
the men he put on the bench were of Italian extraction.

How many men besides Aurelio did he elevate to the judiciary?
Who knows? Logically, one concludes that Aurelio was merely one of
many. It stands to reason that almost every judge elected to the bench
and many who were appointed from 1940 to 1949 at least had to meet
his approval if not get his outright support.

In later years when Mafia or Cosa Nostra had become household
words, a group of Italians formed an organization to protest the link-
ing, by the press, of all those Italian names to the underworld. It was

sort of an Italian anti-defamation league. A friend showed Costello a list of judges who supported the organization and remarked that there were a lot of Italian judges.

"I ought to know, I made most of them," Costello answered with a smile.

The call

In January of 1943, Carlo Tresca, an Italian-language newspaper editor who was an implacable foe and caustic critic of Mussolini, was shot to death by a lone gunman on Fifteenth Street and Fifth Avenue in New York City.

To avid newspaper reader Frank Costello, the murder of a little known anti-fascist could hardly have been a cause for concern. Yet a bizarre chain of events would result — not in Tresca's killer being caught — but in Costello being unmasked as the real boss of Tammany Hall.

Detective seeking to solve the mystery, quickly discounted robbery or something unsavory in Tresca's personal life as the motive. That left them with politics as the only other possibility. As they rummaged about the underworld seeking information, one detective came up with an incredible tale. An informant told him that Tresca's death was ordered by Vito Genovese, then living in splendor in Rome. In having Tresca murdered, Genovese was seeking to ingratiate himself with the Italian Dictator. Since fleeing the United States, the wily Genovese had prospered. He had bought a power plant with the suitcase full of cash he had carried over with him, contributed $250,000 to the construction of a municipal building, and had been decorated with the Italian Fascist state's highest civilian title, that of *Commendatore*. Mussolini himself had pinned the decoration on his breast.

Once detectives had received this information, what happened next was inevitable. They knew that Genovese had ranked above Costello in the hierarchy of the Italian gangs before he ran away. The next logical step was to find out if Costello was involved in the slaying or had information as to who was hired to pull the trigger.

The detectives then went to Manhattan District Attorney Frank Hogan with their information, and he promptly sought and received court permission to put a tap on Costello's phone.

"We really didn't think Costello had anything to do with the murder of Tresca," Hogan recalled, "but we thought we might pick up some information as to the identity of the killer."

✻   ✻   ✻

The information Hogan sought never materialized, but the months of patient listening by detectives paid off in a totally unexpected way. On August 24, 1943, at eight thirty in the morning, Costello's phone rang, and they heard the following conversation take place between Costello and Magistrate Thomas A. Aurelio, nominee of both the Democrats and Republicans for supreme court justice of the State of New York.

Aurelio — "Good morning, Francesco. How are you and thanks for everything."

Costello — "Congratulations, It went over perfect. When I tell you something is in the bag, you can rest assured."

Aurelio — "It was perfect. Arthur Klein (Congressman) did the nominating — first me and then Gavagan and then Peck. It was fine."

Costello — "That's fine."

Aurelio — "The doctor called me last night to congratulate me. I'm going to see him today. He seems to be improving. He should be up and around soon and should take the train for Hot Springs."

Costello — "That's fine."

Aurelio — "*Blank Blank* congratulated me. (*Naming a public official from another county.*) That's a fellow you should really do something for; he certainly deserves something."

Costello — "Well, well, we'll have to get together, you and your Mrs. and *Blank Blank* (*Here he names the wife of the official from the other county.*) and myself and have dinner real soon."

Aurelio — "That's fine, but right now I want to assure you of my loyalty for all you have done; it's undying."

Costello — "I know. I'll see you soon."

The phone clicked on the receiver, and that was the end of the conversation.

Before being picked to run for the supreme court, Thomas Aurelio, who grew up on the East Side and obtained his law degree from New York University, was an assistand district attorney in Manhattan from 1922 to 1931. Mayor Jimmy Walker then elevated him to the bench where he quickly earned the reputation of an uncompromising foe of gangsters, drunken drivers, and Communists who took part in street disorders. In 1935, Mayor LaGuardia reappointed Aurelio — his original appointment was to fill out the term of a magistrate who had died — and praised him mightily for his performance up to that point.

Over the years, Aurelio was the front runner for a nomination to the supreme court, but each time he was beaten out by someone with better connections. Finally, in 1943, his aspirations were sponsored by Dr. Paul Sarubbi, one of the most powerful of the Tammany Hall district leaders. Sarubbi took Aurelio to meet Costello who also pledged his support.

❖   ❖   ❖

A short while before the Democratic Convention, at which the supreme court nominees were to be chosen, Dr. Sarubbi suffered a stroke and became bedridden. The stroke affected only his legs, and he was able to continue to wield his political power from his bedroom. He used a number of young politicos as messenger boys to act as both his legs and ears.

Two days before the convention, to be held in the Girls Commercial High School auditorium on Forty-second Street, Sarubbi's political nose began to itch. He had heard disquieting rumors that some of the support he had lined up for Aurelio was beginning to melt away.

He called in one of his young men and told him to deliver a message. "You go up to Bert Stand at Tammany Hall," he ordered, "and you tell Stand to remember that if he crosses Aurelio he better move out of New York State. Get the message right now. You tell him that if you cross Tom Aurelio, leave New York State."

The messenger found Stand and delivered Sarubbi's message. He didn't have to explain who the message was from. Stand knew.

On the day of the convention, the doctor was still agitated. His physical state made it impossible to ride herd on things personally, and he was still worried that the script wouldn't be followed. He finally asked another district leader, his closest political friend, to do him a favor.

"This is what I want you to do for me," he said. "I want you to get up there at Tammany Hall. I don't want you to leave Bert Stand. Tail Bert Stand. You go with him; you stay alongside of him. Make sure that you tell him that you're going to shadow him and tell him I said,

'It's Aurelio tonight, and if it isn't Aurelio, he better leave town.' There's a lot of shenanigans going on, and I don't like the smell of things."

Dr. Sarubbi had been alerted of the wavering on Aurelio by Socks Lanza who warned that the ringleader of the rebellion seemed to be Stand. Sarubbi knew that if Aurelio was dumped, Costello would be furious. He had given his word.

The leader called in to act for Sarubbi delivered the message and then offered Stand counsel: "Look, Bert, don't be a fool. There are three nominations tonight, and one of them has to be Aurelio. Don't fool around."

Aurelio was nominated by Congressman Klein. Then someone seconded the nomination, and he was one of the three men chosen by the Democrats that night to run for the supreme court. After observing that everything ran smoothly, the district leader sent by Sarubbi grabbed a cab to the good doctor's home to report on the proceedings.

"How did it go?" Sarubbi asked anxiously.

"Like you were there yourself calling the shots," the district leader answered.

"Where are they now?" Sarubbi asked quietly, his voice full of satisfaction.

"Celebrating back in the clubhouse on Second Avenue," was the reply.

Sarubbi then asked the district leader to please get him the clubhouse on the phone because he wanted to congratulate Aurelio. Congressman Klein happened to pick up the phone and he remarked how nice everything had worked out. Justice Aurelio (his election would be only a formality) then got on the phone. Sarubbi held a short conversation with him in Italian and then hung up.

Sarubbi's friend protested. "You know, doc," he said, "you're a funny guy. I love you, but here I go and knock myself out for you and the organization and for everything, and I play cops and robbers for you, and I run up to Bert Stand, and I tell him this, and I tell him that. I come back here. I don't eat. I don't have a drink. I don't even have the chance to smoke a cigarette. I did it all because you're my good friend. I love you, you know, and finally when it comes to the end, you talk to him in Italian. I don't understand Italian."

"I just told him to call up Frank Costello and thank him," Sarubbi answered.

❖   ❖   ❖

The following day Sarubbi's political bird dog paid a visit to the Manhattan Democratic Club on Second Avenue where the celebration over Aurelio's nomination was still going on. The club was crowded

The first arrest — Costello in 1908.

Costello mug shot in 1935.

Left: Joe (the Boss) Masseria.
(N.Y. Daily News Pho)

Below: Big Bill Dwyer at his trial in 1927. (N.Y. Daily News Pho)

Left: Lucky Luciano when he was captured in Hot Springs, Ark.
(N.Y. Daily News Pho)

Above: Vito Genovese at the time o his narcotics arrest.
(N.Y. Daily News Pho)

*Left: Joe Adonis when
he was arrested in 1937.*
(N.Y. Daily News Photo)

*Above: Frank Erickson
being questioned about
the Anastasia murder.*
(N.Y. Daily News Photo)

Dandy Phil Kastel faces the
Kefauver Committee in
New Orleans.
  (United Press International Photo)

Below: Costello's $100 Dinner.
  (N.Y. Daily News Photo)

Dinner & Entertainment
Sponsored by
Frank Costello, Vice-Chairman of
Men's Division, Salvation Army Campaign

Monday, January 24th, 1949 at 6:30 p. m.
at the Copacabana
10 East 60th Street, New York

Entire proceeds for
Salvation Army Association

$100 per person   *Dress Informal*

Costello smiles at Kefauver.
(N.Y. Daily News Photo)

The hand ballet seen by America.
(N.Y. Daily News Photo)

Reporters compare notes on the Costello shooting in front of the Majestic.
(N.Y. Daily News Photo)

Columnist John J. Miller and his wife, Cindy, Costello's dinner companions.
(United Press International Photo)

Costello leaves the hospital after being shot in the head.
(N.Y. Daily News Photo)

*Below: Vincent (The Chin)
Gigante being booked for
attempted murder.*
(N.Y. Daily News Photo)

*Right: A panhandler finds an easy
touch.* *(N.Y. Daily News Photo)*

*Bottom: The Costello home in
Sands Point.* *(N.Y. Daily News Photo)*

Frank and Bobbie relaxing in Sands Point.
(Photo by Newsday)

with political flunkeys, state senators, assemblymen, and political hangers-on. In those days, putting a supreme court justice over was a big thing.

"Abe Rosenthal was the club's district leader," Sarubbi's political confidant said, "and I was amazed to see him shaking hands and taking all the credit. I'm standing right there while all this is going on, and I say to myself, 'Hey, you schmuck, you had as much to do with it as the man in the moon but as long as you're taking the credit, go ahead.' Well, nobody knew that Hogan had the whole thing, and a few days later Mike Kennedy was called into Hogan's office and asked about mob infiltration in Tammany. Kennedy denied any knowledge of anything, and then Hogan asked him who was the district leader of Aurelio's club. He told him Abe Rosenthal. So the next thing you know, Abe gets invited to see Hogan in his office, and he really shits. After all, he took the congratulations that he sponsored Aurelio, and he had nothing to do with it. He never sponsored Aurelio, but because of his ego, he got himself in a lot of trouble.

"He was one of the leaders controlled by Sarubbi, but Costello never dealt with him personally on the Aurelio thing because Costello didn't trust Abe. Rosenthal was even called in by the Kefauver Committee years later, and he was asked if he got any money out of the Aurelio nomination. He didn't get a dime, but no one believed him. Some people say he died over this thing. He was a lawyer and in mortal fear of being disbarred."

*   *   *

Hogan waited several days and then released the taped Costello-Aurelio conversation. Even in a time of war it made headlines. This incontrovertible proof that the judiciary and all it stood for was being perverted by the underworld was serious business.

Aurelio refused to withdraw from the election even after the Democrats and Republicans disavowed his candidacy. He fought a long court battle to keep his name on the ballot, and won. He issued a statement in which he denied any knowledge of Costello's background.

"I have read the newspaper reports in connection with my conversation with Mr. Costello, made public by District Attorney Hogan," his statement said. "I recall such a conversation. During my brief acquaintance with Mr. Costello of approximately six months standing, I knew him to be a businessman of good repute, and I definitely disavow any knowledge of his criminal background."

Hogan launched an investigation which resulted in a public hearing to determine the extent of the influence of the underworld in the political arena. Costello was called to testify.

Hogan brought out that Costello numbered among his good friends the elite of the mobs including Al Capone, the late Dutch Schultz, Lucky Luciano, Socks Lanza, Owney Madden, and Joey Rao.

Costello's lawyer attempted to counter this formidable array of gangland names, and asked him if he didn't also know many respectable people.

"Absolutely," his client answered. "I know some of the finest businessmen in the country. I don't want to mention their names. I don't want to embarrass them."

Costello's lawyer then asked him if it had been his ideal to mix with the better people during the last eight years.

"Nothing but the best," Costello answered.

❋   ❋   ❋

Despite continued pressure to force him to withdraw, Aurelio continued to hang tight. On election day he polled 48,804 votes more than his closest opponent, Matthew M. Levy of the American Labor Party whom the Democratic machine now publicly backed. The whole effect of the scandal was to heavily reduce his expected plurality — that was all. Aurelio then assumed the bench and — in fairness to him — served competently without a hint of doing anything improper. Everyone agrees, even District Attorney Hogan, that he made an excellent judge.

Little changed on the New York political scene as a result of the revelation. Costello continued to be the power behind Tammany Hall, and judges continued to be chosen in backroom deals — but from that time on, everyone was careful about what they said on the telephone.

Capo

The reign of Frank Costello as acting boss of the Lucky Luciano family began sometime in 1937 and officially ended on the night of May 2, 1957, in the foyer of the Majestic Apartments' lobby. By that time, however, the power had long since slipped from his hands, and the shot that deposed him was a mere formality, like the coup de grace at a French army execution.

During this period that he was in power, New York's five Mafia families enjoyed relative peace as Costello's philosophy of working out problems without resorting to violence prevailed. His ability to cool potentially explosive situations and suggest workable compromises was such that he became known for his statesmanship and was called the "prime minister of the underworld."

One example of Costello's method of handling things occurred in 1943, when his boyhood friend and family lieutenant in New Jersey, Willie Moretti, alias Willie Moore, began to act strangely. He was exhibiting the first signs of mental illness brought on by syphillis. Willie, who loved to gamble, began to talk wildly about betting and winning millions of dollars on mythical horse races and also started to ramble on about matters that shouldn't be spoken about in public. Some of the other family capos began to grumble that Willie was a threat to everyone.

Costello, who had been best man at Willie's wedding and who had real affection for him, decided to head off trouble before it arrived. He ordered Willie to take a long vacation out West and hired a male nurse to accompany him. Willie didn't want to go, but when Costello insisted he went.

During the time Willie was away, he besieged Costello with phone calls. As District Attorney Hogan was wiretapping Costello's phone, amused detectives listened as Willie pleaded to be allowed to come home. Costello patiently explained to him that he wasn't well enough yet. He was protecting Willie from himself. He didn't want the local commission, composed of the capos of five families in New York and the one family in New Jersey, to order Willie's execution on the grounds that it was a mercy killing for his and everyone else's good.

❈   ❈   ❈

Costello must have viewed his designation as acting boss by Luciano with something less than enthusiasm. Over the years he had carefully held himself apart from the organization (as the men of the Mafia themselves refer to their secret society) to whatever extent he could and carved out his own empire. When he was elevated to capo, he was already extremely wealthy and controlled a mixed bag of illegitimate and legitimate businesses: Frank Erickson's bookmaking syndicate, the slot machines in New Orleans, Irving Haim's Alliance liquor distributorship, large tracts of New York real estate, part ownership of the Copacabana nightclub, and assorted odds and ends. He preferred the company of the legitimate businessmen and politicians he was courting so assiduously to the suspicious, inbred Mafiosi who sought only their own kind. Being elevated to capo gave him power, but what he really wanted was power in the straight world. Yet he could neither refuse to take over, nor resign from the organization. When you join the Mafia, or Cosa Nostra as Joe Valachi called it, you join for life, and the only route of escape is death.

Costello's vision of the Mafia was that it was a service organization catering to the wants of the public. If there was no demand for these services, the Mafia could not exist. During prohibition there was a public demand for alcohol, so the Mafia made its profits satisfying this need. Gambling, shylocking, even narcotics were all rackets that fulfilled a public need, and the organization catered to what the public wanted. (Costello later changed his attitude towards narcotics and in 1948 issued an order stating that it was forbidden for members of his family to traffic in drugs.)

Costello along with the other leaders of the Mafia, strongly disapproved of naked criminal acts such as robbing a business or a bank at the point of a gun. Murder was used only as a weapon against their own kind, the supreme punishment for breaking sacred rules. When a member became involved in an unlawful activity that was not ordered by the family he was on his own, and if he got caught he received no help from the organization. Anyone arrested while on family business, on the other hand, could be assured of money for a lawyer and that his family would be taken care of if he went to jail. The road to respect and wealth for a member of the Mafia was to carve out a racket for himself and stake claim to a territory that no one had prior claim to. When you did that, as Costello had in bootlegging and slot machines, then you received the backing of the family, and no one dared to try and elbow you out.

                    ❖   ❖   ❖

There was an unlimited supply of rackets in New York. Costello was far from being the only one who was successful. Vito Genovese controlled the Italian lottery before he fled to Italy; Socks Lanza was a power on the waterfront and controlled the unions around the Fulton Fish Market; Tommy Lucchese and Louis (Lepke) Buchalter ran the garment district unions; Willie Moretti had the gambling concession in many areas of New Jersey; Lucky Luciano was involved in narcotics and prostitution; Joe Adonis had the gambling in Brooklyn and was a political power. The list was endless.

The Capo begins as a soldier or button man who is the Mafia's infantryman. The soldier is expected to be available whenever the bosses in the organization require his services. In return he receives the protection of the entire group for his business enterprises. A soldier, for instance, may succeed in putting fifty juke boxes in restaurants and bars in Queens. The racket is his, and the family will back him up if anyone tries to muscle in. If someone else claims the territory, the jurisdictional dispute is settled by the higher ups.

The capo is far removed from most of his soldiers. He carefully protects himself from any illegal act. When he issues an order it is passed down the chain of command, and by the time it is carried out he is as insulated from its consequences as the head of General Motors is from the shipment of a Buick. That is why it is so difficult for the police to arrest a capo.

Joe Valachi, who was a soldier in the family, complained that he never saw Costello. "All he was interested in was making money," Valachi said.

When Costello became acting boss, there were about 450 members of the family. He shielded himself from the day-to-day operations of the organization to a much greater degree than the capos of the

other four New York families. His lieutenants ran the organization:
Tony Bender, also known as Anthony Strollo, ruled in Greenwich
Village; Trigger Mike Coppola in Harlem; Joe Adonis in Brooklyn;
Willie Moretti in New Jersey; Anthony (Little Augie Pisano) Carfano
in the upper Bronx; and Mike Miranda controlled the East Side. These
men only came to him when serious problems arose.

In addition, Costello had strong contacts with gang leaders of other
ethnic groups like Meyer Lansky, Bugsy Siegel, Lepke Buchalter, and
Longy Zwillman.

Often the territories overlapped. Harlem, for example, had at least
three families sucking money out of the black community. Besides
Costello's, there was also the Gaetano Gagliano and Vincent Mangano
families. (Tommy Lucchese later succeeded Gagliano, and Albert
Anastasia succeeded Mangano.) Yet there were no territorial disputes.
It was all one happy family, with all beefs settled on the highest level
of the Mafia.

          ✻   ✻   ✻

On occasion a mob member had to be sacrificed for the collective
good. Such a sacrifice occurred in 1939 when Lepke went into hiding
for his role in several garment district murders performed by Murder,
Inc. Lepke was wanted by Tom Dewey, then Manhattan District
Attorney.

An intensive manhunt was launched which eventually involved the
FBI. Daily headline stories increased the heat, and many of the gang
leaders felt threatened as the police harrassed everyone in their search
for Lepke. FBI Director, J.Edgar Hoover, through his friend, the all-
powerful, syndicated columnist Walter Winchell, had the word passed
to Costello that he would make things very unpleasant for a lot of
other people unless Lepke gave himself up. The sudden focus by law
enforcement on organized crime was most disturbing. Costello met
quietly with the chiefs of the New York mobs, and it was greed that
Lepke had to turn himself in for the good of all concerned.

Lepke was located in an apartment in the Bronx, and Costello dispatched two of his friends. Longy Zwillman and Willie Moretti. The
message they delivered was: "Give yourself up or we will be forced
to take care of you. A deal has been worked out so you won't get the
chair."

Lepke reluctantly agreed. Costello then contacted his buddy Winchell and arranged for Lepke to surrender to him. Winchell, playing
the yarn to the hilt, first issued an appeal over his radio show to Lepke,
asking him to turn himself in and offered himself as the guarantee that
the police wouldn't do anything nasty like shoot him on sight. Several

days later Lepke met Winchell on a street corner in the city, and the columnist had the story of his lifetime.

In the trial that followed, Lepke was convicted and sentenced to die in the electric chair. The execution didn't take place until 1944, after he had exhausted all appeals. Newspaper stories reported that he went to his death denouncing Costello for having betrayed him.

Among Costello's closest friends in the thirties and forties was Generose Pope, a self-made millionaire, contractor, and publisher of the Italian-language newspaper *Il Progresso*. He greatly admired Pope because he was a man who made it legitimately, and Pope returned the friendship. Pope's three sons called Costello "Uncle Frank," and he regarded them as nephews. In later years, when Costello was the subject of unfavorable newspaper stories, he was defended on the editorial pages of *Il Progresso*.

Another close friend of Costello's was Frank Erickson. But their friendship, aside from their business relationship, had a very different character to it. Erickson had a talent for getting into mischief, and Costello had an amused tolerance for his friend's peccadillos. It was almost like an indulgent father for an errant son. He would give him a lecture on the correct mode of behavior in public and then help extricate him from his latest jam.

Erickson was a tall, bald, pudgy man, with a pink complexion and the round face of a cherub. He looked more like a prosperous barkeeper than a bookmaker. He lived in a grandiose style, with a bodyguard, chauffered limousine, and several mistresses.

Lieutenant Rudolph McLaughlin recalls receiving an order one time to look up Erickson. "The order came right from City Hall," he said, "and we traced him to the Fifth Avenue apartment of one of his girlfriend's, a professional tennis player. So we planted ourselves outside and waited for him to come out. He was still living with his wife at the time, and I just don't know what their arrangement was. But she was supposed to be a pretty tough broad, and she didn't care what kind of deal he was in, he had to come home at night to sleep, otherwise she'd raise all kinds of hell.

"Now I don't know how he knew we were there waiting for him, unless it was a tip from someone in headquarters, but suddenly one of Erickson's payoff men arrived at the scene while we were waiting in front of this building. We knew him, and he knew us, and we asked him what he wanted. 'Oh nothing,' he answered, 'but could you just get lost for ten minutes and give Frank a chance to get home because his wife is waiting for him.' We said, 'no good.' But to make a long story short, about four in the morning the chief of the detective division of Manhattan East arrived on the scene and tells us he just got orders from headquarters to give him a shot, walk away, and let him get out. I don't know where the contract came from but it was a pretty good one."

*   *   *

Frank Erickson was born in New York in 1896, a third generation American of Norwegian and Irish ancestry. His father, an electrician, died while he was still a boy, and he grew up in orphanages and foster homes. As a youngster he worked as a bus boy in a Coney Island restaurant. He never forgot the experience, and when he became wealthy always went out of his way to tip the bus boy. A story, probably apocryphal, of how he emerged as a bookmaster is that while working in the restaurant, he used to run bets for customers to neighborhood bookies. One time someone gave him twenty dollars to bet on a horse, and he couldn't make it to the bookmaker in time. Before seeing the bettor, he found out that the horse lost and pocketed the money. After that he booked a few of the bets himself until he built up his bankroll, then he quit the restaurant and went into business for himself.

By 1920 he was a power in the gambling fraternity and by 1930 one of its leaders. He brought merchandising to gambling. When most bookies were content to allow customers to come to them, Erickson pursued the customers. He reminded them by phone, by mail, and by a stream of presents scaled to the action of the customer. The heavy action players received $300 gold tie clips from Tiffany's. Those who were more conservative received $125 gold pencils that read, "Compliments of Frank Erickson."

From 1919 to 1926 he was arrested five times for gambling, and each time the charges were dismissed, or he received a suspended sentence. In 1939, he was arrested in Queens for vagrancy and was so insulted by the charge that he showed up in front of the courthouse in an armored car and was escorted into the courtroom by six Brink's guards. When he was called in front of the magistrate, he dumped securities worth $125,000 in front of the bench to prove he wasn't a vagrant. The case was dismissed.

In 1950, he served ten months on Riker's Island after District Attorney Hogan finally made a charge stick. While on the island, he was placed in a highly desirable job, received use of the warden's office for private meetings, and had 184 special bench visits in which his visitors were allowed to sit alongside him on a bench instead of talking through a screen. This was as many as all the other prisioners were allowed that year.

He died on March 2, 1968, at the age of seventy-two. He suffered cardiac arrest during a bleeding ulcer operation. A saddened Frank Costello attended his funeral.

❖   ❖   ❖

Although he earned much of his wealth from the suckers who gambled, Costello himself was one of the suckers. He loved to gamble and would routinely bet as much as five thousand dollars on a horse race and considerably more on fights. He also bet baseball and football during the seasons and anything else that came along. He was never happier than when he pulled off a betting coup.

No one was more aware of Costello's delight in beating the bookmakers than Gerard (Cheesebox) Callahan, a renegade New York Telephone Company employee, who worked for Costello for many years on a free-lance basis. He was the underworld's "wire man," an electronic whiz who used his talents to fool the police and the bookmakers.

Cheesebox, or Mickey as his friends call him, won fame of sorts when he invented an electronic relay system housed in a wooden cream cheese box which helped bookies escape a bust. The cheesebox was an ingenious device. It enabled a bookie to give a customer a phone number in the Bronx, for instance, yet when the customer dialed the number, the call would automatically be relayed to a phone in Brooklyn. Police were driven crazy by the gadget. They would laboriously trace a bookie's line and then crash the apartment expecting to find phone men and betting slips. Instead they would find an empty room except for a phone and a cheesebox attached. By the time they were able to figure out where the calls were being relayed to, the bookmaker had cleared out. In the days before the development of sophisticated electronic gear, the cheesebox was quite a piece of work.

Mickey Callahan is a likeable, Barry Fitzgerald-type Irishman who drinks Canadian Club neat and doesn't have an honest impulse in his body. He is a schemer who enjoys the twists and turns of making a dishonest buck. He also has a fund of stories worthy of a biographer.

He first met Costello in the early thirties. Costello was in the slot machine business then, and he hired Mickey to "gaff" his machines, adjust them mechanically so the payoffs would be minimal. Mickey also worked for other Italian mobsters and indulged his wry sense of humor by taking advantage of his electronically unsophisticated clients. He would design and build elaborate gadgets and, for kicks, install flashing red, green, and white lights that were there simply for effect.

"That's the colors of the guinea flag," Mickey explained. "I always got more money that way."

Cheesebox began his career by hanging around an Italian restaurant on the East Side that was frequented by mobsters. "Now Joe the Boss started asking me to do little favors for him," he recalled. "They were not big. In other words, just locate somebody for him to do this or that. There were lots of other guys who used to hang around that restaurant, including Costello. He was a pretty likeable guy.

"I observed what Costello said was law. He was a convincer. But he was not bigger than Charley Lucky (Lucky Luciano) or Joe the Boss. In fact, Charley Lucky was working for Joe the Boss. So Frank Costello exchanged telephone numbers with me and said he had a lot of work and he'd like me to do it for him. We agreed and, he started giving me work.

"The work at first wasn't big work. I used to gaff his slot machines. Then I graduated, and he gave me wire work. He'd say that he was convinced one guy was a rat, and he'd give me an apartment number of a home, whatever it might be, and a telephone number. The only thing he didn't supply was the multiple numbers on the poles, in the box. I would put a tap in, and them days — I mean in a tenement or apartment house of wherever it would be — I'd tell him what place he should have somebody rent *an apartment* or where the person could sit. Now I'd pull the line in there and set things up, and of course we weren't as advanced as we are right now, so all I gave the fellow was a headset, and he was on his own. I'd get paid my price, and whatever transpired I'd never know. He'd call me up and say, 'Look, we had that guy dead wrong.' I didn't care. So I'd just take my leads off, and that was the end of the story. When I was working for him he'd give me a tap job about once a month — someone he wanted to spy on. He was very liberal with his money, and our relationship went on for quite a while.

"I knew Willie Moretti, we used to call him Willie Moore before I knew him. Willie Moretti was no more than a stick-up man years ago. He and Costello were both degenerate horseplayers. They were always trying to beat the bookies. Costello used to call me up and say, 'Look, we have to knock this son-of-a-bitch out of the box. This bookmaker, he's no good.'

"So they'd have me tap in on some bookmaker's service line, Nationwide News serviced everybody then, and the bookies would get calls on races from all over the country broadcast right into their offices. My job was to hold up the flashes. I'd cut into the line and imitate the announcer's voice and say something in code, and Costello and Moretti's men would be right in the bookie's office listening. My code would tip them off to the winner. Then they'd bet their lungs and tap the bookie out. I'd get a piece of the action."

Mickey remembers getting a call from Costello one day and being told to meet him in front of the Park Central Hotel on Seventh Avenue.

"When I met him he said, 'Irish, let's take a ride to see Willie.' Well, I knew that was money, so I said okay. Willie Moretti had a place in Deal, New Jersey, and some guy drove us down. We went into Willie's house, in the playroom, and it looked more like a bookmaking place than somebody's home. There were a lot of mobsters sitting around this big long table reading the racing form and studying scratch sheets. Everybody there was Italian, and they were jabbering away at one another, but I understood the lingo pretty good by then. Willie was sitting at the head of the table like a high priest. 'Hey, Irish,' he yelled. 'Hey, Willie Moore,' I yelled back. He had the telephone to his ear, listening to the call of a race. Then Willie says, 'Hey, they're about to start. Who the hell made the bets?' So Costello picks up the phone and calls bookmakers in Cincinnati, Detroit, and Chicago. He bet his lungs. So while this is going on, I took a pair of wires and strung them to the radio's amplifying system, and now Willie doesn't have to hold the phone to his ear. The race call is blasting through. They looked at me like I was God, and everybody said, 'Hey, this guy is great.' They're all happy and excited because the race they bet on is coming up.

"Now they're running at Belmont because that was the track. They get the first call, and the horse they bet on is nowhere. Now everybody is angry looking. I'm standing studying all this. You could read their thoughts in their faces. Another stiff and everybody is thinking of killing the trainer or the jockey or whoever the hell gave them the tip. At the half-mile pole, their horse gets a call — he's third. You could see a few smiles. Now they're at the three-quarter mark, and he's second and moving up. Everybody gets up and starts to scream. They're screaming and yelling in Italian and whipping him home. So I start screaming and yelling in Italian and whipping too. He wins it by a half a length, and now the dance goes on. Everybody singing, laughing, yelling. Just like in the "Godfather" — da-da-da-da — everybody's dancing around the table. I'm dancing. Frank is giving me money. Willie Moore is giving me money. Johnny Caboose, Willie Moore's right hand man, is giving me money."

❀   ❀   ❀

Mickey's relationship with Uncle Frank, as he used to call Costello, lasted right into the middle forties. They parted then because Costello felt Mickey was taking advantage by charging whatever numbers came into his head.

Costello, according to Mickey, wasn't always as affable and friendly as most people thought.

"He was a tough son-of-a-bitch under that smiling, calm face of his," he said. "He could put someone in their place or make his point very clear smiling. In other words, instead of saying, 'I'll break your fucking head,' he'd say, 'You know, that's not nice what you did. People get themselves in a lot of trouble for less than that.' I seen him do it many times."

❋   ❋   ❋

Despite the heavy responsibility of leading the Luciano family and his total involvement in New York City politics, Costello in the forties continued to expand his business interests and ever-widening circle of friends. On the business side, Meyer Lansky and he founded the Emby Distributing Company for the distribution of juke boxes and another firm to handle cigarette vending machines.

Costello also purchased some valuable Manhattan real estate: three buildings in the Wall Street area. The most valuable parcel was a thirteen story office building at 79 Wall Street. The other two were four story office buildings, one at 87 Wall Street and the other at 114 Water Street. He sold all three in 1950 for five hundred thousand dollars.

In Florida, Lansky, who had a genius for finding lucrative investments for mob money, put together a syndicate and established a string of gambling houses in Broward County, which is Fort Lauderdale. The night club-casinos were the Colonial Inn, Club LaBoheme, and Club Greenacres. The syndicate consisted of the Lansky brothers, Costello, Joe Adonis, Frank Erickson, Vincent (Jimmy Blue Eyes) Alo, and Chicago's Jake (Greasy Thumb) Guzik, heir to the old Capone empire. In addition, Costello and Chicago mobster Tony Accardo were the proprietors of a handbook concession in Miami Beach which, according to the Miami Crime Commission, — had a gross profit of ten million a year.

In his effort to gain ever more influential friends, Costello became close with Jack Warner, one of the heads of Warner Brothers, the motion picture company, and with George Wood, New York vice president of the William Morris Agency, talent managers of most of the big names in show business. The trio played golf together, gambled together, and saw each other frequently over the dinner table.

Costello was interested in Hollywood and told friends that at one time he was seriously considering settling there. He made several trips to California to see how movies were made and was treated like royalty by the motion picture executives who had good reason to respect his power. Bugsy Siegel had been dispatched to handle things on the West Coast by the New York mob syndicate in 1937 and, by the early forties, had muscled himself into a position where he controlled several of the unions that the moviemakers had to deal with. Warner Brothers and other Hollywood studios asked and received Costello's help on several occasions in regard to Siegel-inspired labor problems.

❊   ❊   ❊

Costello liked to handle Mafia business at the track, and police often observed him conferring there with Trigger Mike Coppola and Tony Bender. Mafia business also forced him to visit a restaurant in New Jersey once a week. The restaurant also attracted the attention of the New York City police when they spotted high-echelon members of the secret society visiting the rather obscure dining establishment with clockwork regularity. Joe Adonis, Willie and Solly Moretti, Jerry Catena, Tommy Lucchese, Albert Anastasia, Tony Bender, Vincent Alo, Tommy (Tommy Ryan) Eboli were among those who were there most frequently.

The stream of traffic soon made it obvious to Manhattan District Attorney Hogan that Duke's, located in Cliffside Park, directly across the street from popular Palisades Amusement Park, had become the nerve center of organized crime in the Metropolitan area. Here the lords of the underworld, breathing the corrupt New Jersey air, were able to meet in privacy and discuss family business safe from the prying eyes and ears of the more vigorous New York police.

Duke's had a drab front, but inside it had a long mahogany bar and pleasantly decorated booths, and it served excellent food and drinks. It also had a rear entrance — used by the visiting Mafiosi — and two large, sound-proof rooms that served as mob meeting rooms. Many of the local residents, attracted by the excellence of Duke's kitchen, would dine there regularly without any notion that it was the headquarters of the mob.

Costello would visit Duke's only on Tuesdays, when the top leaders would show up for a once-a-week strategy session. Others, like the Moretti brothers and Joe Adonis, made Duke's their headquarters and would be there every day. The police first became aware of Duke's in 1941 and finally closed it down about 1947.

❊   ❊   ❊

Costello's pose as merely an ex-bootlegger and gambler began to wither in the early forties when two incidents focused newspaper attention on his role in the scheme of things. The first of these incidents was the Thomas Auerlio affair in 1943. The second occured in June of 1944, when he alighted from a taxicab at Fifty-ninth Street and Fifth Avenue and carelessly left behind two envelopes containing $27,200 in cash. The envelopes held 271 hundred dollar bills and 2 fifty dollar bills.

The driver, Edward Waters, found them and immediately turned the money in to the nearest police station. The newspapers jumped on the story of how the honest, hard-working cabbie had successfully resisted temptation.

"Are you crazy? What the hell did you turn the money in for?" a detective at the precinct asked Waters.

"I thought it was counterfeit," he answered, attesting to his sanity.

Costello realized he had lost the money almost immediately and did what was probably one of the most stupid acts of his adult life. He put in a claim for it.

The money didn't mean a damn thing to him. He must have known that putting in a claim would make him the subject of a countless number of newspaper stories. His pride was such, though, that he had to continue his charade of being just a gambler and businessman. So he acted out the role to its hilt. If a businessman lost money, he would claim it, naturally. So did Costello.

Mayor La Guardia, seeing an opportunity to make political capital in his role as crime fighter, said Costello wouldn't get the money back until he could prove he earned it honestly.

"What I'm interested in," La Guardia chirped to reporters, "is where did the bum get it and where was he taking it."

(The money had been given to Costello by Dandy Phil Kastel who had made a trip to the city to divvy up the quarterly proceeds of the New Orleans operation.)

Costello was enraged. Here he had lost a large sum of money and instead of having it returned, as would be the case with any other citizen, he was being called a bum in the newspapers. In addition, La Guardia was now saying the money should go to the police pension fund. Costello ordered his attorney George Wolf to file suit in court to force the city to return it.

The Internal Revenue Service didn't waste any time getting into the picture and quickly entered a claim for the money as partial payment of $36,000 the agency said Costello owed in back taxes. The courts would now have to decide whether the $27,200 should go to Costello, the city, or the Federal Government.

In October of 1944, Supreme Court Justice Carroll Walter listened to Costello's contention that $15,000 of the money was earned in his role as president of the 79 Wall Street Corporation, and the additional

$12,200 had been borrowed from a friend whom he declined to name. The court ruled that the entire sum be turned over to the tax man.

After it was all over, Costello admitted to friends that he had allowed his pride to rule his reason. He had received millions of dollars worth of unwanted publicity and wound up with a lawyer's fee for his trouble.

*   *   *

The man with whom Costello had more business dealings than any other over the years was Meyer Lansky. They also had a relationship that went far beyond a balance sheet. Both had the same general philosophy and outlook. They regarded the rackets as a business to be run on strict business principles, and they were both heavily involved in gambling.

They also saw a great deal of each other socially. Lansky's three children called Costello Uncle Frank, and he regarded them with warm affection. Paul Lansky, Meyer's second son, obtained his appointment to West Point through Costello. Lansky also frequently consulted Costello on his personal problems and sought his advice. Lansky once asked Costello to find out if the unpleasant rumors he heard about his daughter Sandy turning into a "swinger," were true. He knew that Costello had a network of informers among the restaurant owners, head waiters, and bartenders in New York's better places who were always anxious to do him a favor. Costello checked it out and found that Sandy had teamed up with Marilyn Doto, Joe Adonis' daughter, and both had a wild reputation at such places as Jilly's and the Harwyn Club. The club owners knew who the girls were and fell over themselves catering to their every whim. He didn't have the heart to tell Lansky, though, and lied to him about Sandy.

*   *   *

Meyer Lansky was born Maier Suchowljansky in 1902, in Grodno, Poland. He arrived with his family in New York in 1911, grew up on the Lower East Side, and went as far as the eighth grade in school.

He was a short, emaciated-looking youngster with a pinched face that gave him a hungry look. He had sharp brown eyes and an insatiable thirst for knowledge that he never lost. When he registered for selective service in 1942, a time when he was already a millionaire and one of the kingpins in the rackets, it was disclosed that he was receiving private tutoring in higher mathematics.

During his teenage years he teamed up with Ben Siegel, and the two were arrested on a felonious assault charge. It was reduced to disorderly conduct, and as the two stood in court, Magistrate McAdoo looked at them and is alleged to have said: "You boys have bugs in your heads."

In this way, so the story goes, the Bugs and Meyer mob was named. The five-foot-four, 120 pound Meyer absolutely doted on his tall, handsome partner. They were a study in contrasts. Meyer was thoughtful and cautious. Ben was impulsive and violence prone. Yet they worked well together. Ben (no one dared call him Bugsy to his face) was the muscle and could use a gun with deadly efficiency. Meyer was the planner, the brains. Between them they became the dominent Jewish mob on the Lower East Side.

During prohibition they went into bootlegging and prospered, forming alliances with Joe the Boss, Luciano, and Costello. It is significant that Lansky and Siegel were given the contract for the slaying of Joe the Boss and Maranzano. Luciano was not an ingrate. As his power grew, so did theirs.

The Costello-Lansky relationship bloomed into full flower during the thirties and forties, and the two of them would often be seen together in various restaurants around town. Toots Shor remembers that Lansky had a great interest in criminal law and that Costello and some of the other racketeers used to kid him about it and call him Clarence Darrow. He was a quietly dressed, somber little man who had become the financial wizard of the mob.

*   *   *

Besides gambling houses in Florida, Lansky is credited with helping to develop Las Vegas through his backing of Bugsy Siegel. He also made the deal with Cuban dictator Fulgencio Batista for the mob-dominated casinos that flourished in Havana before Fidel Castro spoiled it all. After being kicked out of Cuba, Lansky reestablished things on Grand Bahama Island with the Lucayan Beach Hotel. A reformer came along and caused that to blow away too, but not before his investors had made a handsome profit.

Costello invested heavily with Lansky in Las Vegas and Cuba. He was one of the principal financial backers of the Flamingo, the gambling palace that Bugsy Siegel built, and which is acknowledged to be the pioneer hotel that changed a three-mile strip of desert into the gaudy mecca of legalized gambling in the United States. If Siegel can be considered Las Vegas' George Washington, then Costello and Lansky were its Hyam Salomons'.

In late 1969, Lansky fled to Israel after being indicted by a grand jury in Las Vegas for being one of seven persons who skimmed thirty-six million off the top of the gambling take at the Flamingo over a period of years. As a Jew he claimed Israeli citizenship, and the Jewish state had reason to honor his claim despite his reputation. Lansky had donated millions of dollars to Israel during the dark days of its birth when it was being besieged by Arab armies from all directions.

But Israel also had reason to be grateful to the United States, and when Washington asked for his extradition (he fought it successfully for two and a half years), the Israelis booted him out. A two-day flying odyssey followed in which Lansky is reputed to have offered one million dollars to any nation that would give him sanctuary. None did, and he was returned to the United States.

Today he is an extremely wealthy, old man with serious heart trouble who is desperately fighting to keep out of jail. He was recently acquitted of an income tax evasion charge by a Miami jury, but he has another income tax trial coming up in Las Vegas. How he'll fare in Nevada remains to be seen.

Nineteen forty-five was an extraordinary year for the Mafia. Luciano got tired of sitting in his jail cell and asked out. Thomas E. Dewey, the man who had put him behind bars and was by that time Governor of New York, agreed. The only provision was that he insisted Luciano be deported.

The full story behind Luciano's release, which previously has not been printed, had its beginnings, in 1942 when German U-boats sank twenty-one ships off the Atlantic Coast in January, twenty-seven in February, and fifty in March. Worried U.S. Naval intelligence officials suspected that spies on the docks were somehow passing shipping information to the enemy. Then the French liner Normandie, being converted to a troopship, burned at her Hudson River berth. Lieutenant James O'Malley of the Office of Naval Intelligence, acting on orders from his superiors, approached Manhattan District Attorney Hogan and asked to be put in touch with the underworld to enlist their support in securing the New York waterfront. Hogan assigned assistant district attorney Murray Gurfein, now a Federal judge, to help him.

✻   ✻   ✻

A meeting was arranged with Socks Lanza, then under indictment for extortion in connection with the Fulton Fish Market rackets. Lanza, in turn, went to Costello who told him to give the Navy all the help he could. A month later he instructed Lanza to tell Lieutenant Commander Charles R. Haffenden, who was in charge of the project, that the only way to guarantee the loyalty of the entire waterfront was to enlist the aid of the boss, Lucky Luciano, who was still in jail.

Haffenden asked how to go about getting Luciano's cooperation and was sent to see Moe Polakoff, Luciano's lawyer.

After several meetings, Meyer Lansky was brought into the picture because Luciano said he needed him. In addition, Luciano was transferred from tough Dannemora to Great Meadows Prison (then the country club of state prison) to make it easier for everyone to visit.

Starting in May of 1942 and running until May of 1945, Luciano was visited in prison by some of the top mobsters in the East: Lanza at least four times; Lansky about ten times; Mike Lascari of New Jersey, Longy Zwillman's partner, nine times; and Costello, Willie Moretti, and Mike Miranda at least once.

They all fed Luciano information that he relayed to Naval Intelligence. Costello, for instance, detailed possible hiding places on Long Island, because he knew every nook and crany of the area from his bootlegging days.

Just how valuable the information was is unknown. Naval Intelligence, however, appears to have been satisfied because there were no more Normandie incidents.

*   *   *

On May 7, 1945, V-E Day, Luciano applied to Dewey for executive pardon. He based his request for clemency on his contribution to the war effort. Dewey passed the request over to his handpicked parole board.

Lieutenant Commander Haffenden then swore out an affidavit and addressed it to the board. The affidavit attested to the fact that Luciano had used his contacts in Sicily to smooth the way for the Allied invasion, thereby saving many American lives.

Norman Lewis, author of *The Honored Society*, points out that Luciano people in Sicily were told to wear shirts or coats with the letter "L" (for Lucky) embroidered on the back as a sign to the GI's that these were friendly partisans. These partisans were actually the Mafiosi whose power had been undermined by Mussolini. So with the aid of Luciano and the American army, they were put back into the seat of power.

The Americans, though, didn't realize this at the time, so Luciano's release looked like the fair reward for a patriot. The truth of the matter was that the Sicilians hated the Germans and would have cooperated with the Americans no matter what Luciano said.

The real story of Luciano's release, according to underworld gossip and federal investigators close to the situation, was far different from the one officially given. Luciano ordered Costello to get together every bit of dirt he could about Dewey. Costello concentrated on the witnesses at Luciano's trial who had literally buried him. When these witnesses were approached, they recanted their testimony and said they perjured themselves because they were addicts and drugs had been withheld from them by the prosecution. Dewey's staff, they swore, fed them the testimony, and they repeated it on the witness stand.

Once this dossier was put together, Luciano then threatened to go into court with it by suing for a new trial on the basis of the new evidence of perjured testimony. While it probably wouldn't have resulted in his freedom, it certainly would have proved highly embarrassing to Dewey, now firmly eyeing a second try for the Presidency.

Moe Polakoff has told friends: "While there is no question that the information Luciano turned over to Naval Intelligence was useful. That was the excuse given for his release, but certainly not the reason."

The late syndicated columnist Drew Pearson, many years after the event, quoted Luciano as telling him: "They claim I got out because of my efforts to help the navy. That wasn't it at all. I was getting tired of sitting up there in prison and I had my lawyers dig up everything they could on a very prominent official. When they finished they brought me a book. The stuff on him was terrible. So I told the lawyer that if I didn't get out of Dannemora this stuff would be published. I told them to tell him that if they think I was bad they should see the stuff we have on him. That was what got me out."

Costello backed up Luciano's story in private conversations with friends. The main difference in his version is that he claimed credit for engineering the entire thing, including the strategy of using Luciano's war work as an excuse and the recanted testimony of the witnesses for blackmail.

❆   ❆   ❆

On January 3, 1946, acting on the recommendation of the parole board, Dewey granted Luciano a pardon. He was then sent to Ellis Island to await deportation.

While he was at Ellis Island, Frank Costello and Moe Polakoff showed up at the ferry boat slip. *Daily News* reporter Robert Dwyer spotted Costello.

"Hello Frank. What gives?" Dwyer asked.

"Look kid, I'm not making you. You didn't see me, see," Costello answered, after shaking hands with the newsman.

Costello, carrying two large suitcases and Polakoff, empty handed, then were allowed to take the ferryboat to Ellis Island. Dwyer attempted to follow but was kicked off the ferryboat slip three times by the Coast Guard.

On February 9, Luciano was escorted aboard the Liberty Ship *Laura Keene*, docked at Pier Seven, Brooklyn's Bush Terminal. A crowd of reporters tried to follow him aboard the ship, but their way was blocked by about fifty longshoremen carrying menacing-looking bailing hooks. This was the heart of Anastasia country, the area of waterfront ruled by "Tough Tony" Anastasia, Albert's brother.

Harry Ratzke, Immigration and Naturalization's assistant superintendent in charge of security, attempted to clear a way for the newsmen. He was threatened by the dock wallopers and promptly retreated. While this was going on, a farewell shipboard party was in progress aboard the *Laura Keene*. Frank Costello, Longy Zwillman, Mike Lescari, Joe Adonis, and about half a dozen others were giving the boss a proper send off.

As humorist Harry Golden might say, "Only in America."

Don Vitone returns

"I even stuttered when I talked to him."

Joe Valachi

Crowds of cheering and cooperative Italians welcomed the conquering Americans as they marched up the boot of Italy in 1944. Fascism and the adventure with Mussolini were over. The good sense of the Italian people had returned, and they regarded the Americans as liberators, not conquerors.

To the military fell the task of governing the areas freed of Germans. Italians who spoke English were in great demand as interpreters. In the Naples area, the Allied Military Government was delighted to find a short, energetic man who spoke excellent English, who seemed to know everything, and who appeared to be completely trustworthy. He had lived in America for many years before returning to his beloved homeland. The interpreter was Vito Genovese.

In no time he became the indispensable man around headquarters where his duties went far beyond that of a mere translator. He possessed excellent information and supplied the Americans with the names of many local Fascists. He also was knowledgable about black market operations and helped the military police break up several rings. And for all this he proudly disdained pay, an unheard of thing.

Vito Genovese helped make life more pleasant for the officers of the occupying forces. He seemed to have an uncanny knack for coming up with a case of precious scotch or scarce two-inch thick steaks. He entertained many high-ranking officers in his beautiful villa and had an inexhaustible supply of lovely women friends whom he didn't mind introducing to lonely American officers. In their reports these officers described Vito Genovese in glowing terms. "He would accept no pay; paid his own expenses; worked day and night and rendered most valuable assistance to the Allied Military Government," wrote a major for whom Genovese worked.

Then an agent of the Army's Criminal Intelligence Division, Orange C. Dickey, while investigating widespread activities by a highly organized blackmarket ring in the Naples area, made an astounding discovery. The head of this ring, which was stealing army food supplies by the truckload, was Vito Genovese. Surprised, he began checking into the interpreter's background and found that before the Americans arrived, he had traveled in high Fascist circles and had been decorated for his contributions to the cause by Mussolini. Dickey gathered all the necessary evidence, arrested Genovese, and filed a report of his findings to headquarters.

The report proved an acute embarrassment to the high brass. They stared at the evidence in disbelief and did nothing. Frustrated at the lack of action, Dickey reported his findings to the FBI. They expressed an interest in his prisoner, but not for his black-market activities. Genovese, they said, was wanted for murder and ordered that he be returned to stand trial for the 1934 killing of Ferdinand (the Shadow) Boccia.

                    *   *   *

Dickey and an American intelligence officer returned Genovese to America where he was handed over to the King's County District Attorney's office in Brooklyn. Some years later, Dickey described the experience to the McClellan committee.

"At various times I was offered many things," he testified. "At one point I was offered a quarter of a million dollars to let this fellow out of jail. On one occasion, when I was offered another sum of money, I had with me an officer by the name of Lieutenant Dillon."

The key witness against Genovese was Peter LaTempa, a cigar store salesman, who was not part of the murder but had unluckily overheard the plans to kill Boccia. To safeguard his life he was held in jail as a material witness.

While in the cell, LaTempa suffered from gallstone attacks. A physician prescribed medication which he was given daily. On January 15, 1946, LaTempa was given his medicine in a glass of water. After drinking it, he fell ill and quickly died. A New York City taxicologist analyzed his internal organs and reported that he had been given enough poison "to kill eight horses."

An investigation into the murder failed to reveal who was responsible, and with the death of LaTempa the charge of murder against Vito Genovese also died. He walked out of jail on June 11, 1946.

Don Vitone, as Genovese was respectfully addressed by those in the Mafia, was welcomed back with a party in his honor held in the Diplomat Hotel in New York. It was attended by all the East Coast Mafia chiefs. Significantly, Frank Costello led him to the place of honor at the head of the table.

A Justice Department report states that Genovese advised those gathered to pay him homage:

"Let them figure you for a businessman, not a rackets guy."

✳   ✳   ✳

Don Vitone was not an imposing man in appearance. He was short, stocky, had a full face, and amber-tinted glasses. He wore expensive, conservatively-cut clothes and could easily be taken for a successful accountant or small businessman.

His most outstanding feature was the cold, hypnotic stare of his eyes. They seemed to be able to look right through you. In 1959, when he was arrested on a narcotics conspiracy charge by Treasury agents, I had the opportunity to look into his eyes, and even today I can remember the experience vividly. They were expressionless, completely void of pity. The eyes of someone who killed whenever something or someone was in his way.

✳   ✳   ✳

Don Vitone was a Neapolitan by birth and came to New York with his family in 1912. His father, who ran a small contracting firm, settled in Queens, but Vito preferred the atmosphere of the Lower East Side's Little Italy, and he was placed with relatives who lived in the area.

He was caught stealing vegetables off a pushcart when he was sixteen. The peddler held him by the arm and began screaming at him. Young Vito pulled free, stared at the peddler, and solemnly warned him: "Don't ever touch me again; you can call the cops, but I'll kill anyone who puts a hand on me." There are old men on Mulberry Street in Little Italy who swear the story is true.

In 1917, he was sentenced to sixty days in jail for carrying a gun. He was arrested again the following year on a felonious assault charge but was freed when the victim refused to testify against him.

During the prohibition years he was charged with homicide twice, but there was no firm evidence, and he was released. He was also questioned in several other killings. Those were the years in which he and Luciano worked together as a team and in which they both rose to prominence under Joe the Boss. He was always the number two man to Luciano and held that position when Joe the Boss and Maranzano were killed.

Vito became rich during the early thirties when he captured control of the Italian lottery. With his profits he bought into a number of Greenwich Village nightclubs, several of them catering to homosexuals.

His first wife, a plain, simple girl, Anna Ragone, died of tuberculosis in 1931. The following year he married again, choosing Anna Petillo Vernotico, a distant cousin twelve years younger than he. At the time of the marriage, Anna had been a widow just twelve days. Her husband, Gerardo Vernotico, was found murdered on the roof of a tenement just a few doors away from a Genovese-owned business on Thompson Street. He had been shot, stabbed, and strangled with a clothesline. Underworld sources say that Genovese had him killed because he had fallen in love with Anna.

The love affair didn't last. In 1952, Anna gathered up enough courage to sue for separation and asked $350 a week in support. Vito refused. The affair was aired in court in Freehold, New Jersey, and Anna told stories of her husband seducing her women friends and beating her. One time, she told the court, he punched her so hard in front of guests that two of her teeth fell out.

What interested authorities more, however, was her description of her husband's wealth. She claimed Vito was worth thirty million and had money stashed away in vaults in New York, New Jersey, Naples, Paris, Switzerland, and Monte Carlo. She said his wealth came from narcotics, gambling, liquor, and extortion and that he owned two dog tracks in the South and a string of nightclubs in Greenwich Village. She said that while he was in Italy, she personally ran the Italian lottery racket, and it threw off profits of between twenty thousand and thirty thousand dollars a week.

When he fled to Italy, she testified, he carried $750,000 in cash in a suitcase, and right up until World War II she would visit him there regularly bringing as much as $100,000 in cash to replenish his supply.

Why didn't Genovese have Anna killed or accede to her modest demand of support? Joe Valachi supplies the answer. He said that Genovese loved Anna and that when they were in prison together he would see tears roll down his cheeks as he talked about her and her betrayal. As for the money, Valachi described Genovese as being the tightest man in the mob. "He wouldn't go for nuthin'," is the way Valachi put it.

*   *   *

When Don Vitone returned, Costello handled him the way a snake charmer handles a cobra — warily and with extreme respect. He took pains to see that Genovese did not feel he had been shunted aside in his absence. Don Vitone slowly took over control of the family. Costello made no protest, content to take a backseat role. He explained that he had only been a caretaker in Genovese's absence.

The reins of power had shifted over the years and Don Vitone noted the fact. He saw that Costello had formed alliances with Joe Adonis and Albert Anastasia and that the organization needed and respected him. He observed Costello's political power and his growing wealth and influence. For someone who wanted all the power for himself, the situation was intolerable. Still, Don Vitone had to act with caution, solidify his own alliances, and then chip away at the weakest links of Costello's empire.

"Well, when he came back, he was mumbling and grumbling, and he was giving hell to Tony Bender," Valachi told the McClellan committee." 'You allow these people to sew up everything and tie up everything,' but Tony told him, 'Well, you told him (sic) to make the worst of things so that is what I have been doing.' "

Genovese complained that Costello, Moretti, Anastasia, and Adonis had everything sewed up. There was no room for him to move.

*   *   *

Don Vitone's return came at an unusual time in Costello's life. He was in his middle fifties and beginning to question the values and course of his life. The Mafia, with its medieval blood oath, its violence, its ignorance, and its members who were most often little better than thugs, contrasted sharply with the legitimate world in which he spent so much of his time. He had shaken the poverty of his heritage long ago and would have liked to have retired from the secret society. Yet he knew this was impossible. The ties between the Mafia and its members were much stronger than those of a Roman Catholic marriage: there were no special dispensations for annulments. There was not even a separation.

He had begun to suffer periods of depression and insomnia. Most of his life was over, and like many men who reach his age he thought about death and the meaning of his life. Was it all a waste? When he was gone, would only the fact that he had been a racketeer be remembered?

In an attempt to deal with the depression and the questions he was asking himself, Costello, in 1947, secretely began seeing a psychiatrist regularly. He told no one about it. Not even his closest friends.

The psychiatrist was Dr. Richard H. Hoffman, a well-known shrink with a Park Avenue clientele. Costello had met Dr. Hoffman during one of his long walks in Central Park. The two had become friendly, and Costello decided to seek help with his problems.

Dr. Hoffman treated Costello for two years or so. The relationship ended when the newspapers found out about it, and the psychiatrist admitted he was treating Costello. He said that he had advised him to mingle with a better class of people. An angry Costello immediately broke off the relationship and denied he was a patient. Hoffman, he said, used to ask his advice about patients and found it most useful. As for mixing with better people, Costello said he had introduced Hoffman to a better class of people than Hoffman had introduced him to.

Costello had been embarrassed by the psychiatrist's revelations and lashed out angrily. The truth of the matter was that Dr. Hoffman treated him for more than two years. He listened to Costello tell how he had hated his father and what it was like growing up in East Harlem. He listened to Costello describe how he had been made to feel inferior because he was Italian and how deep down inside he still felt inferior despite his accomplishments. Then there was the image the press projected of him — story after story in which he was called a gangster and accused of every crime imaginable. It was true that he had never sold any bibles, and sure he had been a bootlegger and was involved in gambling, but if he was guilty of wrongdoing, so was everyone else who took a drink during prohibition or ever made a bet with a bookie. He had never killed anyone. He had never had anything to do with heroin. On the contrary, he had done whatever he could to prevent violence.

Dr. Hoffman told him he should widen his horizons and change his image. He should make new friends and open up areas of life that might give him satisfaction to explore. There was a sameness about his friends and business associates. As for his image, well, there was a lot he could do there. A man with his talent for organization could do many things — become involved in charity, for instance. Many men had changed their image and received immense satisfaction through charitable work.

❋   ❋   ❋

In January of 1949, Costello took on the responsibility of raising money for the Salvation Army. After being appointed a vice-chairman

of the organization's men's division, he sponsored a fund-raising dinner
at the Copacabana. All told, about 150 persons attended and each
contributed one hundred dollars to attend the charitable affair.

✻　　　✻　　　✻

The invitation sent out by Costello read:

Dinner and Entertainment
Sponsored by
Frank Costello
Vice-Chairman of Men's Division
Salvation Army Campaign
Monday, January 24, 1949 at 6:30 p.m.
Copacabana
Ten East Sixtieth Street, New York
Entire Proceeds for
Salvation Army Association
$100 per person. Dress informal.

The menu consisted of fresh fruit cocktail, hearts of celery, ripe and
green olives, salted almonds, chicken okra soup, sirloin steak, new
string beans saute' mixed green salad, creme glace' petit fours, and
demitasse. Attached to each menu was the following statement:

"I deem it a great honor and privilege to take part in the 1949
Salvation Army campaign and to sponsor this dinner and entertainment
on its behalf.
"For the generous contributions of my many dear friends to this
great cause and for their assistance in making this affair possible,
thanks from the bottom of my heart."

Frank Costello
Vice-Chairman, Men's Division

✻　　　✻　　　✻

The affair obviously meant a great deal to Costello, but it turned
into a fiasco and a source of painful embarrassment to many of those
who attended. The newspapers received a tip that Costello had sponsored the Salvation Army campaign dinner and had a field day with the
story. Editorial writers raised the question about the propriety of a
respected charitable organization allowing a notorious racketeer to
raise money that was almost certainly tainted. Reporters carefully dug
up the names of the guests to see who was breaking bread with Frank

Costello. The guest list included people from his three worlds: the rackets, politics, and business.

Among those who attended were: Vito Genovese; Dandy Phil Kastel; Frank Erickson; Manhattan Borough President Hugo Rogers; Congressman Arthur Klein; Tammany Hall leaders Carmine DeSapio and Francis Mancuso; Tammany secretary Sidney Moses; former Tammany leader Clarence Neal; Supreme Court Justices Thomas Aurelio, Anthony DiGiovanna, S. Samuel DiFalco, Morris Eder, and Algron I. Nova; Judge Thomas Downs of Queens County Court; Judge Lewis J. Capozzoli of City Court; Special Sessions Justice Joseph Loscalzo; Gene Pope Jr., youngest son of Costello's close friend; Dr. and Mrs. Harold Hoffman; and Mr. Howard Chandler Christie, the well known painter, and his wife.

"It was a lovely affair, and I never met so many judges in my life," Mrs. Christie gushed to reporters.

Not everyone who attended the fund raising affair was invited. Detectives from the Intelligence Division of New York City's Police Department managed to slip in as guests. From the intelligence gathering point of view, the trouble they went through was well worth it. They observed the effusive welcome Costello reserved for Vito Genovese and how he led him to the head table to sit in the place of honor.

"He practically kissed his ass in front of everyone," the detectives reported.

The significance of it all was unmistakable. In the authority conscious Mafia that could only mean one thing: Don Vitone had replaced Costello and was now the boss in the family. This was the first knowledge that police had of the changing order of things.

When the story of Costello's charity dinner broke in the newspapers, the politicians and judges ran for cover. Many of them denied any knowledge of who had sponsored the affair even though the invitation clearly stated the information.

C. Frank Cramer, director of the Salvation Army, at first said that he didn't know that Frank Costello was *"the Frank Costello."* Then he changed his tactics and defended the fifteen thousand dollars the dinner had raised.

"We will take anybody's money to further our good work," he said and then added, "The money paid by the 150 guests isn't necessarily Costello's."

Mrs. Jackson A. Dyckman, director of the women's division of the organization, was much more honest. "We hope we can meet a Frank Costello on every corner," she said. "We need the money, and that is the prime object, not where it comes from."

Shortly after, Costello resigned as vice-chairman.

*   *   *

Late in 1946, the underworld was electrified by the news that the boss, Charley Lucky, was back. He had quietly slipped into Cuba with the knowledge and help of Cuban government officials. Meyer Lansky had arranged things, and Luciano quickly established himself in a penthouse suite of a luxury hotel, just ninety miles away from the shores of Florida.

In early 1947, what seemed to be the entire hierarchy of the mob went south to greet Charley Lucky. Luciano's old family was represented by Costello, Genovese, Moretti, Adonis, Little Augie Pisano, and Mike Miranda. The capos of the four other New York families also traveled to Cuba: Joe Profaci, Joe Bonanno, Tommy Lucchese, and Joe Magliocco. Chicago was represented by Tony Accardo and the Fischetti brothers, Joe and Rocco. Meyer Lansky, the man who had made it all possible, was also there.

It was party time, and the mob chiefs were entertained in fine style. The Fischetti brothers brought singer Frank Sinatra with them to greet Luciano. Sinatra had reason to pay homage to the boss. His career had been helped considerably by Willie Moretti when he was a kid singing with the Tommy Dorsey band. In fact, when Luciano's apartment had been searched one time by the Italian police in Naples, they found a gold cigarette case with the inscription: "To my dear pal Lucky, from his friend, Frank Sinatra."

Besides fun and games, the mob chiefs also had business to discuss. The big problem was what to do about Bugsy Siegel who was defying syndicate orders and acting as if he were in business for himself. To begin with, Bugsy had initially sunk three million in syndicate money into the building of the Flamingo Hotel in Las Vegas and had ran out of cash before it was completed. He then borrowed another three million — from anyone he could — much of it from Lansky and Costello. The Flamingo at that point represented a six million dollar investment, an unheard of figure in those days.

While this was serious, the final straw was when Siegel refused an order to merge two mob-controlled racing wire services — one owned by the Chicago mob and the other by the New York mob — in Las Vegas because it was more profitable for him personally to force bookies to buy both. Siegel didn't own the wire services (Trans-American and Continental), he was merely managing them. Yet he was so desperate for money because of the Flamingo, he ignored repeated warnings. Finally, in a pique of anger, he sent back word to New York that

he was boss in the West and that no one was going to tell him what
to do.

After reportedly resisting the final solution to the problem, Luciano
is said to have finally agreed that Siegel would have to be eliminated
for the good of everyone.

❊   ❊   ❊

While all this was going on, Luciano's suite was being observed by
agents of the Federal Bureau of Narcotics. They quietly kept a watch
on his visitors, careful not to give themselves away. The penthouse
suite was proving to be a valuable source of intelligence.

The game of cat and mouse came to an end when the late syndicated columnist Robert Ruark received a tip on Luciano's new-world
hideout. He printed the news that Charley Lucky was back in business in Havana. Harry Anslinger, head of the Bureau of Narcotics,
then did the only thing left for him to do: he pressured the Cuban
government to kick Luciano back to Italy. At first, the Cubans refused.
Then Anslinger, backed by Washington, threatened to cut off all American medical supplies to the island if Lucky didn't go. Lucky went.

He returned to Italy, his Cuban idyll over. It was the last time Luciano strayed from the shores of the land of his birth. He died of a
heart attack on January 28, 1962 at the Naples Airport. He had gone
there to meet a film producer interested in doing his life story. His
death at sixty-five, Italian police said, occurred just as they were about
to arrest him for running a huge international drug ring that had smug-
gled $150 million worth of heroin into the United States in the previous
ten years.

The Havana decision concerning Bugsy Siegel was carried out on
the night of June 20, 1947. Siegel was sitting on a couch, in front of
a large window, reading a newspaper in the living room of the sump-
tuous Beverly Hills home he maintained for his girlfriend, Virginia
Hill. Virginia, who was knowledgable about mob decisions and affairs, had fled to Paris. She knew Siegel had been sentenced to death
and didn't want to be in the area when it occurred — not because she
was afraid, but because she loved him.

❊   ❊   ❊

Virginia Hill was an Alabama-born, tempestuous, green-eyed, auburn-haired beauty who knew her way around the bedrooms of a score
of racketeers. She had tried suicide several times while involved with
Bugsy. In May of 1947, just a month before Siegel was killed, she
was taken to the hospital after swallowing a bottle's worth of sleeping
pills. Doctors pumped out her stomach, and she woke up to find Siegel

by her side talking glibly to several physicians about how he would donate a new wing to the hospital in appreciation for saving her life.

Virginia, in front of the doctors (and newspapermen who had sneaked along), shouted: "Give them the Flamingo for a wing. To hell with that dump. Get out, Ben, before you're dead."

❋   ❋   ❋

Allen Smiley, one of Siegel's closest pals, was in the house with him and sat at the other end of the couch. While they both sat there quietly, someone armed with a 30-30 carbine sneaked into the hedges in front of the window and fired three shots into Siegel's head. The slugs smashed his nose, tore out one eye, ripped his cheeks apart, and neatly removed a section of vertabrae in his neck.

Thirty-minutes after Siegel was slain, three men, Moe Sedway, Morris Rosen, and Gus Greenbaum, walked into the Flamingo and announced that they were now giving the orders.

The hand ballet

Late in 1950, a traveling troupe of players from Capitol Hill in Washington, D.C., known officially as the Special Senate Committee to Investigate Organized Crime in Interstate Commerce, began a road tour of fourteen American cities. More commonly known as the Kefauver committee, after its chairman, Senator Estes Kefauver of Tennessee, the committee threw a powerful searchlight on the widespread hold organized crime had on life in the United States. The American people — through the relatively new medium of television — watched in fascination as revelations made it abundantly clear that there were two national governments in the United States: one in Washington and one in the underworld.

Nowhere was the morality play that unfolded a bigger smash hit than in the nation's capital of sin — New York City. Housewives abandoned their chores and sat fascinated in front of their TV sets, women crowded into TV-equipped bars, businessmen and officials cancelled appointments so as not to miss one of the daily televised performances. It was one of the first real-life dramas to be shown on the home screen, and its occurrence marked TV's coming of age. From that time on, its devastating power became apparent to everyone.

Frank Costello was the undisputed star of the play, and his expressive hands, with nails buffed daily by a manicurist to mirror-like brightness, became its symbol. He was given top billing by the committee

161

when it issued an interim report describing him as "the most influential underworld leader in America."

Before Costello's testimony began, attorney George Wolf protested vigorously against his client being shown on TV. The committee instructed the TV cameramen to obey the request, and they then did the flecting his inner turmoil under hammering cross-examination told of his hoarse, whispery voice with seemingly disembodied hands reflecting his inner turmoil under hammering cross-examination, told an eloquent story on the home screen. When the questions were rough, Costello crumpled a handkerchief or rubbed his palms together or interlaced his fingers. When he became impatient, he grasped a half-filled glass of water or beat a silent tattoo on the table top or rolled a little ball of paper between his thumb and forefinger. Sometimes he would split the side pieces of his glasses lying on the table. When he made a point, the index finger of his right hand would point straight out, and when he attempted to control his hand movements, the fingers would tear at each other.

The suddenly grown-up medium created other stars: Senator Estes Kefauver, a tall, lanky, homespun character, gained so much national exposure that he was able to seek the Democratic nomination for President; Senator Charles W. Tobey of New Hampshire, a tart New Englander with a talent for emiting shock and indignation, became the nation's conscience; Rudolph Halley, the committee's chief counsel from New York City, short, dark-haired, intense, and with a high-pitched voice that betrayed a slight lisp, won fame as a hard-driving prosecutor with his bulldog tenacity during cross-examination.

Other members of the committee who never reached star status but were important minor players were Senators Herbert R. O'Conor of Maryland, Alexander Wiley of Wisconsin, and Lester C. Hunt of Wyoming.

Time — March 13, 1951, about ten-thirty A.M.

Place — A courtroom in the United States Court House, Foley Square, New York City.

Scene — The courtroom is overflowing with press and spectators. The senators sit on leather-covered chairs placed on a raised platform behind the bench usually occupied by federal judges. The bright TV lights give the large room with its high ceilings a false sense of being bathed in sunlight. A recess is about to end, and the babble of all the voices talking at once rises in intensity. The roar subsides for a moment and then picks up again as Frank Costello and attorney George Wolf walk to the witness table. Costello walks slowly, almost ponderously, in a sort of stiff-shouldered gait. He appears impassive, his facial expression is set in rigid lines. For his initial appearance, he wears a beautifully tailored, conservatively cut, powder-blue suit with matching shirt and tie. As he and Wolf seat themselves, Senator O'Con- or, acting as chairman this day, pounds his gavel for silence. A manuso- leum-like stillness descends as Costello raises his right hand and solemnly swears to tell the truth.

❊   ❊   ❊

Before the questioning begins, George Wolf rises to address the com- mittee. He strenuously objects to the TV cameras, saying, "Mr. Costello doesn't care to submit himself as a spectacle." He argues that the intru- sion of TV would interfere with his client testifying properly. Senator O'Conor orders the TV people not to show Costello's face during the proceedings. Wolf then asks permission to read a statement for his client who is suffering from laryngitis. Permission is granted.

The statement is an attack on the many newspaper charges — based on a March 1, 1951 interim report by the committee — in which Cos- tello was named as the head of one of the two major crime syndicates that are said to have the nation by the throat. The statement vigorously denies that there is any truth to the allegation and eloquently says:

"Give me, I ask you, this last opportunity of proving that your charges against me are unjustified and should be retracted. Confront me with evidence if you have it; if the charges are based on inferences, let me know what these inferences are. Then give me the right to publicly reply to your evidence or construe your surmises.

"I am not only asking that you respect fundamental rights and princi- ples, I am begging you to treat me as a human being."

❊   ❊   ❊

(Costello's stubborn pride in not wanting to appear as a criminal before the entire nation has resulted in his refusing to follow the advice of his lawyer by invoking the protection of the Fifth Amendment. He is intent on maintaining some facade of respectability and on showing the American people that he has nothing to hide.)

❊   ❊   ❊

Halley begins by plunging right into Costello's criminal background*.

Halley — "Have you been known under any other names other than Frank Costello?"

Costello — "Well, when I was a boy I believe my mother's maiden name was Saverio; not that I used it, but they called me that."

---

*Throughout, the testimony has been edited because of space limita- tions, but in no way has its thrust been changed.

Halley — "Have you used any other names?"

Costello — "Not to my recollection."

Halley — "Have you ever used the name Castiglia?"

Costello — "Not since I have been in America."

Halley — "Did you use it before you came to America?"

Costello — "Well, I couldn't have used it. I was only two years old."

Halley — "So you never used the name Castiglia?"

Costello — "Not that I remember."

Halley — "But you did use the name Saverio?"

Costello — "Well, I might have used it, yes; I might have, when I was a boy."

Halley — "Well, you used it after you were a boy, did you not?"

Costello — "Yes."

Halley — "Now, what do you mean when you say you might have used the name Saverio? Don't you know very well you used the name Saverio?"

Costello — "I might have used it; yes."

Halley — "Well, you are not using the English language when you say you might have. That means nothing."

Costello — "I'm sorry, I'm not a college man like you, Mr. Halley."

Halley — "You were convicted of a crime under that name, were you not?"

Costello — "Thirty-five, thirty-six years ago; yes."

Halley — "You have been asked about your conviction on many occasions, have you not?"

Costello — "Well, I have; yes."

Halley — "Now, getting back to Saverio, do you recall whether or not you were ever convicted in the State of New York in the year 1915 for possession of a revolver?"

Costello — "I was convicted for a misdemeanor."

Halley — "Were you convicted for possession of a revolver?"

Costello — "That's right; yes, sir."

Halley — "And on that occasion did you use the name Frank Saverio?"

Costello — "I imagine I did then; yes."

Halley — "Do you remember ever having applied for your naturalization?"

Costello — "Yes."

Halley — "Do you remember being asked, in the course of your naturalization proceeding, whether you ever used any alias or other name?"

Costello — "I wouldn't remember that."

         *   *   *

In the first hour of questioning, Halley establishes the following: every bit of information would have to be pulled out of Costello; the witness used an alias in the past; he has a criminal background; he lied during his naturalization proceedings.

Halley's intent is to show that Costello committed fraud when applying for citizenship so as to lay the foundation for a future deportation case. Most of the morning is spent on all the circumstances surrounding the naturalization proceedings. Costello's answers are weak, and Halley says his intent is to show the entire affair has the elements to "obtain naturalization by fraud."

Tobey — "Well — I am just thinking out loud now — if it is a fact that there was a conspiracy between the parties here involved to break the laws and transgress the laws of this country, and if at a later date he was made a citizen, and if a false statement was made in that situation there, is not the man who made the false affidavit as susceptible to the deportation from this country as one who falsified the records?"

Halley — "That is my thinking sir."

         *   *   *

Halley continues to pound at Costello's naturalization proceedings and delves into his bootlegging activities during the period in which he applied for citizenship. Costello denies he was in bootlegging prior to 1926 and says his acquittal of the charges when he was indicted with Big Bill Dwyer in 1925 is proof he wasn't a bootlegger until later.

After laying the foundation for future deportation proceedings, Halley switches his focus and asks Costello for a complete financial statement of his assets. Costello refuses and invokes the Fifth Amendment. Halley reminds him he had promised to furnish the committee with a complete listing of his assets when he appeared in executive session previously.

Costello is on the horns of a twin dilemma: if he submits a false statement, he is subject to being hit with perjury charges if the committee can prove he's lying; if he submits a true one, it is as good as handing himself over to the Internal Revenue Service. That is why he changes his mind and invokes his constitutional rights not to incriminate himself.

A long legal argument follows in which Halley argues that Costello has waived his right to invoke the Fifth because he has already answered questions in regard to his financial assets in executive session. Wolf, in turn, argues that his client has a perfect right to change his mind. The committee takes the entire matter under advisement and promises a ruling after the luncheon recess.

       ❊   ❊   ❊

(As the luncheon break begins, Costello walks directly behind Kefauver where American Broadcasting Company TV cameraman Louis Tyrrell is operating camera number two.
"Hey, kid," he says. "Remember, no face. Only the hands."
"Anything you say, you're the boss," Tyrrell answers.
Tyrrell, now a well known TV sports producer, recalls that when the hearings switched to Washington, Jake (Greasy Thumb) Guzik also approached him and said: "Hey, only the hands. Just like Frank.")

At the start of the afternoon session, the committee rules Costello has waived his right to invoke the Fifth Amendment on his assets and orders him to answer the question. He refuses. The consequences of the refusal can be profound. If he is found guilty of contempt of the Senate committee, a jail term can result.

Halley then asks Costello about his known assets: the Wall Street real estate and the Louisiana Mint Company. Costello answers this time — part of his profits from these enterprises have been declared on his income tax returns. He maintains that Phil Kastel is really the boss of the New Orleans slot machine operation, and he is merely a silent partner.

The next subject is Costello's 1949 income tax return. It opens up a bag of worms. Included in the return is the sum of fifteen thousand dollars, paid Costello by George Morton Levy, head of Long Island's Roosevelt Raceway. Costello testifies that he was paid fifteen thousand dollars a year by Levy, from 1946 to 1950, to keep bookmakers away from the track.

Halley — "Do you know anything about the bookmaking situation at Roosevelt Raceway?"

Costello — "No."

Halley — "Or at any harness track?"

Costello — "No."

Halley — "Prior to this occasion in 1946, had you gone into the question of bookmaking at the harness track with Levy?"

Costello — "No; not to my knowledge."

Halley — "Had he been previously consulting you what to do about bookies at Roosevelt Raceway?"

Costello — "No."

Tobey — "Well, you were paid sixty thousand dollars, weren't you, fifteen thousand dollars a year; is that right?"

Costello — "That's right."

Tobey — "But you did take sixty thousand dollars for doing nothing?"

Costello — "That's right, I did."

Tobey — "Isn't that kind of synonymous with taking candy from a child?"

Costello — "No. I know a lot of lawyers that get a fifty thousand dollars fee that's worth only fifteen hundred dollars."

Tobey — "We aren't talking about lawyers."

Costello — "Then why talk about me."

        ❄   ❄   ❄

(Costello's mysterious relationship with Roosevelt Raceway that hasn't been satisfactorily explained to this day. George Morton Levy still maintains that he paid Costello the sixty thousand dollars because a state harness official had a fixation about bookmakers and imagined that he saw them all over the track. To satisfy him, Levy says, he hired Costello who had the reputation of having influence with bookmakers. Levy says the state official seemed to be satisfied from that time on.

Those who are knowledgable about harness racing in the late forties, when there wasn't betting large enough to attract bookies, consider the explanation completely ridiculous. A more plausible one might be that Costello earned his money because of his political influence. The tracks are at the mercy of state legislators and often seek to have legislation passed beneficial to them. Costello had many state legislators in his hip pocket, and Levy, an astute operator, must have been aware of that.)

        ❄   ❄   ❄

Halley switches to a new topic — he attempts to show that Costello is an underworld boss. Using the information obtained during Manhattan District Attorney Hogan's tap on Costello's phone in 1943, he delves into the time Willie Moretti went to the West Coast for his health.

Halley — "Didn't you send him to California because he couldn't keep his mouth shut?"

Costello — "Absolutely not. I kept nobody in California."

Wolf — "May the witness explain about that subject matter, Mr. Halley?"

Halley — "Surely. Go right ahead. That is a fine suggestion."

Costello — "I might have suggested that he should take a rest and go up to recoup, maybe, in Florida, California, or somewhere. What privilege have I got to send him away?"

Halley — "Well, you were his boss?"

Costello — "Boss of what?"

Halley — "Did he ever call you up and say, 'Hello Chief?' "

Costello — "I called him, 'Chief' too."

Halley — "I haven't found any conversations in which you called him 'Chief.' "

Costello — "I called him 'Chief Meyers.' I called him 'Chief Meyers' when we were kids."

The question of whether Costello is Moretti's boss or not is Halley's last subject of the day. Before adjournment, Senator O'Conor requests Costello and Wolf to reconsider the refusal to answer the question about net worth. He warns that if Costello refuses to answer, the committee will have to consider whether to issue a citation for contempt.

❖   ❖   ❖

In the morning session of March 14, Halley opens by bringing up the subject of the New Orleans operation, and when he fails to obtain any tangible results, he switches to a new topic. He wants to know if Costello ever worried about his phone having a wire tap on it.

Halley — "Did you ever do anything to find out if you had a wire tap on your wire?"

Costello — "No; it wasn't necessary."

Halley — "Did you ever pay anybody to check over whether you had a wire tap?"

Costello — "No, sir; absolutely not, never paid anyone."

❖   ❖   ❖

(A telephone company employee, James McLaughlin, would testify later in the hearing that he had been paid a number of times to check Costello's phone to see if there was a tap on it. As a result of his testimony, the committee will cite Costello for perjury.)

Halley continues to go over much of the ground covered at least once since Costello began to testify: New Orleans, the Beverly Club, Roosevelt Raceway, and his relationship with Willie Moretti. The subject matter has diminishing returns, but Halley is tenacious and spends time wringing out whatever small concession he can from the witness. Costello's face and voice show the effects of the relentless cross-examination. His facial lines are deeply set from fatigue, and his voice is weaker and more gravelly. At the luncheon recess the committee excuses Costello until the next day to accommodate other witnesses.

In the afternoon session of the following day, March 15, George Wolf rises to address Senator Kefauver before the questioning of his client begins. He complains that the television lights make the crowded courtroom hot and uncomfortable and says that Costello is suffering from a severe throat inflammation and laryngitis.

"Now he has reached the end and the limits of physical and mental endurance. He cannot go on. He desires to defend himself and wants the opportunity to do so," he tells Kefauver.

Halley counters by saying that Costello has lied throughout his time under examination and that if had told the truth, the questioning might well be over.

"Now, Mr. Chairman," Halley says, "I believe the witness must continue to testify, must answer questions on the four subjects which were stated as the subjects upon which the committee wanted detailed information at the end of last session. They were: his activities, his legitimate business, and illegitimate business; his assets and net assets; his criminal associates, the people with whom he has associated before coming in front of this committee to testify; and finally, his political connections, which are perhaps the most important subject matter before this committee."

Wolf persists in his request for an adjournment and says it might require several weeks for Costello to regain his health. Halley reminds Kefauver that the committee is out of business in two weeks, and the chairman orders the questioning of Costello to continue.

"Senator, I am in no condition to testify," Costello tells Kefauver. "You heard my statement through Mr. Wolf, and I stand by it, and under no condition will I testify from here in, until I am well enough."

Kefauver — "You refuse to testify further?"

Costello — "Absolutely."

Kefauver — "You ask questions Mr. Halley, and we will see."

Halley — "Before I start, I think I should say, Mr. Chairman, that for a sick man, Mr. Costello is a very astute witness in my opinion, for the last two days, and a very difficult witness to cross-examine."

Costello — "Am I a defendant in this courtroom?"

Halley — "No."

Costello — "Am I under arrest?"

Halley — "No."

Costello — "Then I am walking out."

Before he walks, Costello listens as first Kefauver and then Halley warn him that he is risking arrest, a possible jail sentence, and being brought forcibly back before the committee to testify. He answers that he must think of his health first and walks. Bedlam breaks out in

the courtroom as newspapermen rush to their phones to report the
headline news that Costello has walked out on the Kefauver committee.

*   *   *

*("That time he walked out on the Senate committee, well, that very
evening he was in my restaurant," Toots Shor recalls. "I started to
holler at him, call him, 'You dumb guinea bastard, why did you do
that, you had the whole country on your side. You can't walk out on
a Senate hearing like that.'*

*"He just looked at me and said, 'I had to. I have to find out first
what O'Dwyer is going to say.'*

*"Christ, everyone knew that he and Mayor O'Dwyer used to see
each other all the time. All that the committee knew about was that
one meeting, and Frank had to see if O'Dwyer would stand up.")*

*   *   *

Costello faces the committee again on the afternoon session of March
16. Senator Kefauver says that Costello's physician has been questioned
and is of the opinion that since he has no fever he should be able to
testify an hour a day without harm to himself. Wolf protests that his
client is too ill to answer questions, but Kefauver instructs Halley to
go ahead. From the first question it is obvious the committee has
figured out what is really troubling Costello.

Halley — "Mr. Costello, did you have a meeting with William O'Dwyer
in the year 1942?"

Costello — "I refuse to go further with the questioning — answering
the questions — until I feel fully well and capable."

Halley — "Mr. Costello, do you know James Moran?"

Costello — "I don't care to answer any questions."

Kefauver — "It is not a question whether you care to answer them,
Mr. Costello."

Costello — "I don't feel I am fit to answer questions today and
answer them truthfully and sensibly."

Halley — "Mr. Chairman, in view of the fact that the witness has
created an issue, I would like to ask for a stipulation so that the committee may appoint a physician who would be permitted both to ex-
amine Mr. Costello and consult with the physicians who have already
treated Mr. Costello."

Wolf agrees, and Kefauver so rules. Kefauver then reminds Costello that he is still under the committee's subpoena and tell's Wolf
that in his opinion his client's refusal to answer questions is contemp-
tuous of the Senate. Costello is excused, and the clerk calls the next
witness.

(Television makes Costello a celebrity. He is recognized instantly when on the street or in a public place. When he dines in a restaurant, people approach him for his autograph. Cigarette companies offer him large sums of money to display a package of their brand on the witness table for his hands to toy with while testifying. He refuses and remains loyal to English Ovals. He has become the symbol of the underworld and hates it.)

❊   ❊   ❊

On March 19, the afternoon session, Costello's health has recovered sufficiently for him to resume testimony. By this time former Mayor Bill O'Dwyer has made his appearance before the committee. Kefauver notes that the testimony of Costello and wire tap expert James McLaughlin conflict and remarks that one of them must be lying. He says he is forwarding the record to the Department of Justice to determine who has committed perjury.

Halley then questions Costello about O'Dwyer's visit to his home in 1942. Costello tells the same story as O'Dwyer. He stoutly maintains that the occasion was the only time they ever met and that O'Dwyer was there on Air Force business.

Costello's memory of the O'Dwyer visit, however, is very sketchy, and he is unable to satisfactorily explain why Tammany Hall boss Mike Kennedy and other Tammany leaders were there. Halley then goes over the formidable list of Tammany leaders who are friends of Costello and asks him if he is a politician. Costello says he isn't a politician, just a friend of politicians.

Halley — "We haven't quite developed the extent of your friendship with these various leaders yet, as least here at the public hearing. But you and I have talked about it a bit.

"I wonder if at this point you might explain to the committee what was the basis of your ability to persuade these politicians?"

Costello — "Well, I can't readily explain that, Mr. Halley. The idea is that I have been living all my life in the neighborhood, in Manhattan Island. I know them, know them well, and maybe they got a little confidence in me. And if I use a little judgment and say, 'You should do this because he would make a good leader, an honest leader.' I don't know; I can't explain that."

Halley — "Well, it goes further than that, doesn't it, Mr. Costello?"

Costello — "Oh, many of us have lived in New York all of our lives."

Halley — "I think you have testified that you haven't even ever voted. Is that right?"

Costello — "That's right."

Halley — "You are not a member of any political organization?"

Costello — "No, sir."

Halley — "You never were?"

Costello — "No."

Halley — "It is very difficult for me to understand how you would be the man who would be able to sway the election of a Tammany leader, as you did on the occasion of 1942, under these circumstances.

"Can't you enlighten the committee on the sort of influence, the reason why these people have faith, confidence in you?"

Costello — "I don't believe I can, Mr. Halley."

Halley — "Do they fear you?"

Costello — "Why should they fear me?"

Halley — "Well, do they?"

Costello — "Well, you know they don't."

✽   ✽   ✽

Halley continues to hammer away at Costello's many friends in Tammany Hall. The Judge Aurelio incident is gone over in detail. Through all the questioning, Costello insists his advice is sought merely on the basis of friendship. Still, Halley achieves what he is seeking. To anyone listening to the testimony, it is clear that Costello, during the forties, was the dominant force in New York City Democratic politics.

The session ends as Senator Tobey remarks that he is greatly satisfied that the witness' voice has returned, and Costello is excused until the following day.

On March 20, the afternoon session, Costello is the witness again. Halley continues to concentrate on politics, and the names of numerous judges and political leaders and their relation to Costello come under scrutiny. Costello continues to deny he is in the business of making judges and political leaders and tells Halley, "Since the Aurelio case, I burned my fingers once, and I never participated in any candidates."

An exchange between Halley and Costello is representative of the tenacious quality of the questioning:

Halley — "Of course, you knew Judge Savarese?"

Costello — "Well, I met him."

Halley — "You don t mean you met him. He is a very good friend of yours, isn't he?"

Costello — "Well, yes. I would say he is a friend."

Halley — "You don't want me to pull out those phone taps and go through this the hard way?"

Costello — "You have been doing everything the hard way with me, Mr. Halley."

Halley — "We can keep it up indefinitely. But it is a fact, is it not, that Saverese was a very good friend of yours?"

Costello — "Well, he has been to my home."

The questioning continues in this vein with Halley's questions assuming more than he really knows and Costello's answers refusing to concede more than he believes Halley is able to prove. Each name brought up is a contest of wills. The session ends with the subject of Costello and his political associates still a hot topic before the committee.

❖   ❖   ❖

March 21, in the morning session, Halley returns to Costello's businesses, starting from the time he manufactured Kewpie dolls, bootlegged, ran the slot machine racket, and developed his real estate enterprises and going up to recent times when he became involved in the manufacture of electric broilers. The final topic of the afternoon session arises when Halley delves into Costello's underworld associations. He asks about the Havana meeting with Lucky Luciano.

Halley — "How did that come about?"

Costello — "I was in Miami at the time, and I went to Cuba for a couple of days, and I believe I was there just a day or two.

"I was checking out of the hotel; I was flying back, and in the lobby I met Charley Luciano."

Halley — "And he rode out to the airport with you, is that right?"

Costello — "He did; yes."

Halley — "What did you talk about?"

Costello — "Well, I wouldn't exactly know the right words, but we spoke of health, America, and Cuba, and what not in general. General conversation."

Halley — "Did you talk about business matters?"

Costello — "No."

Halley — "Or anything pertaining to gambling?"

Costello — "No."

Halley — "Or anything pertaining to the drug traffic?"

Costello — "No. That's ridiculous, Mr. Halley."

Innuendo and guilt through association are Halley's only weapons as he cross-examines Costello about his underworld friends. His knowledge of the scheme of things in the underworld is as limited as the files of federal and local law enforcement agencies. It will be another ten years before Joe Valachi decides to talk and make everyone aware of what really goes on. Some of the better known racketeers that Halley links Costello with through cross-examination are: Willie and Solly Moretti, Longy Zwillman, Jerry Catena, Carlos Marcello, Little Augie Pisano, Joe Adonis, Bugsy Siegel, Meyer and Jake Lansky, Charley Fischetti, Al Capone, Jake Guzik, and Tony Accardo.

The final blow, after having made seven separate appearances before the committee, is struck by Senator Tobey who asks Costello why he decided to become an American citizen.

Costello — "Why? Because I live in this country."

Tobey — "During these years since you have been here, have you prized the privilege of being a citizen of the United States?"

Costello — "I believe I have."

Tobey — "Do you appreciate the rights that are yours as an American citizen?"

Costello — "I do."

Tobey — "Has this country come up to your expectations?"

Costello — "Yes."

Tobey — "When you signed or had someone sign your naturalization papers, what did you promise to do as a citizen of the United States?"

Costello — "Well, I promised to obey naturally."

Tobey — "Obey what?"

Costello — "The Constitution."

Tobey — "And the laws?"

Costello — "That's right."

Tobey — "All right. Have you always upheld the Constitution and the laws of your state and nation?"

Costello — "I believe I have."

Tobey — "Have you offered your services to any war effort of this country?"

Costello — "No."

Tobey — "Bearing in mind all that you have gained and received in wealth, what have you done for your country as a good citizen?"

Costello — "Well, I don t know what you mean by that."

Tobey — "You are looking back over the years now, to that time when you became a citizen.

"Now, spending twenty-odd years after that, you must have in your mind some things that you have done that you can speak of to your credit as an American citizen. If so, what are they?"

Costello — "Paid my tax."

It was Tobey's parting shot, an attempt to humiliate Costello. As a man who was far from unmindful that the entire nation was watching his performance, the crusty old New Englander was playing his role as the nation's conscience right up to the hilt.

＊   ＊   ＊

Costello never forgot the treatment he received at the hands of the Kefauver committee. He harbored resentment against Kefauver until his dying day and once passed on information to his friend, columnist Drew Pearson, that Kefauver had an interest in gambling houses in Tennessee. Pearson checked the information out and found nothing to substantiate the charge. Costello firmly believed that the members of the Kefauver committee were hypocrites, using him as a stepping stone to further their political careers.

In later years he told friends that during the hearings, Kefauver once asked to see him alone, and he complied. Kefauver first assured Costello that nothing said between them would ever be repeated or used in anyway. Then he asked:

"How can we curb gambling in the United States?"

"Senator," Costello answered, "if you want to cut out gambling there's just two things that you need to do."

"What's that?" Kefauver asked eagerly.

"Burn the stables and shoot the horses."

Uncle Frank's friends

The varied affairs of Frank Costello ran like a connective thread through the eight days of public and three days of private hearings held by the Kefauver Committee in New York City in 1951. The forty witnesses at the open hearings included federal, state, and local law enforcement officials, politicians, businessmen, racketeers, and a mob playgirl who seemed to have jumped out of the pages of a Hollywood script.

The affairs included Costello's legitimate businesses, slot machines, bookmaking, rum running, naturalization, political influence, relations with political bosses and notorious gangsters, and net worth. The testimony pertaining to politics was particularly fascinating to the public because it provided the man in the street with an insight into how the city really worked. Of the sixteen districts in Manhattan, Costello admitted to varying degrees of intimacy with Tammany leaders in at least ten districts.

The testimony of Costello's friends and associates helped sketch out the unique position of hidden power and prestige that this unusual man held in both worlds. It is significant, for instance, that in 1942, Bill O'Dwyer, a man who earned his reputation as the prosecutor of Murder, Inc., had to go to Costello's home when he sought political support rather than Costello having had to seek out O'Dwyer's aid. O'Dwyer denied he ever sought Costello's political help, but the facts of the visit spoke for themselves.

WILLIAM O'DWYER: Silver-haired, distinguished looking, with a gift for histrionics and rhetoric, O'Dwyer was the United States Ambassador to Mexico at the time of his appearance before the Kefauver committee. He had been appointed to the post by President Truman when he had resigned from the office of mayor in 1950. He began with a long and impassioned statement defending his administration and noting its accomplishments. It was not unlike a lecture by a professor before a not-too-bright class of undergraduates on the realities of life in government. His theme was that rather than being dominated by Costello and his associates, he had been an ardent foe of the racketeers.

The theme didn't last long. Perhaps the most damaging piece of testimony to O'Dwyer's reputation that came out while he was under cross-examination was his admission that Irving Sherman was a good friend whom he saw frequently. Sherman, a gambler with strong underworld links, was Costello's political messenger boy. O'Dwyer insisted that Sherman had never asked him for anything and that he knew him only as a public-spirited businessman.

Halley found it difficult to understand how a man with O'Dwyer's background as a prosecutor could be so naive about Costello's real role in the underworld for so long.

Halley — "I just have this list of six, and I remember you had a reason for not including Costello. I think he was in another department."

O'Dwyer — "The main reason is that I never did find his name mentioned in connection with any murder in Brooklyn."

Halley — "I think you pointed that out."

O'Dwyer — "And at no time at all was his name mentioned at all in the investigation, as I recall it, except in the turning in of Lepke, and there were several names mentioned in that besides his."

Halley — "I think you pointed out that Costello was the man who ordered that Lepke be turned in to the law enforcement officers?"

O'Dwyer — "No; I didn't know enough about him for that, but that he was the man who made arrangements to turn him in."

Halley's point was well taken. O'Dwyer's contention that he regarded Costello as merely a gambler and businessman hardly stood up in view of the fact that he knew Costello was powerful enough to force or at least make arrangements for a top mob figure like Lepke to hand himself over to the police.

Halley spent most of his time questioning O'Dwyer about his 1942 visit to Costello's apartment. Throughout, O'Dwyer stoutly maintained that his only motivation was Air Force business and that he thought Costello might be of help in a serious situation. When Senator Tobey

implied through questioning that O'Dwyer was being less than candid
in his answers, the former mayor turned into the attacker and made
accusations of his own. He said that he had heard that Tobey had
solicited contributions for a previous senatorial campaign from bookmakers in New Hampshire and New York. O'Dwyer later apologized
to Tobey for making the charge and explained it all away by saying
it had been provoked by the heat of the moment.

Halley, however, was not about to be sidetracked. He returned to
the point of O'Dwyer's appearance before the committee by asking
him if he was embarrassed when he arrived at Costello's home and
found it filled with Tammany politicians.

O'Dwyer — "Embarrassed?"

Halley — "Yes, by any political implications because of the presence of these particular people at this place where you were going
to have a conference?"

O'Dwyer — "Do you live in Manhattan?"

Halley — "Yes."

O'Dwyer — "Nothing ever embarrasses me that happens in Manhattan."

❀   ❀   ❀

O'Dwyer denied that he had ever met privately or in a group with
Costello again, although he said he had a faint recollection of one
other meeting but couldn't remember any details and thought he
could be mistaken. (Costello insisted they had met only that once.)
Further testimony made it clear, however, that O'Dwyer and Costello
didn't have to meet to communicate. Irving Sherman saw James Moran,
O'Dwyer's confidant and bagman throughout his political life, with
all the frequency necessary.

In his second appearance before the committee, O'Dwyer made
the rather mind-boggling statement that the "man who is elected to
run the City of New York hasn't too much time for politics." Its equiv-
alent might be a cook saying he hasn't time to step into the kitchen.
Halley, after remarking that he didn't know what was meant by that,
brought out the following: O'Dwyer had appointed former Manhattan
Borough President Hugo Rogers, one of Costello's closest political
confederates, to a top job in the Traffic department; supported Samuel
DiFalco, a protege of Costello's close friend Generoso Pope, for a
berth on the supreme court; and appointed Joseph Loscalzo to the
court of special sessions, despite the fact that Loscalzo's name had
come up during the Aurelio phone conversation and that he had sought
Costello out on a golf course to solicit his political help.

O'Dwyer's explanation that he was unaware that any of these three were connected with Costello in any way was a weak defense for the man who had spent much of his life in the murky depths of New York City politics and claimed to be an implacable foe of the underworld. By the time his cross-examination was over, his reputation was heavily tarnished, and an unmistakable aroma was attached to his entire tenure as mayor.

❊   ❊   ❊

MEYER LANSKY: The financial genius of the underworld took his first appearance before the Kefauver committee so casually that he didn't even bother to bring his lawyer with him. When Kefauver reminded him that he had the right to legal counsel, Lansky answered that he didn't "think it was necessary." Unlike Costello, he wasn't concerned about what conclusions the public might draw from his refusal to answer questions. He invoked the Fifth Amendment in regard to all questions asked about his business activities. He admitted that he had known Costello and most of the other top names in the mob for many years.

The committee instructed Lansky to return with Moe Polakoff, his attorney, the following day because he was running a risk of being cited for contempt. When they appeared, a heated exchange developed between Polakoff and Senator Tobey which accurately depicts the atmosphere of the hearings.

Tobey — "You were a counsel for Luciano?"

Polakoff — "I was."

Tobey — "How did you become counsel for such a dirty rat as that? Aren't there any ethics in the legal profession?"

Polakoff — "May I ask who you are, sir?"

Tobey — "My name is Senator Tobey. That isn't germane to this hearing but just a question of human interest. There are some men beyond the pale. He is one of them."

Polakoff — "May I answer?"

Tobey — "Go ahead."

Polakoff — "I don't want to get into any controversy with you about that subject at the present time, but under our Constitution every person is entitled to his day in court — ."

Tobey — "I see."

Polakoff — "Whether he is innocent or not. When the day comes that a person becomes beyond the pale of justice, that means our liberty is gone. Minorities and undesirables and persons with bad reputations are more entitled to the protection of the law than are the so-called respectable people. I don't have to apologize to you — ."

Tobey — "I didn't ask you to."

Polakoff — "Or anyone else I represent."

Tobey — "I look upon you in amazement."

Polakoff — "I look upon you in amazement, a Senator of the United States, for making such a statement."

Tobey — "Let me say something to you. If I were counsel, and that dirty rat came in, I would say, 'You are entitled to representation, but you can't get it from me. I will have no fellowship with you. Get out of my office, and find your representation somewhere else.' "

Polakoff — "That is your privilege."

Tobey — "Exactly."

Polakoff — "But it is not your privilege to criticize someone else."

One would expect criticism of an attorney for representing an infamous client from the unsophisticated public, unschooled in law, but coming from a Senator, it was an incredible exchange that can only be explained in relation to the temper of the times and Tobey's holier-than-thou mind. In today's world, he would have been clobbered with protests from every lawyer's group in the nation for criticizing an attorney for defending an unpopular client.

*   *   *

The committee took the legal position that Lansky — under investigation by the Internal Revenue Service — had to answer general questions about his business interests without giving the amount of his investments or profits, otherwise he would be cited for contempt. Polakoff asked for time to research the legality of the ruling, and Lansky was excused until such time as he would be recalled.

In his third appearance, Lansky was questioned in detail about his meeting with Luciano in Havana in 1947.

Halley — "What did you talk to Luciano about when you saw him in Cuba?"

Lansky — "Mr. Halley, I couldn't even recall what I talked about. I know it was nothing of importance."

Halley — "Purely social?"

Lansky — "Purely social. What else could I talk to him about?"

Halley — "Did it have anything to do with business matters whatsoever?"

Lansky — "No, no."

Halley — "Whether legal or illegal?"

Lansky — "No business, illegal or legal, with him."

Halley — "What did you do when you saw Luciano in Havana?"

Lansky — "Gee, I can't recall. I don't know."

The entire line of questioning was an exercise in futility. Lansky maintained that his relationship with Luciano in Cuba was purely social, and there was no way in the world Halley could dispute this contention. Lansky was finally excused from the hearing. He left as unperturbed as the first time he had entered.

※   ※   ※

WILLIE MORETTI: An expansive little man in a loud suit, he provided the comic relief the hearing had needed all along. At the time of his appearance, his counsel warned the committee that his client had been suffering from a "severe illness for many years" which had affected his mind. On this day, however, Willie Moretti seemed to be as sane as his inquisitors.

Moretti testified that he was a gambler and owed his good fortune in life to his amazing luck in picking horses. He assured the committee that he had an infallible system of his own. He also admitted knowing Costello, Genovese, Adonis, Zwillman, and every other big name in the rackets for many years.

Halley — "Well, aren't these people we have been talking about what you would call racket boys?"

Moretti — "Well, I don't know if you would call it rackets."

Halley — "How would you put it?"

Moretti — "Jeez, everything is a racket today."

Halley — "Well, what do you mean by that."

Moretti — "Everybody has a racket of their own."

Halley — "Well, some of them are lawful and some are not. Are these fellows in the gambling racket? Would you call it that way?"

Moretti — "If you want to call it a racket, call the race track a racket, too; that is legitimate, isn't it?"

Halley — "Well, we are talking about illegitimate rackets."

Moretti — "The stock market is a racket, too."

Halley — "Well, it is legal, is it not."

Moretti — "Well, why not make everything legal; let the Government control it."

※   ※   ※

Willie Moretti may have been suffering from paresis, but he still was crafty and clearly got the better of the exchange with Halley. He said he met most of the people he was asked about at the track, and when Halley asked him if they weren't considered the mob, he answered, "They call anybody a mob who makes six percent more (sic) on money." Halley then shifted to the famous mob hangout, Duke's Restaurant, located in Cliffside Park, New Jersey.

Halley — "Does Frank Costello go there?"

Moretti — "Not too often."

Halley — "But he is there once in a while; is that right?"

Moretti — "Yes."

Halley — "Now, what do you people talk about at Duke's? Do you just pass the time of day or is any business done?"

Moretti — "Just pass the time of day; no business transactions."

Halley — "None at all."

Moretti — "None."

Halley — "How often in the course of a week do you go to Duke's ordinarily?"

Moretti — "Three, four times a week probably."

Halley — "Are there any other people that you would like to tell me about who you see at Duke's?"

Moretti — "I think I told you enough."

❀   ❀   ❀

Halley, delighted at the expansive and chatty answers he was getting from Moretti, continued to question him about the people he knew. Moretti assured him that he just automatically met these people because "well-charactered people don't need introductions." Besides people always surrounded him at the race track because he won all the time.

Halley then brought up the subject of the Mafia. Until Joe Valachi talked in 1961, no mob member ever had admitted publicly that such an organization even existed. Moretti may have been somewhat mentally ill, but he wasn't completely crazy.

Halley — "Did you ever hear of the Mafia?"

Moretti — "Whom?"

Halley — "Mafia?"

Moretti — "Read about it."

Halley — "You mean in the newspapers?"

Moretti — "Yes, sir."

Halley — "Never talked to anybody about it?"

Moretti — "No, sir."

Halley — "Do you know anything about it yourself?"

Moretti — "No, sir."

Halley — "Have you heard about the Unione Siciliana?"

Moretti — "Just in the newspapers."

Halley — "You are not a member of either the Mafia or Unione Siciliana?"

Moretti — "What do you mean by a member, carry a card with Mafia on it?"

Halley — "No, I am not being humorous now."

Moretti — "I mean to be a member you've got to carry a card. You've got to be initiated."

Halley — "And do you know anybody or have you ever known anybody who did?"

Moretti — "How could I know if it don't exist?"

❋   ❋   ❋

Willie Moretti left with the praise of the committee ringing in his ears. Kefauver complimented him for his forthrightness, and Tobey said his frankness was "rather refreshing." He really hadn't told the committee a thing, but he had had such a good time under cross-examination that everyone felt he was being candid.

"Thank you very much," Willie responded to the praise. "Don't forget my house in Deal if you are down on the shore. You are invited."

❋   ❋   ❋

JOE ADONIS: Born Joseph Doto, Senator Kefauver's description of him when he appeared before the committee was: "Slick, smooth; an expensively tailored figure with iron-grey hair pomaded into a Hollywood-style hairdo. What Adonis thought about Kefauver and the committee he made abundantly clear by his voice which betrayed a sneering attitude and by his refusal to answer questions that couldn't possibly have incriminated him. He took the Fifth Amendment when he was asked if he had ever been a bootlegger, even though his record clearly showed that he had been convicted and had been fined one hundred dollars for being one.

"At the present time criminal charges and investigations are proceeding against me in the State of New Jersey," Adonis said, explaining why he was refusing to answer most questions. "Such charges have also been presented against me in the State of New York. The Federal Government is engaged in an extensive investigation of my tax returns and of all income I have from any source."

Adonis admitted that he knew Costello but refused to answer whether he had ever been in business with him. Halley then took him through the usual route of famous names: Luciano, Genovese, Moretti, Lansky, etc., etc. Adonis agreed that he knew them but invoked the Fifth Amendment on any question beyond that.

Halley — "Is it not a fact that you and Meyer Lansky were partners at the Arrowhead Inn?"

Adonis — "I refuse to answer on the grounds that it might tend to incriminate me."

Halley — "Were you a partner in the Green Acres Club?"

Adonis — "I decline to answer on the ground that it may tend to incriminate me."

Halley — "Were you a partner at the Club Boheme?"

Adonis — "I refuse to answer on the ground that it may tend to incriminate me."

(All three clubs mentioned above were in Florida's Broward County.)

※   ※   ※

And so it went for the entire time he was under cross-examination. Joey A, as he was called by the politicians in Brooklyn, gave the committee as little as possible. When he was asked why he moved from Brooklyn to New Jersey in 1944, he answered: "I like the climate there better." At the end of his questioning, Kefauver warned him that as a result of his refusal to answer questions that had no relevancy to the possibility of incrimination, he would recommend that he be cited for contempt.

(Adonis was later cited for contempt of the Senate, but he went to jail after being convicted on gambling charges in New Jersey before he could be tried on the contempt case. He later agreed to being deported and spent the remainder of his life in Italy, first returning to his home town of Montemarano where he received a hero's welcome. He died of pneumonia in 1971, and his body was then flown to New York for burial in a family plot. He was sixty-nine.)

※   ※   ※

VIRGINIA HILL: Statuesque, auburn-haired, pretty as a Hollywood starlet, with grey-green eyes and an upturned nose — she was suspected of being more than a plaything for the mob. Rumors had it that Virginia Hill was also a courier and had transported large sums of money from one section of the country to another. Whatever the case, she lived in high style and casually gave parties in Hollywood and Sun Valley that cost as much as twelve thousand dollars each.

She was the daughter of an Alabama share cropper and left home to seek fame and fortune in the big city when she was seventeen. The big city she chose was Chicago, and when she arrived in 1934, the Chicago World's Fair was going on. She got a job at the fair as a waitress and was promptly discovered by a Capone-connected bookmaker named Joe Epstein. From that point, she widened her horizons and became friends with the Chicago syndicate bosses: the Fischetti brothers, Tony Accardo, and Frank Nitti. From there she went to New York where Joe Adonis took an interest in her welfare for a while. Then she met Bugsy Siegel and went to California with him.

In a committee executive session, Senator Tobey professed not to understand why all the men she knew were so willing to give her expensive presents and large sums of money.

"Young lady, what makes you the favorite of the underworld?" Senator Tobey asked.

"Senator, I'm the best goddamned cocksucker in the world," Miss Hill replied.

✿   ✿   ✿

On the day of her public hearing before the committee, Miss Hill — then in her fourth marriage, this time to an Austrian ski instructor named Hans Hauser — swept into the courtroom wearing a wide brimmed hat and a platinum mink stole. Directly behind her were a horde of reporters and photographers. A volatile and unpredictable woman, she was the living reality of a tabloid newspaperman's dream. Kefauver attempted to call off the hounds.

Kefauver — "Now, gentlemen, let us give Mrs. Hauser a chance to accustom herself without too many flash bulbs."

Halley — "Mrs. Hauser — ."

Mrs. Hauser — "Make them stop doing that."

Kefauver — "All right, let's not flash any more bulbs."

Mrs. Hauser — "I'll throw something at them in a minute. I hate those things."

Halley — "Now, Mrs. Hauser, most witnesses have had their pictures taken, and they have stopped as soon as they started to testify."

Mrs. Hauser — "I know, but most of them never went through with these bums what I did."

✿   ✿   ✿

Halley began by taking her back to the Chicago World's Fair and asked her to tell about her financial affairs and contacts with gangsters she might have had since then.

Mrs. Hauser — "Well, I worked for a while. Then the men that were around that gave me things, they were not gangsters or racketeers or whatever you call these other people.

"The only time I got anything from them was going out and having fun, and maybe a few presents. But I happened to go with other fellows.

"And for years I have been going to Mexico. I went with fellows down there. And like a lot of girls that they got. Giving me things and bought me everything I want.

"And when I was with Ben, he bought me everything."

Halley — "By 'Ben', you mean Ben Siegel?"

Mrs. Hauser — "Yes; and he gave me some money, too, bought me a house in Florida. And then I used to bet horses."

When Halley asked for more definite information about her income, she explained that she was able to maintain her style of life through gifts and tips on horses that seemed always to win. At one point Halley called Siegel, 'Bugsy.' She firmly corrected him, saying: "Ben is his name."

Halley — "Now you met Siegel about 1942 or 1943; is that right?"

Mrs. Hauser — "I think so; I don't know the exact time. I met him here in New York."

Halley — "And had you previously known Joe Adonis?"

Mrs. Hauser — "Yes."

Halley — "Did Adonis ever give you money?"

Mrs. Hauser — "No."

Halley — "And how long did you know Adonis — for how many years, say, before 1945."

Mrs. Hauser — "Well, I don't know exactly. That must have been in 1942 or 1943 that I met him."

Halley — "And Adonis never gave you any money?"

Mrs. Hauser — "No. He took me out or something. But he never gave me money."

Halley — "Through Adonis you met Costello?"

Mrs. Hauser — "I met them both at the same time."

Halley — "Did you ever get money from Costello?"

Mrs. Hauser — "No."

Halley — "Did you ever get money from Meyer Lansky?"

Mrs. Hauser — "I never got money from any of those fellows."

Halley — "From none of those fellows?"

Mrs. Hauser — "From none of those fellows, none of those that I've been reading about, or none that I knew. They never gave me anything."

＊   ＊   ＊

Virginia Hill Hauser vehemently denied that she had ever been a money courier for the mob, calling the report a "lie." She said that she had never heard Costello or Adonis talk business in front of her and that all she knew about Siegel's business was that he was deeply involved in the building of the Flamingo in Las Vegas.

Mrs. Hauser, having contributed little but glamour to the hearing, was excused by the committee, and, as she left the courtroom, many of the reporters and photographers promptly trailed after her. As she waited in front of the elevator bank for an elevator, the reporters began to bombard her with questions. Her response was to whirl around and plant a gloved fist in the face of Journal American reporter Marjorie Farnsworth. The photographers continued to hound her in the street where she sought refuge in a cab. Her parting remark to her tormentors was the sincere wish that each and everyone of them would fall victim to the atom bomb.

(On March 24, 1966, Virginia Hill Hauser was found dead in the bed of her Spokane, Washington home. The coroner ruled that her death was caused by an overdose of sleeping pills.)

The target

Frank Costello emerged from the Kefauver committee hearings as the best known racketeer in the nation and the number one target of the Justice Department. The word was out: "Get Costello!" The Federal Government moved on three fronts: the contempt of the Senate charge; income tax evasion; denaturalization.

He didn't stand a chance against the unlimited resources and awesome power of Washington. During the fifties and early sixties, he was in and out of the courts and jail as often as a Times Square prostitute. He became philosophical about it all and often remarked that publicity had made him a symbol as easily recognizable as a Coke bottle.

The irony of it all was that the Government was behind the times. The real power had shifted into the grasping hands of Vito Genovese. Costello was still an advisor and commanded a great deal of respect, but the constant glare of the spotlight had eroded the power he had built on political contacts and relative anonymity. After the Kefauver hearing he was too well known, and while he still wielded enormous political power, the politicians had to be more circumspect about being seen in his company.

✿　　　　✿　　　　✿

In tracing the history of Costello's rise from comfortable obscurity into a television star, the turning point, without a doubt, was District

189

Attorney Hogan's release of the Aurelio phone call transcript in 1943. That focused national attention on Costello, and he became the prey of the headline hunters. A public official seeking publicity only had to accuse him of something to be assured a banner headline. Although many of the charges were without foundation, Costello had become libel proof. Anyone could accuse him of anything without worrying about the consequences.

✵   ✵   ✵

Following the Aureilio affair, Mayor LaGuardia's pressure on the police to harrass Costello became so intense that several detectives decided to plant betting slips on him and then arrest him as a book-maker. Costello received a tip from a friendly cop in on the scheme and pondered what to do about it. On the day he knew the plant was scheduled to take place, he went to a tailor and had all the pockets in his suit sewn shut.

The attempted frame took place while he sat with friends in a Long-champ's Restaurant on Broadway. When the detectives ran up against the sewn pockets, they realized they had been out-foxed and walked away.

✵   ✵   ✵

Late in 1943, *The New York Times* carried a story which said that Costello was on the blacklist of the Federal Narcotics Bureau as one of the financiers of the drug trade. While Costello may indeed have been on a Narcotics Bureau blacklist, he didn't deserve to be. He never had been involved in any way with narcotics, and there wasn't a shred of evidence to substantiate the charge. Costello denied his involvement, but no one paid any attention to the denial.

The charge emerged again in December of 1946 when Garland H. Williams, New York Supervisor of the Narcotics Bureau, accused him of being the "mastermind and absolute ruler" of a sinister gang of young Mafiosi operating a multi-million dollar drug market in Harlem. Williams said that Costello's organization had nationwide ramifications and extended as far South as Louisiana.

Livid with rage, Costello decided to try and do something about the accusation this time. He took the rather unusual step — considering his position in life — of calling a press conference in the office of attorney George Wolf. Nattily dressed in a blue suit and red tie, Costello told reporters he had dispatched a letter to District Attorney Hogan that said:

"I am shocked by the horrible charges referring to me in the press.

I demand the opportunity of branding them false before a grand jury where I will submit to examination without delay and waive immunity.

"I have no recollection of ever having met any of the individuals reported to be under arrest in the narcotics investigation. At no time, directly or indirectly, have I been the boss or connected in any way with any Harlem gang or racketeers; at no time either directly or indirectly have I ever been connected with any organization known as Mafia."

Under questioning by reporters he went on to say: "To my mind there is no one lower than a person dealing in narcotics. It is low and filthy trading on human misery. Anyone who knows me knows my opinion of narcotics and the low opinion I have of people dealing in it or with it."

❋   ❋   ❋

Costello's indignation was real. Joe Valachi told the McClellan committee that in 1948, Costello, warned that anyone in his family caught dealing in drugs would have to face a family trial after the Government trial. The profits from heroin were so large and tempting, however, that he couldn't enforce the rule. Members of his family continued to deal in drugs despite his opposition.

Valachi wasn't the only one who said Costello wasn't involved in drugs. I interviewed both Federal and local law-enforcement officials and in each case was told that there never was any evidence implicating Costello in the heroin trade.

❋   ❋   ❋

The practice of dragging Costello's name into something just to make the press pay attention continued. In April of 1947, Vice-Admiral William W. Smith, investigating war profiteering, charged that Costello was the man secretly behind the Aero Dynamics Research Corporation, a firm accused of operating falsely as a nonprofit research organization to dodge taxes.

"As far as I'm concerned, it's the biggest fish story of all time," Costello said.

No one believed the denial, even though it was true, and Costello began to loom larger and larger as the man who was behind everything. (What was happening was that informers decided to cash in on the Government's desire to link Costello to criminal activity, and they earned their bread by feeding officials false information.) The officials, in turn, willing to believe anything the informers fed them, shot from the hip, satisfied they were aiming in the general direction of the target.

An insight into how Costello had mushroomed into the ogre of crime in the United States was reflected in an off-the-record interview Attorney General Tom Clark granted *New York Post* reporters Oliver Pilat and Irving Leiberman in 1947. A memo on the interview quotes Clark as calling Costello the "nearest thing to Capone we have today."

"He (Costello) hasn't killed as many people as Capone, but I want to get rid of him," Clark said.

The Attorney General let the reporters in on a secret. Costello's background was being combed carefully by the Justice Department to see if a case could be made to deport him.

Costello was guilty of many things, and the Government had a perfect right to try and get rid of him, but he wasn't guilty of murder. That was the one thing that the New York cops, who knew him best, never suspected Costello of being involved in. They knew he always tried to avoid violence. Yet Clark, who had available to him the files and records of the FBI, was willing to imply to reporters that Costello was a killer.

A much more accurate evaluation of Costello's activities was compiled by Virgil W. Peterson, operating director of the Chicago Crime Commission, in 1949. In a confidential communication to the office of New Orleans Mayor Morrison, Peterson wrote:

"Frank Costello, in my opinion, is undoubtedly the number one gang leader in America today. In addition to his power among the underworld, the insidious influence which he exerts on the government is the most dangerous aspect of his activities.

"He and his gang have contacts all over the United States and they have worked very closely with other criminal gangs such as the Capone syndicate in Chicago. Wherever they operate, they always exert a tremendous amount of political influence.

"For many years, Frank Costello was the most powerful figure in Tammany Hall, New York, but that influence has not been confined to New York.

"Frank Costello has his finger in so many underworld activities but, unfortunately, there is seldom any record available to prove such connections.

"Costello and his mob have had control of gambling in Broward County, Florida, for many years. When the county operates at full blast there are fifty-two gambling houses open during the season."

Peterson's evaluation of Costello's activities was quite accurate and pointed out the two areas of his involvement: gambling and political corruption. He was not into heroin and disdained violence.

Many of the people who knew and dealt with Costello during the years he wielded immense power say he kept the lid on things and kept New York from turning into a shooting gallery like Chicago.

"I know what you've heard about him," said a newspaperman who was close to Costello in the thirties and forties, "but believe me when I tell you he was a force for good around this town. If he hadn't been around there would have been a lot more killing and rough stuff. He kept the animals in line. He had so much power and prestige that he could settle a tense situation with a phone call."

✻   ✻   ✻

By the fall of 1951, Vito Genovese was firmly in command of the Luciano family. But this wasn't enough for Don Vitone. He secretely wanted to be *capo di tutti capi,* boss of all bosses, something no man had ever been in the Mafia in America. The lessons of the past served his ambition well. As one of those responsible for the death of Joe the Boss and Salvatore Maranzano, he knew perfectly what dangers such ambition faces, but the Byzantine complexity of his mind was perfectly suited for the endless plotting and slow building of alliances for such a project. He was both patient and cunning. He knew that before this power he coveted could be grasped, certain men must first be eliminated. Only then could he reach for the prize in safety.

Willie Moretti, who had carved out his own empire in New Jersey, provided Genovese with an excuse to take one firm step towards his goal. The wise-cracking Mafia lieutenant's mental condition had deteriorated again. He had become friendly with a number of New Jersey reporters and was threatening to hold a press conference about gambling operations in New Jersey. The capos were upset about all the publicity Willie was receiving, and they feared he might lose control of his tongue.

Don Vitone exploited the situation and began agitating that Moretti was losing his mind and should be hit. He told Joe Valachi, "If tomorrow I go wrong, I want you to hit me in the head too." Moretti was a danger to everyone, he said, and argued for a "mercy killing" for the good of everyone in the organization.

Don Vitone kept silent about the benefits he would reap if Moretti were eliminated. The power of Costello, who argued against violence, would be eroded further; Moretti was Costello's close ally with ties that went back to childhood; Moretti's gambling rackets would fall into the hands of the family; Moretti could be replaced with Jerry Catena, Genovese's underboss.

In the Italian section in Hasbrouck Heights, where Moretti lived when he wasn't at his beach home in Deal, many people remember the chatty little man with a great deal of affection. He was godfather to so many kids there that he was nicknamed "Cump," short for compadre, godfather. Willie went with his wife to mass every Sunday and contributed to every charity in town. He often sent one hundred dollar bills in anonymous envelopes to people being evicted or ill.

Singer Frank Sinatra, a native of the area, also has good reasons to remember Willie Moretti with affection. He was his good friend and sponsor and the man who helped launch him on his fabulous career. In 1950, Willie became upset when he read that Sinatra was divorcing his wife Nancy, for Hollywood actress Ava Gardner. He promptly dispatched the following telegram:

"I am very much surprised what I have been reading in the newspapers between you and your darling wife. Remember, you have a decent wife and children. You should be very happy. Regards to all. Willie Moore."

❋   ❋   ❋

Genovese called for a meeting of the capos of the New York-New Jersey families. At the meeting he successfully argued for the elimination of Moretti. Costello could do nothing. Only the time and place remained to be chosen.

On October 4, 1951, Albert Anastasia, who then lived in Fort Lee, New Jersey, awoke complaining of back trouble. He phoned Moretti and said that his chauffeur was not available and asked to borrow Moretti's to drive him to the hospital. Moretti readily agreed. Anastasia was driven to St. Mary's Hospital, located in Passaic, New Jersey, where he created a disturbance because the x-ray technician wasn't present. Anastasia insisted his back be x-rayed and made certain everyone in the hospital was aware of his dissatisfaction. He was elaborately establishing his alibi.

Later that morning, shortly before eleven-thirty A.M., Moretti walked into Joe's Elbow Room, his new hangout since Duke's had been closed down. The restaurant was on Palisades Avenue, close to where Duke's had stood.

Willie had company that day. When he walked in he was greeted by four men, and after they all shook hands they sat down together at a table. They chatted amiably in Italian for a few minutes, and then one of the men asked the waitress to see the menu. Believing that they were going to order lunch, she walked into the kitchen to get silverware for the table. As she gathered the silverware, she was startled by the sound of several shots. Frightened, she peered out through the kitchen's swinging doors and saw that all but one of her customers were gone. Wille Moretti, fifty-seven, one hand clutching his chest, his legs apart, his feet pointing at the door, lay on the floor. Blood still flowed from wounds in his head and formed twin pools.

✻   ✻   ✻

Shortly after the murder of Moretti, John Robilotto, better known as Johnny Roberts, a soldier in the family then headed by Albert Anastasia, had a cup of coffee with Joe Valachi in a restaurant. After a few minutes of small talk, Valachi mentioned a hat carelessly left behind by one of Moretti's killers. Roberts admitted that he had been there that day but assured Valachi that the hat wasn't his size, meaning that he wasn't the forgetful one.

✻   ✻   ✻

In October of 1952, the Government moved on the first of its three-pronged attack on Costello. He went on trial in Manhattan Federal Court on the contempt of the Senate charge. Attorney George Wolf built his defense on the contention that Costello was a special target of the Kefauver committee, and that the contempt citation had resulted from unfair treatment. Eleven of the twelve jurors voted for conviction, but there was a lone holdout, and the trial ended in a hung jury. Another trial was quickly scheduled, and this time Costello was convicted. He was sentenced to eighteen months in jail.

On August 22, 1952, for the first time in more than thirty-seven years, Costello was back in prison. He was sent to Lewisburg, in Pennsylvania, where he became number 20125. After several months there, he was transferred to Atlanta, then transferred again to Milan, Michigan, where he finished out his term. He was a model prisoner and, with time off for good behavior, was released on October 29, 1953.

✻   ✻   ✻

Even before Costello began serving his time on the contempt of the Senate conviction, the Internal Revenue Service was hard at work seeking a way to put him in jail for a much longer stretch. The plan was to make a tax case against him. It was a rather formidable task. As most men in his position, Costello carefully matched his recorded expenditures with his declared income. He was careful not to write checks for large amounts, paid cash for bills whenever feasible, and operated most of his enterprises under fronts.

He had had two close calls with the tax man in the past, the first brush dating back to 1932. At that time he had hired George Morton Levy as his attorney, and a settlement was arranged with Albany and Washington. Costello had neglected to file income tax returns between

1919 and 1932. This little oversight could have resulted in his going to jail, but the tax people were more interested in money then than in incarcerating him, and Levy was able to settle with the state for $350,000 and an undisclosed amount with the feds.

The second close call had come in 1939 when he went on trial and was acquitted of income tax evasion charges in New Orleans. Since that time, Costello had been extremely cautions in covering his fiscal tracks. He knew it was just a matter of time before the Government tried again.

In the summer of 1952, the Intelligence Division of the Internal Revenue Service in the New York area received orders from Washington to go all out on trying to make a case against Costello. This time there was no question of a settlement. The Justice Department wanted Costello in jail.

The agents assigned to the case, Wilfred Leath and John R. Murphy, began by analyzing his returns which showed that he had reported an average yearly income of thirty-nine thousand dollars from 1946 to 1949. They reasoned that their best chance was to try and make a net worth case against him, attempting to prove that he lived on a much higher scale than his declared income. To do this, they had to prove he spent a lot more than he was telling Uncle Sam about.

They routinely checked every bank Costello and his wife were suspected of doing business with. They visited Costello's tailor, his barber shop, the restaurants he frequented. They traveled to New Orleans and his vacation spots in Hot Springs, Arkansas and Miami Beach. Every piece of mail sent to him was recorded by the post office in the hope that this would lead to a Costello expense. Despite all the work, however, nothing concrete turned up. The agents were stymied.

A careful accounting of Costello's known assets in New York, Kansas, Texas, Louisiana, and Florida showed him to have an estate valued at $206,819. Mrs. Loretta Costello's assets, which included two automobiles and two fur coats, were placed at $59,155.

None of this was out of line with what Costello declared his income to be. There were no yachts costing a fortune or purchases of jewelry. Still, they weren't trying to trace every dime that flowed through Costello's hands. They knew that was impossible. All they wanted to do was prove he had a substantial amount of undeclared income — enough to send him to jail.

A small break came when the agents decided to concentrate on following the trail of Mrs. Costello's checks. Frank Costello was an indulgent husband and allowed his wife to have charge accounts at many of the elegant Fifth Avenue shops. She bought her hats at Hattie Carnegie and her dresses at a number of the exclusive little shops that attract the wives of the wealthy. It was not unusual for her to spend as much as six hundred dollars for a gown. She bought minor jewelry at Tiffany's. This, coupled with his expenditures for custom-made suits that cost three hundred fifty dollars, thirty-five dollar shirts, and one hundred dollar monogrammed silk pajamas, added up to a pattern of living that just wasn't possible on an income of thirty-nine thousand dollars a year. Yet it all added up to less than ten thousand dollars. Nothing that could be taken before a jury to get a conviction.

Then one of the agents decided to play a hunch. He traced a five dollar check issued by Mrs. Costello to a flower shop. A check of the flower shop's records showed that the flowers had been sent to St. Michael's cemetery in Astoria, Queens.

At the burial grounds, the agent discovered that Mrs. Costello had purchased a plot that cost $4888. Further inquiry revealed that the plot had been paid for in cash, with Costello using his wife to conceal the transaction. On the plot itself, the agent discovered an impressive marble mausoleum built in the style of a Greek temple. He then sought out the mausoleum contractor to find out what this impressive monument cost.

The contractor was found, but he had no record of putting up a mausoleum for a man named Costello. His records showed that the structure had been erected for an elderly man named Amilcare Festa, who lived near Costello's mother in Astoria. Upon being questioned, Festa admitted that the mausoleum wasn't his. He was an old man, he explained, and he had been given a chance to earn some money. He didn't ask questions and just did as he was told.

The agents applied pressure to the old man, and he cracked. He said a young man had approached him and asked that he hire a contractor and have the mausoleum erected. He was also given a set of blueprints that were to be strictly adhered to.

"If you need money," the young man cautioned, "you call this number." Festa was handed a slip of paper that contained a number where he could reach Costello.

The next day a messenger delivered an envelope containing thirty $100 bills. This was followed by further cash deliveries of $5000 and $5615, making a total outlay of $13,615. That cash outlay, plus the cash outlay for the plot and other things to do with the cemetery added up to $23,503 in unexplained cash, however more important, it showed an elaborate scheme to hide substantial sums of cash being spent.

Another small bonanza for the agents turned up when they checked a flower shop owned by Costello's pal, bookmaker Frank Erickson. A check of the ledger revealed a customer "C., Frank." This turned out to be Costello. He spent two thousand dollars a year in Erickson's shop.

✤   ✤   ✤

In April of 1954, after two years of painstaking detective work by the agents, Frank Costello went on trial on income tax evasion charges in Manhattan Federal Court. He was accused of conspiring to hide $51,095 of his income over the four years that the indictment covered. The prosecutor opened by saying he was ready to show that Costello spent substantially more on rent, clothes for himself and his wife, nightclubs, restaurants, plush Florida hotels, and an expensive mausoleum than his declared income.

In all, 144 witnesses were called and over 500 documents introduced as evidence by the Government. Amilcare Festa turned out to be one of the key witnesses against Costello. Also called were many of the sales persons who waited on Mrs. Costello in the Fifth Avenue shops she frequented. They all helped prove the case against him beyond a reasonable doubt.

✤   ✤   ✤

During the trial, Costello's attorney told him that the three hundred fifty dollar suits he wore had a bad effect on the jury and suggested he wear something else in the courtroom.

"What should I wear?" Costello asked.

"Buy yourself a suit from one of those plain-pipe clothes racks," the attorney said.

"I'm sorry, but I'd rather blow the goddamn case," Costello answered.

✤   ✤   ✤

The verdict was never really in doubt. The jury pronounced Costello "guilty," and the court leveled the toughest sentence the law allowed — five years and a thirty thousand dollar fine. It was a stunning blow, and Costello sat at the defense table for several minutes while the enormity of what a five-year term means to a sixty-three-year-old man sunk home. Newsmen at the trial reported that tears came to his eyes. Appeals were filed immediately, and a dejected Costello walked out to the street where he was besieged by the press. Before getting into an automobile, he offered the newsmen a comment and some advice: "I think this is a political thing: a lot of guys trying to get ahead by climbing on my back. And that's the way the world goes." He then added: "I want to give you fellows some advice. Remember this — when you spend money, spend cash and don't have any checks. If

your wife has any money, have her declare it right away, or they will
be after you."

❈   ❈   ❈

Over the next two years, Costello kept his battery of attorneys
busy fighting the execution of the sentence. When the Court of Appeals refused to overturn the conviction, the case was carried to the
United States Supreme Court. In agreeing to review Costello's case,
the Supreme Court said the review would be limited to one question,
the main basis of the appeal: whether a defendant can be required to
stand trial when only hearsay evidence was presented to the grand
jury that indicted him.

While awaiting the Supreme Court ruling, the Government began
questioning Costello in preparation for starting denaturalization proceedings against him. This was the final straw. In what was an extraordinary move for a man of Costello's pride, his attorney went before
a lower court and introduced evidence that he was sick, suffering
from an ulcer and melonoma of the left temple, notoriously one of
the most fatal forms of cancer. (The ulcer contention was based on
fact, the melonoma on fantasy.) The attorney told the court that Costello would agree to voluntary deportation if the five-year sentence
were suspended.

This must have been one of the most embarrassing and depressing
moments of Costello's life. His pride was such that his wife didn't
know he had a bridge in his mouth until after he died. For him to
plead for mercy on the grounds that he was sick and old and to agree
to be thrown out of the country was completely out of character. He
loved New York; loved to walk the dirty, crowded streets; knew its
history; and could point out its landmarks. Once when Albert Anastasia attempted to persuade him to move to New Jersey, Costello
remarked, "The place is too corrupt for me." Italy was a foreign country to him. While he was proud of his Italian heritage, he was as much
a native of the curious, polyglot society of the New York experience
as Huckelberry Finn was of Hannibal, Missouri. Yet at his age he
knew that going back to jail might mean that he would spend his
last days in a cage. Above all else, he didn't want to die in prison.
His pride rebeled at the thought.

The Government refused the offer, and when the Supreme Court
upheld his conviction he had reached the end of the line. On May
14, 1956, dressed in a grey suit with a pencil stripe, grey-figured
tie, and a grey snap-brimmed hat, he walked into the United States
Marshal's office in Foley Square at 3:25 P.M. and surrendered him-

self. He had been given until four to turn himself in. He posed willingly for photographers, refused to answer questions put to him by
reporters, and appeared resigned to his fate. He was then handcuffed
and taken to the Federal House of Detention on West Street.

Costello was sent to the Federal Penitentiary in Atlanta, where he
quickly adjusted to the routine of prison life and was treated like an
elder statesman by the other prisoners. He hadn't, however, given up
hope of getting out. He hired a new lawyer, Edward Bennett Williams
of Washington, who had a nationwide reputation as a criminal lawyer
and a knack for breathing new life into cases that were dead.

After studying the record of Costello's tax trial, Williams filed an
appeal on the grounds that the evidence presented against Costello
was tainted because much of it was gathered through illegal means.
The Court of Appeals agreed to review the case, and Costello, after
serving eleven months of his sentence, was released on twenty five
thousand dollars bail pending the outcome of the decision. It all seemed
like a miracle, and Costello hailed Williams as his knight in shining
armor. A warm relationship, based on mutual respect and personal
affection, developed between the two men. It lasted for as long as
Costello lived.

*   *   *

*Before being released from Atlanta, Costello contacted friends in
New York and requested they take Bobbie to dinner on the day he
was due to come home. He didn't want his wife to see him until he
had rid himself of all traces of the prison. When he reached the city,
he first went to his apartment and changed into a fresh suit and shirt.
Then he visited the Waldorf barber shop where he had a haircut,
shave, manicure, and sunray lamp treatment. Feeling like his old self,
he took a cab to the midtown restaurant where Bobbie and a few
friends awaited him, kissed her lightly on the cheek, and began to talk
as casually as if he had been held up a few minutes in a traffic jam.*

*   *   *

Costello immediately picked up the threads of his normal routine.
Mornings he visited the Waldorf and held court, afternoons he usually
visited the Biltmore steamroom, and evenings he dined out with friends.
Meanwhile, Williams and attorney Jake Kossman of Philadelphia fought
to upset the tax conviction. The charge of tainted evidence had raised
a serious Constitutional question, and it seemed likely that the issue
wouldn't be decided until it had been bucked up to the Supreme Court.

*   *   *

Vito Genovese was less than ecstatic at Costello's return. His am-

bition to be boss of all bosses made him decide that Frank Costello was expendable. He began a whispering campaign on how all the publicity Costello was receiving was bad for the organization. After he was shot in the head, Costello became convinced that the treacherous Don Vitone was in back of his tax troubles and had fed the Government information to get rid of him. He didn't think it was a coincidence that he was shot less than two months after his release from jail.

❖   ❖   ❖

The Court of Appeals denied Costello's appeal for a new trial, and it then traveled its logical route to the Supreme Court where Justice William O. Douglas signed an order continuing Costello's bail. This meant that he would be free until the highest court in the land handed down a decision.

The final ruling on the bid for a new trial was reached in October of 1958. It went against Costello, and he was ordered to surrender himself once again to serve the time he still owed on his sentence. The legal maneuvering of his attorneys had given him an eighteen-month respite. He obeyed the court order and was sent back to prison. In June of 1961, after serving forty-two months of his five-year term, he was released from Atlanta. As usual, he had been given the maximum time off for good behavior.

Deportation, the third of Washington's three-pronged attack, began in September of 1956. The entire proceedings were a tangle of legal moves that resulted in three separate Supreme Court decisions. It began when Costello was brought from Atlanta to Manhattan Federal Court to stand trial on deportation proceedings. Looking haggard and complaining that he suffered from heart trouble, Costello made it clear that he was no longer willing to voluntarily leave the United States. "Your honor," he told the court, "I am still very ill, but I cherish my citizenship. My sentence in my condition is equivilent to a life sentence, but I still want to retain my citizenship."

Federal Judge Edmond L. Palmieri dismissed the action, ruling that the Government's case was tainted by wire tap evidence. This time Washington appealed and won. The entire case was then carried all the way to the Supreme Court where Palmieri's decision was upheld. Attorney General William Rogers then ordered the Justice Department to seek new grounds to strip Costello of his citizenship.

The Justice Department found the new grounds, and after more court appearances, Costello was denaturalized for concealing his bootlegging activities when he was naturalized in 1925. The Supreme Court upheld the order in February of 1961, and at that time it appeared certain that Costello would be deported to Italy upon his release from prison. At the heart of the Supreme Court's decision was the question of whether there was "willful misrepresentation and fraud" when Costello listed himself as a real estate operator when he applied for citizenship. The majority of the court thought so, but a minority decision, written by Justice Douglas, thought otherwise. He said that bootlegging itself was not a ground for denying naturalization to an alien in the twenties.

"If it were," wrote the great civil libertarian, "it would be an act of hypocrisy unparalleled in American life, for the bootlegger in those days came into being because of the demand of the great bulk of people in our communities — including lawyers, prosecutors and judges — for his products."

Costello thought that Douglas had written one of the great legal opinions of our time. It was pretty much the rationalization he had used much of his life when explaining why he went into bootlegging and gambling. There was a public demand, and he merely filled that demand.

The minority opinion, though, didn't alter the facts of the situation he faced. Unless Williams could produce another small miracle, he would be facing an unwanted ocean trip when he was released from prison.

The Italian Government took note of Washington's plan to return Costello to the land of his birth and protested. A foreign ministry spokesman, with impeccable logic, pointed out that Costello was about as Italian as East Harlem.

"Italy should not be expected to carry the burden of a man who was born in Italy, lived here only a short time, and then spent most of his life in the United States," the spokesman said. "It's not blood that makes a man a criminal; it's society, and we definitely do not want to pay for such men."

Edward Bennett Williams, encouraged by Douglas' dissenting opinion, fought the legality of the deportation order. After losing in a hearing before the Board of Immigration Appeal, he again took the legal route that led to the Supreme Court. What he was doing was saying that Immigration's deportation order was not legal. To most legal observers, Williams was skating on very thin ice, and his maneuverings were viewed as merely delaying tactics. But in February of 1961, in what was considered a major surprise, a six to two Supreme Court decision overturned the deportation order. The Government finally threw in the sponge, and Costello, after eight years of battle, was assured that he could stay in the United States for as long as he liked.

The aftermath

Frank Costello wasn't given time to dispute the decision to kill him.

The pistol, fired at point-blank range, seemed to explode in his face like a giant firecracker at the exact moment he whirled to look at his assassin in the foyer of the Majestic's lobby. The .32 caliber bullet pierced his scalp just behind the right ear and then curved around to the nape of the neck, neatly splitting the skin wherever it touched. Then it slammed into the marble wall behind him, ricocheted around the small foyer, and fell to the floor spent. As Costello staggered backwards, holding his head, the bulky gunman rushed out the door, brushing aside the badly frightened doorman, Norval Keith.

Phil Kennedy heard the shot clearly as he sat in the cab Costello had just left. The cab was facing downtown, waiting for a red light to change at Seventy-first Street and Central Park West, when Kennedy reacted to the sharp crack of the shell's detonator cap. He vigorously pushed open the cab's passenger door, striking it hard against a car parked at the curb, and ran the fifty yards or so to the Majestic's entrance. As he ran, he saw out of the corner of his right eye the blur of a long, black Cadillac in low gear, moving fast with its lights out, heading downtown. The Cadillac raced through the red light. It contained the fat gunman who was convinced that he had successfully carried out his assignment. He had seen Costello stagger, clutch his head, and the first flow of his blood.

Inside the Majestic's lobby, Phil Kennedy found Frank Costello sitting on a black plastic bench holding a blood-soaked handkerchief to the right side of his head.

"Are you all right, Uncle Frank?" he asked anxiously.

"I'm okay," Costello answered.

Kennedy looked at the profusely bleeding wound and asked the doorman to try and reach one of the physicians who lived in the building, but Noval Keith was in a complete state of panic and wasn't capable of rational response.

"Come on, I'm going to get you to the hospital," Kennedy said. Costello made no protest.

He helped the surprisingly calm Costello to his feet and hailed a passing cab. The driver of the cab they had arrived in had become frightened and had driven off without getting paid.

"Roosevelt Hospital and step on it," Kennedy ordered.

Kennedy knew better than to ask Costello questions about who did it. If Uncle Frank wanted him to know something, he would volunteer the information.

"Is there anything you have on you that you want me to hold?" he asked.

Costello thought for a few seconds and shook his head. Despite his outward calm, however, he wasn't thinking clearly. The events of the preceding minutes had shaken him up a lot more than his tightly-controlled face revealed. He had forgotten about the slip of paper delivered to him at the Waldorf barber shop that morning.

"Contact Bobbie and tell her what happened," Costello requested.

"I'll do it first thing," Kennedy promised.

The cabbie made it to Roosevelt Hospital, about a mile away on West Fifty-ninth Street, in less than two minutes. Costello was given immediate treatment in the emergency room.

Police began to arrive at the hospital minutes later. Kennedy went to a phone and called Monsignore. He decided to call Gene Pope and have him tell Bobbie so she would have someone at her side when she received the shocking news. Kennedy explained to Pope that Frank had been shot in the head but that he was all right. He assured him it was just a superficial flesh wound and that Frank had said to tell Bobbie. Pope said he would break the news as gently as possible.

By this time it was about eleven-fifteen P.M. Events had moved so swiftly that it was only thirty minutes since Costello had left Monsignore. Besides Pope, still with Bobbie were Enquirer columnist John J. Miller and his wife Cindy, and Al and Rose Minaci. Pope, of course, was the only one who knew what happened.

He walked back to the table and asked for the check immediately. It was time to go home, he said. No one thought anything about the suddenness with which he cancelled the after-dinner party.

"I'm going to take Bobbie home," he told Miller. Since Pope didn't have his car, and it had been the custom for Miller to drive Frank and Bobbie home after one of their dinners, the columnist was somewhat surprised. Still, he wasn't about to question his publisher about it, and it didn't enter his head that anything was amiss.

Alone in a cab with Bobbie, Pope told her that Frank had had an accident but assured her he was all right. When he said he had been shot, she became extremely agitated. Pope thought it best for her to go home and wait for Frank. She insisted on going to Roosevelt Hospital, fearful that she wasn't being told the truth about the extent of his injuries.

At Roosevelt Hospital she saw her husband for a few minutes, and he calmed her down. He then told her to go home because it would be a long night for him with the police and the press.

The police were already beginning to push Costello for answers. They wanted to know who had shot him and why. Costello observed the time honored Mafia code of silence.

"I didn't see nuthin'," he told the detectives over and over again. "I was facing the other way when I was shot."

Detectives wanted to know why anyone would want to kill him.

"I haven't an enemy in the world," he said.

Having Costello under medical treatment provided detectives with a golden opportunity. They searched his jacket to see if anything he was carrying shed any light on the questions they wanted answers to. They found a small slip of paper with some interesting figures written on it. They also discovered $3200 in cash, mostly in hundred dollar bills, in his pockets. One of the detectives decided Costello would never complain and pocketed $2400. The cop was right. Costello ignored the loss.

❊   ❊   ❊

At about 12:05 A.M., Cindy Miller, alone in her apartment on East End Avenue, while her husband made the rounds of nightclubs to pick up Broadway gossip, heard a bulletin on television that Mafia chief Frank Costello had been shot in the head in an unsuccessful attempt to kill him. She immediately called John on his car phone.

As she was dialing, the door bell of her apartment began to ring insistantly. It was detectives, sent to question her.

After hearing from Cindy, Miller decided that the best thing he could do was to see if Bobbie needed help. He figured that Bobbie was home by this time. He drove to the Majestic and observed on the street what he thought was the most amazing thing in the world: Bobbie walking her two dogs while a crowd of photographers and reporters formed a circle around her.

Miller parked in a bus stop, burst through the circle, and in an agitated voice said, "What the hell are you doing here with the two dogs and all these people following you?"

Bobbie, obviously glad to see him, explained: "I had to walk the dogs. I couldn't leave them alone tonight. We were out too late."

Miller led her by the arm and put her and the two dogs in his car. He then drove to the West Eighties where she was able to finish walking her pets without being harrassed by newsmen. After talking to her for a few minutes and determining she was in control of herself, he drove back to the Majestic. Then he hurried over to the West Fifty-fourth Street station house, the precinct where he knew police would bring Costello for further questioning.

He found Costello in the precinct's detective room, more agitated than hurt. His head was swathed in bandages, his suit was bloody, and his hat bore a hole where the bullet had passed through.

"He wasn't shaken up or nervous or anything," Miller recalled. "He looked, to be blunt, pissed off."

"How are you, Frank?" Miller asked.

"Aaah, this is a big deal over nuthin'," Costello answered.

Costello then began to berate himself for being stupid.

"He was just simply furious at himself," Miller said, "for going into a momentary state of panic over all the blood and everything and allowing himself to be taken to the hospital. He just couldn't get over the fact that the whole thing never would have had to get in the newspapers. The wound was so minor.

"It was insane, of course, because you can't have a bullet fired in the lobby of one of the best buildings on Central Park West and not have it get into the papers — especially if you're Frank Costello. Still he was convinced that no one in the world had to know about it if he hadn't gone to the hospital. Plus the fact that the police had taken his belongings which he was very upset about; and later everyone found out why. He had intricate things in there."

The slip of paper that interested detectives and upset Costello so much was written by hand and read: "Gross casino wins as of 4/27/57,

$651,284. Casino wins less markers (I.O.U's), $434,695. Slot wins, $62,844. Markers, $153,745." The figures obviously referred to the take of a casino. But what casino and where was it located? And how long a period of time did those figures represent?

"Come on, Frank. You know its just a matter of time before we trace it down."

"I won't answer any questions about it until I see my lawyer."

"Is the casino in Vegas?"

"I told you, I'm not goina talk about it."

"Do you own the casino, Frank?"

"Since when is it legal to go into my pockets without a search warrant?"

Detectives also continued to question him about the more pressing subject at the time — who shot him and why? Costello wasn't any more helpful on this subject. He hadn't seen anyone, and he couldn't guess who would want to kill him. Detectives knew he was lying and pointed out that he couldn't have received that kind of wound unless he was looking directly into the barrel of the gun. After several hours, covering the same ground, they said he could go home. They had found Norval Keith, the doorman, to be much more cooperative. He had gotten a good look at the gunman and provided detectives with a description. He was over six-feet-tall, fat, maybe two hundred and fifty pounds, young, and had a funny waddle when he walked.

Costello knew instinctively that Don Vitone was responsible for the shot being fired at him. He was the only one with the power to order his execution. He also knew Don Vitone's motivations: greed and power. The death of Frank Costello would mean that Don Vitone could confiscate his business interests and advance his ambition to become *capo di tutti capi*. Someone of Costello's prestige was always dangerous to a man of ambition.

❖   ❖   ❖

A week before Costello was shot, according to Joe Valachi, Vito Genovese, Tony Bender, and Vinnie Mauro held a strategy meeting. Genovese said he had received some interesting information; Frank Costello had turned informer for the Government. That was why Costello had been released. The story of him getting out while his tax case was being appealed was just a clever cover. Costello had turned into a stool pigeon because he was old and sick and couldn't take it anymore. He ordered Mauro to have Costello hit.

(High Justice Department sources say there is absolutely not one word of truth to the rumor that Frank Costello became a Government informer. How the rumor started is unknown.)

Mauro approached Valachi and told him of Genovese's orders. He had been chosen as the hit man, he said. Valachi became angry because he wasn't asked to the meeting and told Mauro, "Count me out." Then, Valachi said, a Bender soldier, Vincent (The Chin) Gigante, a hulking ex-boxer, half-witted, and ambitious, was given the contract along with Tommy (Tommy Ryan) Eboli and Dominick (Dom the Sailor) DeQuatro. Valachi said that Gigante had target practice daily in a Greenwich Village basement, preparing for his big opportunity.

❊   ❊   ❊

Costello walked out of the precinct in the early hours of the morning, unseen by the hordes of reporters and photographers waiting to talk to him. They were directly across the street, talking among themselves, and had neglected to watch the doors of the precinct. Paul Serafine, an Associated Press reporter, was just arriving on the scene to relieve a colleague when he spotted Costello walking slowly towards Eighth Avenue. He raced after him and stopped Costello before he could hail a cab.

"Frank, we have an office right across the street from the precinct," he began smoothly. "Let's go in there where you can give us a statement without creating a mob scene on the street, otherwise we're just going to hang around your house and bother you, you know that."

Serafine thought Costello was about to agree to the suggestion when the other reporters spotted them and came galloping. After about thirty seconds of pushing and shoving, Costello said that he was sorry but that he had "no comment" and hailed a cab. He then went home.

❊   ❊   ❊

The story heated up. The doorman positively identified the twenty-nine-year-old Gigante as the gunman from a mug shot. Police promptly sent out an alarm to have him picked up, but The Chin went into hiding and couldn't be found.

Meanwhile, in New Orleans, Metropolitan Crime Commission head Aaron Kohn read the story of the attempted assassination of Costello with extreme interest. When he reached the part about the curious slip of paper that contained those mysterious figures, he did some adding of his own. He knew that Dandy Phil Kastel had recently shipped silverware, glasses, and china from the shuttered Beverly Club to the Tropicana, a lavish new hotel and casino in Las Vegas that had reputedly cost $50 million to build. The Tropicana had only recently opened. Kohn relayed his information to Manhattan District Attorney Hogan.

A check of the Tropicana's receipts for its first twenty-four days of business showed that every figure written on the paper found on Costello matched. Through handwriting analysis, Hogan was even able to identify the man who had written the figures. He was Mike Tenico, married to Dandy Phil Kastel's niece. Tenico had worked in the Beverly as an accountant before being shipped to keep track of things at the Tropicana.

The revelation that Costello was a secret partner in the Tropicana caused an investigation to be launched by the Nevada authorities. State law specifically forbids anyone with a police record from having a financial interest in a casino. The mob, however, had always easily been able to circumvent this prohibition by using fronts.

The shooting not only put Costello back in the headlines but also caused him a great deal of personal inconvenience. It began with the police insisting that two detectives guard him around the clock to prevent any further assassination attempts. Costello protested, but he was given no choice in the matter.

"I wish they'd leave me alone," he told a reporter. "I don't need protection from the Police Department or anyone else.

"When I chase them from my door, they go down and sit in the lobby like they own the place. The tenants then complain. It doesn't look good to have police hanging around the lobby.

"I've lived here for eighteen years and never had any trouble until those cops started coming around. All they are doing is embarrassing me."

❊   ❊   ❊

A number of tenants in the Majestic, upset over all the publicity and the daily invasion of reporters and photographers, wrote letters of complaint to the landlord asking that Costello be forced to move. Each complaining tenant, in turn, received a letter from the landlord saying that anyone who wasn't happy with the situation in the building was free to break the lease and move. Mr. Costello was a perfectly respectable tenant, the landlord's letter said.

❊   ❊   ❊

On May 7, just five days after the attempt on his life, Costello was hauled before the grand jury to answer questions. He was interrogated by Al Scotti, Hogan's chief assistant.

"We had him before the grand jury for about an hour," Scotti recalled. "He was impeccably dressed, and his finger nails were well manicured. I happened to glance at them because I was mindful of his appearance before the Kefauver committee when his hands were shown. It aroused my curiosity. Frankly, if you hadn't known who he was or his background, you would have the impression that this man might have been a business man, a law-abiding businessman.

"He seemed to be in complete control of himself, and he answered certain questions directly, although I had my reservations as to whether he was answering them truthfully. There was no need for him to be evasive when he chose to answer because he knew the facts I had in my possession through the form of my questioning. He knew I was in a position to disprove what he was saying.

"I didn't ask him about the motivation behind the attempt on his life because I felt that would be useless — an exercise in futility. I do recall that he became quite disturbed when I confronted him with that piece of paper, and he took the Fifth Amendment on all questions concerning it."

Scotti then granted Costello immunity in regard to the questions about the paper, and when Costello still refused to answer he was hauled before General Sessions Judge Sherman. Edward Bennett Williams defended him and argued that the slip of paper had no relevancy to the attempt on his client's life and that it had been seized illegally. Scotti countered by arguing that it may very well have triggered the assassination attempt if it could be shown that there was a disagreement over the casino's proceeds; and in relation to the contention that the paper was seized illegally, Scotti maintained that Costello's jacket was on a chair in the hospital when it was searched and not on his person, therefore, it did not represent illegal seizure. Judge Sherman ruled in favor of Scotti, and Costello was brought back before the grand jury to face the choice of answering the questions or going to jail for contempt of court.

Williams pleaded with Costello to obey the court order, but he remained true to his code. If he talked, he would have had to name every member of the mob who had an investment in the Tropicana. For Costello the choice was really no choice at all, and he was sentenced to thirty days on Riker's Island, New York City's penal institution in the East River. He served fifteen days and then was released because of time off for good behavior and the fact that Williams was fighting Sherman's ruling all the way to the Supreme Court. The state court's ruling was upheld, but Costello was never asked to serve the few additional days of time he owed.

✽   ✽   ✽

While on Riker's Island, Costello was given a complete physical examination by prison doctors and a United States Public Health Service non-verbal intelligence test. The physicians found that he was suffering from chronic constipation, a cough, a right inguinal hernia, and an inactive duodenal ulcer. Also noted on the health record was

*pally caused his husky voice. The doctors wrote that in 1933, he un-
derwent radiological treatment for a throat condition termed "malig-
nant."*

*In regard to his complaint about a heart problem, doctors found that
he was suffering from a "mild and genial syndrome" of arteriosclerosis.
At the time he weighed 168 pounds, and his blood pressure was 140/90.*

*His score on the intelligence test, as noted by the psychiatrist who
administrated it, was a surprisingly low 97. While this was considered
average, one would have expected a man with Costello's reputation to
have scored much higher. In retrospect, however, most psychiatrists
today will concede that intelligence tests really don't accurately mea-
sure people who are not in the mainstream of our society. They are
designed by people who have no idea of what life is like in the ghetto
and underworld. Everyone who has met Costello agrees that he was a
clever and extremely competent individual, so it must be concluded
that his IQ of 97 was hardly an accurate reflection of his mental capacity.*

✣   ✣   ✣

Meanwhile, police continued to search for Gigante. The Chin went
on a crash diet to alter his appearance and then presented a slimmed
down version of himself to the authorities. He turned himself in with
a lawyer at his side and insisted that he was innocent of firing the
gun aimed at Frank Costello's head. No one believed him, of course,
but proving he was the gunman had its difficulties. Costello continued
to maintain that he hadn't seen who had shot him which meant that
the entire case against Gigante rested on the shaky identification of
Norval Keith, an innocuous little man who was admittedly blind in
one eye.

General Sessions Judge Muller presided at the Gigante trial. The
Chin was defended by Maurice Edelbaum, an experienced and expensive criminal lawyer, who took full advantage of his absolute certainty that Costello would refuse to identify his client under any and
all circumstances.

Judge Muller helped the prosecution when Keith took the stand by
asking him to read the court clock, located on a wall about sixty feet
away. The doorman read it without the slightest hesitancy, and this
knocked out Edelbaum's planned line of attack. He was ready to in-
troduce medical testimony that Keith's eyesight was so poor that it
was completely unreliable.

When Costello took the stand, Edelbaum treated him roughly. The
attorney took him all through the Kefauver committee revelations to
firmly impress upon the jury that whoever had attempted to kill Costello was really doing the community a service. He then asked Costello
to put on his glasses and look Gigante over carefully. Costello com-

plied and, in answer to a question, swore that he had never seen Gigante before.

"Do you know any reason why this man should seek to take your life?" Edelbaum asked.

"No reason," Costello answered.

Then leaning towards the witness box, Edelbaum shouted, "You know who shot you. You know who pulled the trigger that night. Why don't you tell the jury who it was?"

Costello remained silent.

(Edelbaum later told a friend, "I would have dropped dead if he answered.")

The defense was effective, and Vincent (The Chin) Gigante, believed by the police, the underworld, and probably even his lawyer to be the person who shot Costello, was declared by a jury innocent of committing the crime.

✻   ✻   ✻

The Chin is still alive but, according to underworld sources, is suffering from a mental condition and frequently regresses back to childhood. His brother, Mario Gigante, is reputed to be a power in the old Luciano family nowadays. Another brother, Father Louis Gigante, is a much beloved and politically active priest in a Puerto Rican section of the Bronx.

✻   ✻   ✻

Not everyone in the Mafia was willing to swallow Don Vitone's charge that Costello was a Government informer. Albert Anastasia, a Costello ally who was capo of a powerful family, openly accused Don Vitone of a serious breach of the organization's rules. No one was safe, Anastasia argued, if Genovese could attempt to kill Costello without getting the approval of the national commission first.

The situation between the Genovese and Anastasia families became tense. Genovese ordered his soldiers to stay away from anyone connected with Anastasia. For the first time since the days of Joe the Boss and Salvatore Maranzano, war threatened.

Don Vitone began to make a case against Anastasia. He accused him of breaking the rules in many areas. He accused him of selling memberships in the organization like a Tammany politician peddling judgeships and of moving into areas where he had no jurisdiction: lucrative gambling areas in the Caribbean and Florida where Meyer Lansky administered things for the benefit of everyone. He pointed out that Anastasia had become a capo after he arranged for the mysterious disappearance in 1951 of Vincent Mangano, one of the original bosses of New York's five families.

Genovese made up his mind to act when he heard alarming reports that Costello was meeting secretly with Anastasia. He grew fearful that his own death was being plotted. In a countermove, he cautiously reached out to Carlo Gambino, one of Anastasia's lieutenants. He asked for his backing in the Costello matter, and in return he offered to elevate Gambino to capo. Anastasia would have to eliminated first, of course, but that could be arranged. Gambino decided that to refuse the Genovese offer would mean that he too would go on the purge list. Don Vitone was all powerful, and Gambino was ambitious. He agreed to help eliminate Anastasia.

Killing Anastasia presented many more difficulties than the attempt on Costello's life. He was always surrounded by two bodyguards and lived in a mansion in Fort Lee, New Jersey, protected by a wire fence and vicious dogs. The "Mad Hatter," as Anastasia was called in the underworld, "killed left and right" and was regarded by Genovese as an extremely dangerous foe.

❋   ❋   ❋

An example of the impulsive, dangerous, psychopathic character of Anastasia was given by Valachi when he told the McClellan committee about the March 2, 1953 slaying of Arnold Schuster, a twenty-four-year-old Brooklyn clothing salesman. Schuster, a crime buff, had recognized gentleman bank robber Willie Sutton changing a car battery on a Brooklyn street. He notified police and Sutton was arrested.

Anastasia watched Schuster being congratulated for his act of good citizenship over television and became enraged. He stood up in front of the TV and shouted, "I hate squealers." Then he ordered Frederick (Chappie) Tenuto, one of his gunmen, to have Schuster hit. The young salesman was shot to death as he walked home. Anastasia then began to worry about the wisdom of his impulsive act. Tenuto was the only one who could link him to the slaying, he reasoned, and solved that problem by personally killing Tenuto to make certain his lips were sealed.

❋   ❋   ❋

On October 25, 1957, at about ten-fifteen A.M., Albert Anastasia entered the Park-Sheraton Hotel barbershop on Seventh Avenue and Fifty-sixth Street, accompanied by his two bodyguards. He seated himself in chair number four, loosened his tie and belt, and closed his eyes as the barber covered his face with a hot towel. His bodyguards, lounging just outside the shop, suddenly disappeared.

The barber had just lathered Anastasia's face when two men, one stout and the other thin, walked in from the hotel lobby. Before entering the barbershop they drew scarves — tied around their necks — up around the lower portion of their faces. Without hesitating a moment, they strode up behind Anastasia and fired bullets from .32 and .38 caliber guns into the back of his head. The powerfully-built Mafia boss bolted out of chair number four and crashed forward into a counter filled with lotions. He then toppled to the floor dead while his killers continued to fire bullets into his back. Then they walked out and made their getaway.

※   ※   ※

Crazy Joey Gallo, according to informer Sidney Slater, a Gallo associate, took credit for blowing Anastasia away. Slater told District Attorney Hogan that two days after the Anastasia slaying, he ran into Gallo and four members of his mob in a nightclub. When the sensational events of the past week came up in the flow of normal conversation, Gallo, according to Slater, laughed out loud and bragged, "From now on, Sidney, you can just call the five of us the Barbershop Quintet."

※   ※   ※

Following the Anastasia killing, Costello sued for peace. Ralph Salerno, an organized-crime expert for the New York City Police Department at the time, explained why.

"He was a real smart guy with a touch of statesmanship, and he realized the best thing for him to do was give up," Salerno said. "He didn't need money. He had more money then he could ever spend in his lifetime. I don't think he had any kind of feeling of passing on the power in a dynastic sort of way because he didn't have any children. So he made a very, very smart move. I think the rest of his life proves it. He lived to a nice, ripe old age and died in bed. And even the mob guys will tell you in retrospect, 'it was a wrong move to get a guy like Genovese in there.' So he still had all the respect in the world."

Don Vitone agreed to allow Costello to live, but first he humbled him. He stripped Costello of all his gambling interests in Las Vegas, Florida, and the Caribbean and even made him give up his piece of the Copacabana. He also reduced Costello to the status of a soldier in the organization without any rights or standing whatsoever. Finally, he extracted a pledge from Costello that he would never again become involved in any of the rackets as long as he lived.

Costello never voiced a word of complaint except to say that he had made a mistake in judgement on Genovese.

"There was no change in him at all that I can recall," a close friend of Costello's said. "The only thing that you did notice was that never

again did the names of Genovese, Mauro, or Eboli come up in his
conversation. Before he was shot they would come up in the course
of normal gossip, but after the shooting he never mentioned them
again. Actually, they were conspicuous because of their absence. It
was as if he had wiped them from his memory."

                    *   *   *

The sudden eruption of violence in New York stirred the concern
of the rest of the Mafia leaders around the country. Genovese, anxious
to calm things down and wishing to preserve the illusion that he had
been forced by circumstances to break the organization's rules, pressed
for a meeting of all the national leaders. After some discussion about
the site (Genovese preferred holding it in Chicago, but Stefano Magaddino, Mafia boss in the Buffalo-Toronto area, preferred to be closer to
home), it was agreed to hold the conclave at the home of Joseph Barbara, Magaddino's lieutenant. The meeting, which has become famous
as the Apalachin Conference, was held on November 14, three weeks
after the death of Anastasia. A total of fifty-eight top level Mafia delegates gathered in the tiny upstate New York community of Apalachin.
They included twenty-three from the New York City-New Jersey area,
nineteen from the rest of New York State, eight from the Midwest,
three from the West, two from the South, two from Cuba, and one
from Sicily.

In testimony before the McClellan committee in 1963, Attorney
General Robert F. Kennedy, told why the meeting was held:

"We know now that the meeting at Apalachin was called by a leading racketeer in an effort to resolve the problem created by the murder of Albert Anastasia. The racketeer was concerned that Anastasia
had brought too many individuals not worthy of membership into the
organization. To insure the security of the organization, the racketeer
wanted these men removed. Of particular concern to this racketeer
was that he had violated commission rules in causing the assault, the
attempted assassination of Frank Costello, deposed New York rackets
boss, and the murder of Anastasia."

Kennedy was, of course, referring to Genovese. Another aim Genovese had in calling the meeting was to lay claim to the title of *capo
di tutti capi* in the New York City area. As Valachi pointed out at the
same hearing, Genovese already controlled the Lucchese and Gambino
families as well as his own. What he sought at Apalachin was the
recognition and legitimization of his power by the commission. Once
this was accomplished, it was just a matter of time before every Mafioso
in the nation would recognize him as the boss of all bosses.

                    *   *   *

The Mafia chiefs were given little time to ponder over their problems thanks to the great detective work of Sergeant Edgar L. Croswell of the New York State Police. Croswell was keeping an eye on Barbara because the Mafia lieutenant had beaten a murder rap. Croswell was anxious to catch him doing something illegal. He became suspicious when Barbara ordered huge quantities of meat in town and made a large number of reservations at nearby motels. When he spotted the arrival of many faces he recognized from his study of Mafia families, Croswell correctly concluded that something big was up. He then notified his superiors, and after it was certain that all the guests had arrived, roadblocks were set up by the troopers to cut off all possible escape routes. When the state cops hit, a number of the Mafia chiefs, including some who were elderly and no longer fleet of foot, headed for the woods. All fifty-eight were rounded up, including the cream of the New York City delegation. Genovese, Jerry Catena, Joe Profaci, Joe Bonanno, Mike Miranda, and Carlo Gambino were among those caught like fish in the police net.

Outside of disrupting things, causing a great deal of embarrassment and harrassment, there was little police could do to the delegates to the Apalachin convention. They all said they were there to visit Barbara because he was sick and needed cheering up. The raid made headlines in newspapers across the nation and demonstrated once and for all that the Mafia was real and did exist.

*   *   *

The final event triggered by the attempt to kill Costello occurred more than two years after the shot was fired. Its victims were Little Augie Pisano (Anthony Carfano) and Janice Drake, the blond and beautiful wife of comedian Alan Drake.

Pisano, an aging and independent Mafia lieutenant, had been close to Costello since the days of Prohibition. He was intensely loyal to Costello and openly expressed his indignation over the way Genovese was handling things. Don Vitone took offense, and Little Augie was added to his purge list.

Little Augie's unforgivable act of defiance apparently came sometime between the shooting of Costello and the murder of Anastasia. Don Vitone called a conference of the upper echelon of his family in a midtown hotel. Everyone obeyed the summons except Little Augie. Genovese noted his absence and warned Little Augie's close friend, Tony Bender: "If he dosen't come in, you'll be wearing a black tie." Bender sent soldiers out to look for Little Augie, and he was brought to the meeting. While he bowed to the authority of Don Vitone, his attitude and tone of voice left little doubt as to how he really felt.

What saved Little Augie for a while was Don Vitone's preoccupation with consolidating his empire and his wish not to upset the national commission with a killing that wasn't really important to him at the time. Later, however, these problems were no longer in the way, and Don Vitone ordered that Little Augie be hit.

September 25, 1959 was Little Augie's last night on the town. It began at the Copacabana where he had drinks with Janice Drake. Exactly what their relationship was has never been made clear. Augie had helped her husband in his career, and she was at least grateful to him for that. She was a stunningly beautiful woman, and it is possible, but highly improbable, that she was merely a flamboyant symbol that the chesty little mobster liked to have around. It enhanced his image.

While they were at the Copa, what seemed like a chance meeting with Tony Bender resulted in a dinner party with Bender and others at a nearby restaurant called Marino's. During the dinner party, Little Augie received two phone calls. The second call caused him to leave Marino's in a hurry. He left with Janice holding onto his arm.

At about ten-thirty P.M., some forty-five minutes later, they were found in Little Augie's black Cadillac on a dark and quiet street in Queens, close to LaGuardia Airport. Both were sitting upright in the front seat, their heads tilted towards each other, like high school kids who had been petting and then had fallen asleep. Detectives poked a pencil into a small, almost bloodless hole on the left side of Little Augie's head to determine the angle at which the bullet had entered his skull. Mrs. Drake had a similiar wound on the right side of her head.

Police later theorized that the killers had hidden in the back seat of the car and then forced Little Augie to drive to that quiet street in Queens. Mrs. Drake, they said, was killed simply because she happened to be along.

✧ ✧ ✧

A Justice Department report, based on the questioning of Joe Valachi, says that the execution of Little Augie was delayed because he was so frequently in the company of Tony Bender. The hit men asked Genovese if it was all right to also hit Bender, but Don Vitone balked at the suggestion. By September of 1959, however, Bender was aware that his friend was marked for death and willingly played a role in setting him up.

In an unrelated matter, Bender himself was the victim of a gangland execution in April of 1962. The hit was ordered by Genovese from his cell in the Atlanta federal prison. Bender simply disappeared after telling his wife that he was going out for a pack of cigarettes. Underworld rumor has it that the body of the thin, mournful-looking Mafia lieutenant was disposed of by a junkyard crusher and wound up as part of a cube of steel.

The man (Part I)

The late Alicia Patterson, founder of the highly successful Long Island newspaper *Newsday*, was about to order lunch in the Waldorf-Astoria's Peacock Alley when she was approached by a stranger.

"I'm a neighbor of yours in Sands Point," Frank Costello said in his raspy voice, not yet made infamous by the Kefauver committee hearings. "Why don't you and your husband come to my house for cocktails some time. Maybe you'll find you'd like to invite me to your house."

Mrs. Patterson accepted the invitation and brought with her one of her reporters and his photographer wife. They arrived in front of Costello's red-brick Colonial, surrounded by blooming fruit trees and spring flowers, on an exquisite day in May of 1950. The lovely old house was set on two acres, modest by Sands Point standards. As they drove up their host, dressed in a short-sleeved sport shirt and slacks with knife-like creases, waited outside to extend his welcome.

All three were charmed by the natural and unpretentious manner in which Costello and Bobbie entertained. They had come out of curiosity and were a little apprehensive. Costello quickly put them at their ease and invited them to sit on the patio and enjoy the sparkling day. Then he openly called his bookmaker and bet one thousand dollars each on the Giant and Yankee baseball games and on the feature race at Belmont.

"I always got to have action," he confessed. Then added, "If we get bored I've got the Yankees on radio, the Giants on television, and they've just started televising the races."

No one was bored. They had an interesting and pleasant afternoon, delighted to have been in the company of this seemingly friendly and gentle man who was reputed to be a vicious criminal. They found Mrs. Costello as charming and sweet as the wives of their next door neighbors.

The visit of *Newsday's* publisher gives an insight into Costello's aspirations and personality. It was not an isolated incident. He was constantly attempting to show respectable society that he had neither horns or was an ogre. This is what made him so different from the other leaders of the Mafia. They craved only the company of their own kind. One cannot imagine any set of circumstances under which men like Genovese and Anastasia would seek out the company of the publisher of a powerful newspaper.

The trio from *Newsday* were hardly the only ones Costello charmed. He successfully seduced tough and skeptical cops, judges, politicians, businessmen, show business personalities, and about everyone else he came in contact with. He was so different from what everyone imagined. There was never any of the menace that his reputation led one to expect. He had a keen sense of humor and a mocking, realistic outlook on life that he presented in a down-to-earth fashion. Women were delighted at his impeccable manners. He was always the first one to stand when a lady walked into a room or excused herself from the dinner table. He always knew the correct fork to use and never used offensive language in front of women. He also had a finely honed sensitivity to the feelings of others, and it would have been unthinkable for Costello to say or do anything that would embarrass someone in his company. If it wasn't for his East Harlem diction, one would have imagined his background to have been very different.

❖   ❖   ❖

Costello's attitudes and values were a curious conglomerate picked up from the tail end of the Victorian period and then filtered through the realities of life as he saw it. His thinking reflected his shrewd observations on the nature of people gathered on the streets of New York and shaped by his Italian-peasant heritage. He eagerly accepted new ideas and scientific data and at the same time would cling to some incredibly backward view of the nature of things.

He was suspicious of men, for instance, who didn't cheat on their wives because he thought it wasn't natural. At the same time he strongly disapproved of those who openly paraded a mistress in public. This, he said, showed a lack of respect for the institution of marriage. While he literally had thousands of friends, he subscribed to the Italian-peasant attitude of "lontano," which means you allow no one to get closer to you than arms length.

In his mind everything had an angle to it, and he was especially suspicious of name droppers. If someone were to say that he knew Frank Sinatra, for instance, Costello was apt to answer, "I know you know Sinatra, but does Sinatra know you." He carried vast sums of money in his pockets. The right pocket contained his spending money and the left his loaning money. When he loaned money to someone he didn't know very well, he would include an extra one or two hundred dollar bills in the amount, making it seem as if he had made a mistake in counting out the sum. He claimed that he could learn a lot about a man's character this way. If the borrower called his attention to the "oversight," he would go up in Costello's estimation. If not, then Costello would just forget about it, feeling he had learned something significant at a cheap price. He claimed he had uncovered a lot of four-flushers in this manner.

His mind was willing to accept the relatively new science of psychiatry, yet at the same time he was convinced of the veracity of an Italian folk tale dealing with the male ejaculatory process. Costello firmly believed that every male was born with a certain number of "bullets," as he called it, and that if you used up these bullets too soon — whether you were twenty-five or seventy-five — that was the end of it. When he was in his seventies he assured friends that he still had lots of bullets left.

Although he was responsible for the wholesale corruption of politicians, judges, cops, and officials, what he admired most was integrity in a man. Integrity to him, however, was something that occurred between people on a one-to-one basis. He considered that he had a great deal of integrity because he always kept his word. He also greatly admired loyalty and success.

His prejudices were the prejudices of his age. He hated homosexuals (couldn't stand to have one in his presence), and he disliked blacks and gypsies. His attitude towards gypsies was developed in his childhood. His mother had apparently frightened him when he was a boy with stories about how gypsies kidnapped children. When he grew up he recognized that these stories were untrue, but he continued to dislike the sight of gypsies anyway.

The Costello personality was especially effective in masculine society. He was a man's man with the knack of striking just the right chord with males from every walk of life. Despite the unpleasantness of having a bodyguard forced upon him, he could joke with the young, good-looking detective assigned to protect him from future assassination attempts, saying, "Gee, what's a nice-looking kid like you doing on the job? I know it doesn't pay many bananas. Must be tough with a family. Maybe you ought to get in my racket." With another detective he struck a serious note by confiding that he was thinking of going to Berlitz to learn how to speak English correctly. Still another cop, who went on vacation and hadn't seen him in a while, recalled asking Costello how things had gone in his absence. "Lousy," Costello answered in mock seriousness. "My wife had to go on medicare."

"He was fun to be with," a veteran detective who had been assigned to guard him said. "He was a very human guy, and everyone liked him. He didn't want us around, but there was nothing he could do about it. So he accepted it with a certain amount of grace. It made things easier for everyone."

Following the attempt on his life, Costello was also tailed by agents of the Federal Bureau of Investigation and the Intelligence Division of the Internal Revenue Service. Often when he went for a walk in Central Park it would look like a parade.

The IRS agents were especially annoying to him. They had received a tip that he was going to flee the country if the Supreme Court ruled against him on his tax appeal case and he had to return to jail. The agents assigned were told to make certain this didn't happen. There was never a word of truth to the rumor, but the IRS agents regarded the possibility as real and shadowed him with zeal.

No attempt was made to hide the fact that they were following him. One IRS agent was so intent on not losing Costello that he followed a cab he was in too closely. When the cab was forced to make a short stop, the IRS agent's car rammed into the cab's rear. Costello climbed out of the cab with a worried look on his face and gently admonished the agent who was driving. "Gee, let's not have any accidents," he said. "It's not worth anyone getting hurt over this. I'll give you a list of every place I'm going to so you don't have to worry about losing me." When IRS agents would follow him into an expensive restaurant, he'd send the waiter over with drinks or invite them to join his table. Other times his mood would change, and he'd play little games by suddenly hopping out of a cab and disappearing down a one-way street. This would create havoc as one agent had to jump out of the trailing car while the driver raced around the block. Often after showing the agents how easy it was to lose them, he would suddenly appear out of nowhere and wave to them so they would know he was still around.

IRS agent Seymour Bard, one of those assigned to keep watch on

Costello in the late fifties, recalled being part of a team that followed the aging Mafia leader to a doctor's office on the East Side. By then everyone knew Costello's habits pretty well, and when several hours passed without him coming out, panic set in.

"No one wanted to be the agent who lost him when he skipped the country," Bard said. "That would have been the end of your career. So when several hours passed, and he didn't come out of the doctor's office, we were afraid that somehow he had given us the slip. It was way past his normal bedtime, and we couldn't imagine what he was doing in the doctor's office so long."

The agents frantically checked Costello's apartment building and found out that he hadn't shown up at home. Unable to think of anything else to do, Bard and another agent grimly decided to continue to wait in front of the physician's office. Their perserverence paid off when Costello finally walked out in the small hours of the morning. The next day they found out through one of his attorneys that the doctor was a close friend and that he had used the office as a trysting place.

The IRS agents who followed Costello day after day said he bore up under the pressure with dignity and patience. "He was really a nice guy," they all agreed.

                ❋   ❋   ❋

Toots Shor, who knew Costello quite well, said that the qualities he admired Costello most for were his low-key approach, the fact that he was a good gambler, and his sense of propriety.

"He didn't let you know he was a big shot," Shor said. "He had a lot of power in those days, yet he never let you know he was Frank Costello. He acted like just another guy. He sat around and talked sports like we all did. He was a gambler, and everyone knew he was a gambler, and he would bet. He was one of those guys who bet big. He'd bet to get hurt. He was one of the biggest betters in the fights, and in those days — in the thirties and early forties — everybody bet. He'd love to bet and talk sports, and he'd come around and talk fights to me because I knew all the fighters.

"In all the years I knew him — and I go back to the twenties with him — I never saw him yell at anybody. I never saw him raise his voice. He was always nice and decent, and when I got my own saloon and it became a popular place to go he'd always come in and always with his wife. I never saw him with anybody but his wife. He had too much respect for her to be seen with someone not his wife. I liked that about him too."

A newspaperman who knew Costello said: "He had a sort of dignity about him. He'd walk into a room and everyone knew he was the boss, in a nice way. He didn't abuse the power. He had a sort of presence about him that everyone liked. He was a nice man."

A retired police inspector, "He really ruled the underworld out of respect rather than fear."

Costello honestly felt that his reputation was ill deserved. He felt that the rackets he was involved in should have been legal, and when off-track betting came to New York City he remarked, "Now its legal, but when I did it they made me a criminal." He had an amoral attitude towards the role he played in corruption and rationalized that this was part of the realities of life and that everyone was out to make a buck. A criminal to Costello was someone who dealt in heroin or held up banks or was involved in extortion. Bribing a cop or running a slot machine racket was acceptable.

Costello was friendly with some of the best known newspapermen in the nation. Men like Walter Winchell, Damon Runyon, Drew Pearson, and Bob Considine. Through them he played over and over his two pet themes: poverty and environment forced him into the rackets; his sinister reputation was caused by bad publicity.

Winchell, in an interview, asked him what he thought his first mistake was. Costello answered: "If you call it a mistake, I guess it was being born of poor parents and being raised in a tough neighborhood. If things had been different, I might have gone to college and been sitting up there with Mr. Kefauver. But I can honestly say that since I'm old enough to know right from wrong, I've tried to live a good life. I've been married to the same girl for thirty-five years. How many of my critics can match that?"

In an interview with Considine, he said: "If you say I was or am a racketeer, I guess you'll be right. But for a long time I've been trying to figure out just what a racketeer is. I never went to school past the third grade, but I graduated from ten universities of hard knocks, and I have decided that a racketeer is a fellow who tries to get power, prestige, and money at the expense of entrenched power, prestige, or money.

"Maybe I don't make it clear, but I figure that if I'm a racketeer, so are let's say editors. They'll print your articles in the hope of getting circulation from rival newspapers, for circulation means power, prestige, and money.

"I'm circulation."

In an interview with *Newsweek Magazine*: "Right now I'm cleaner than ninety-nine per cent of New Yorkers. Now I don't want you to get the wrong impression — I never sold any bibles. They are all with their shotguns waiting for me to come out of my hole like a rabbit. You think I could get away with anything? It's ridiculous.

"I'm like Coca-Cola. There are a lot of good drinks as good as Coca-Cola. Pepsi-Cola is a good drink. But Pepsi-Cola never got the advertising Coca-Cola got. I'm not Pepsi-Cola. I'm Coca-Cola because I got so much advertising."

In the view of a close friend — despite his protestations to the contrary — Costello really enjoyed all the publicity that gave him almost celebrity status. What he didn't like was the notoriety that accompanied it.

"If he could have controlled the notoriety he really would have loved it," the friend explained. "The fact that he had no control over it, that it got into areas that were uncomplimentary and was out of step with the image he wanted, that's the part he didn't like."

Even many years after the Kefauver hearings, people would come over to Costello's table at a restaurant and ask him for his autograph. He always signed in a good-natured manner, sometimes asking why it was wanted. When he was told because he was a celebrity, he'd beam and sign with a flourish.

What Costello really wanted, his friends agree, was to be acknowledged as a highly successful businessman, not a criminal or a hood. His conversations would often center on his legitimate enterprises and his friendships with legitimate businessmen like Bernard Gimbel or Jack Warner. While he might mention Luciano, Lansky, or Genovese on occasion, it was just in passing conversation, and his friends knew better than to probe.

"You instinctively knew that this was a forbidden area, and you never asked questions beyond what he would volunteer," said columnist John J. Miller.

✳   ✳   ✳

Still the fact remains that the Costello who preached against violence and yearned for respectability was able to maintain friendships with some of the most violent and most disreputable men in the nation. The same Costello who, in his own words, was friends with "some of the biggest men in the country," was also closely connected, for instance, to a pathological killer like Albert Anastasia.

Which then was the real Costello? Was it the affable, immensely likeable man who charmed the publisher of *Newsday* and so many others he came in contact with, or was it the Mafia leader who ran the most powerful family in New York City for so many years? One can only speculate.

Actually, there was no contradiction in the two faces of Costello. It was all one face. People tend to see evil in absolute terms. The Genoveses and Anastasias of any society are clearly recognizable and easy to hate. Their violent transgressions shock us all. Who in a civilized society does not condemn murder? The corrupters, on the other hand, stir the passions less. Bribery has its human elements. Do any of us feel criminal when we pay a cop ten bucks not to write a ticket or cheat on our income tax? The answer, of course, is no. Yet it can be argued with considerable justification that the real danger to the fabric of society comes not from the Anastasias or Genoveses, but from the Costellos. Bribing a politician or subverting a judge does more to rip society's fabric than violence. We can deal with the purveyors of violence, but the corrupters are something else again. They threaten to change us.

It is in these terms we must view Costello. He was a master corrupter and, therefore, much more dangerous than Genovese or any of his kind. This was what he never understood. He felt because he was good to his wife, gave vast sums of money to charity, and avoided violence, he had lived a good life. He died feeling this way.

Costello was a highly adaptable individual. He could have been plunked down in the midst of a group of Hottentots and found some common thread of agreement. The men of the Mafia were hardly Hottentots to him. On the contrary, in his younger years his attitudes coincided with theirs, and his connection with the secret society made it possible for him to do well in the rackets. Costello needed the Mafia, and the Mafia needed Costello. In his later years, however, when he had all the money he had ever hoped for, his membership in the organization became an embarrassment to him. Yet there was little he could do about it. He couldn't just quit as if he were resigning from the Knights of Columbus or some other fraternal order. All he could do was use his influence to keep violence to a minimum and order that his family keep away from the heroin traffic because he thought it was personally reprehensible.

*   *   *

The rise to power of Vito Genovese was matched by a corresponding lessening of Costello's influence. By the time he was shot, his power in the Mafia had waned considerably. Many students of the secret organization believe that at the time of the shooting Costello was searching for a way to retire.

"In many ways Genovese did him a favor," says a Mafia expert in the New York City Police Department. "Costello was tired of it all and wanted out. The unsuccessful attempt on his life was his ticket out. It provided him with the excuse. If he didn't want out he would have fought back."

His relationship with Genovese didn't end, however, when the gunman missed his mark. He and Genovese settled their differences in Atlanta federal prison where Costello was sent to finish the time he owed in his income tax conviction. Genovese was sent there for dealing in heroin in 1959.

Joe Valachi discovered they had kissed and made up when he shared a cell with Genovese in Atlanta. One time he casually mentioned that he had heard that Joe Pagano, a member of the family, owned Costello's piece of the Copacabana. Genovese became furious and asked Valachi what he meant. The surprised Valachi answered: "That's what I heard."

"Where did you hear it?" Genovese demanded to know. Before he could receive an answer, he said: "With my permission, I want you to tell everybody. I am giving you permission. You go tell everybody that Frank Costello — I gave him back the Copacabana, that Frank Costello owns the club."

(Vito Genovese, who believed that every man died the sort of death he deserved, died in prison on February 14, 1969, of congestive heart failure brought on by terminal cancer. He was seventy-one.)

Frank Costello was both self-conscious and proud at the same time about his lack of education. Like so many self-made men, he often remarked about his lack of schooling, but underlying the reference was a strong sense of pride in what he had accomplished despite his background. He read a great deal — mostly on current events — and had what he thought were astute opinions on most everything.

His speech was an odd combination of New York slang with an occassional new word he had picked up thrown in. If he were discussing someone he didn't like, for instance, he might say: "He has a supercilious attitude and is a stool pigeon besides."

When Costello sat down to dinner with friends, he'd invariably pick out some topical thing, often the top new story of the day, then he'd go around the table and solicit everyone's opinion. He'd want to know how you figured it. Then he'd give his opinion on the subject and invariably it was some elaborate theory he had worked out to fit the known facts. His theories were often quite good, but at times they would be rather far-fetched.

When President Kennedy was shot, for instance, he was convinced that it was an elaborate plot engineered by Bobby Kennedy to capture the Presidency. The assassin, he insisted, was just the patsy. His theory neatly fitted his opinion of the President's younger brother whom he considered to be a ruthless opportunist.

He was always fascinated by the underlying facts of a situation. A person climbing a mountain didn't interest him, but the psychological aspects of why that person wanted to climb that mountain interested him a great deal. He was turned on by the motivation of an act rather than its actual accomplishment.

His thoughts on modern America were those of an old-fashioned moralist convinced that our current society is heading for extinction. He had read a great deal about the Roman Empire and said that America was following the same pattern. A civilization crumbles, he said, with the moral decay of its youth. He firmly believed we were following this path and pointed to the rise in homosexuality, promiscuity, and pornography as proof of his theme.

He was especially upset about the hard-core porno movies being shown, and told Broadway columnist Earl Wilson of his horror at innocently walking into one.

"I wondered how I can kill a half hour, and I'm thinkin' of going into Alexander's store to walk around. I never been in the store. I turn on Lexington Avenue, I think its 59th Street, and I see a theater there in a brownstone house.

"I think how can there be a theater in a brownstone house? The admission is three-dollars. I went inside, and I want to tell you — never in my life did I see anything like that!

"They're doing things in that picture I never even talk about or think about. This guy does things with two girls, and then there's two guys with two guys, and all I'm thinkin' is I don't want anybody to see me.

"I'm squirmin' around, I put on my glasses, pull up my coat collar, and walk out of there like a real Dillinger. It was the worst thing I ever saw in my life."

Costello was especially critical of the official toleration of the sex shops in the Times Square area and complained bitterly that Broadway had been ruined, taken over by pimps and prostitues who made it impossible for decent people to go there. He strongly approved of the law and order theme and was critical of the police for not doing their job. He felt that street crime had changed the quality of life in the city and blamed much of the situation on the soft-headed liberals. In his view the bootleggers and gamblers of his day really didn't hurt anyone.

During his lifetime, Costello gave vast amounts of money to charity,

most often anonymously. Each year he would quietly hand Walter
Winchell one hundred thousand dollars or more in cash for the Damon
Runyon Cancer Fund. Winchell would acknowledge receipt of the
money over his radio show by announcing that the huge amount was
from an anonymous donor. The Legal Aid Society was another of
Costello's favorite charities. His courtroom battles had made him ap-
preciative of the need of legal counsel for anyone accused of a crime.

Often he handed out money impulsively to panhandlers, persons
who had met with misfortune, or someone with a hard luck story. One
time he ran across a black woman in the street who was crying because her pocketbook had been snatched. Costello handed her a fifty
dollar bill.

Another time a disheveled-looking youth stopped him in front of a
restaurant and asked for carfare to get home. He lived in New Jersey
and needed a couple of dollars.

For some reason or other, Costello was intrigued with the youth's
song and dance. He asked him if he were willing to take a gamble.
The youth said that he had gotten into trouble gambling and didn't
want to gamble anymore.

"I'm going to reach into my pocket," Costello told him nevertheless,
"and pull out a bill. Whether it's a one or a hundred it's yours."

Costello fished into his pocket and came up with a twenty dollar
bill. He gave it to the youth who grabbed it and ran. A friend with
Costello remarked that that was one lucky panhandler.

"Nah, he's a loser," Costello answered. "That's the only twenty
I got in my pocket. Everything else is hundreds."

Typical of the way Costello handed out huge sums occurred in
the Copacabana lounge one afternoon. Hearst humor columnist Bugs
Baer, his wife, Louise, and Julie Podell, the Copa's owner of record,
were sitting at a table. Nearby, at another table, sat Costello sipping
a drink. The Baers knew Costello, but not well. It was no more than
a nodding acquaintance.

Mrs. Baer, a former showgirl who still showed traces of her former
beauty, was then suffering from the ravages of the heart disease that
later killed her. At the time she was actively involved in raising money
for a heart fund which later developed into the American Heart Association. She was discussing her fund-raising problems with Podell.
After a few minutes, Podell excused himself and sat down to chat
with Costello. He returned a little while later and handed Mrs. Baer
a check for ten thousand dollars. It was from Costello, and on back of
the check he had written, "For Mrs. Baer's charity." He didn't even
know its name.

Another of Costello's attractive qualities was his loyalty to friends.

His close friendship with *National Enquirer* publisher, Gene Pope Jr. had its roots in Costello's friendship with Generoso Pope Sr. When the elder died, Costello took the youngest son of his friend under his wing and helped him in every way he could. First he used his political influence and had Mayor O'Dwyer appoint Pope to the Board of Higher Education so he would have a title with prestige. Later, when Pope became the publisher of the *Enquirer*, he backed him with money. In the early fifties, the *Enquirer* had trouble meeting its payroll and was in danger of going under. Each week, Costello would loan his young friend ten thousand dollars to meet operating expenses. Pope would repay the loan promptly the following week in two five thousand dollar installments as revenue from newsstand sales rolled in. Costello continued to loan Pope money for his payroll even when he was in jail. Bobbie or Big Jim O'Connor would deliver the cash. The *Enquirer* today is quite successful with a weekly circulation said to be in excess of four million. Attempts are also being made to change its image from wild sensationalism to a more conservative and respectable view of the news. The fact remains, however, that Costello was its godfather.

Pope wasn't the only one Costello took the trouble to help while he was in jail. He was especially fond of Edward Bennett Williams, and when the attorney visited him in his cell one time, Costello noticed that he seemed perturbed about something. Costello asked him what the problem was, and Williams explained that he and his wife were taking her parents out that night to celebrate their thirty-fifth wedding anniversary, and he had promised to get tickets to *My Fair Lady*. The tickets hadn't come through, and now he was facing having to disappoint them.

"Mr. Williams, you should have told me," Costello said. "Maybe I could have helped."

Williams said that it just hadn't occurred to him that a man in jail could get tickets to one of the hottest Broadway musicals of all time. The subject was then dropped.

Late that afternoon, after Williams had returned to his hotel room, he heard a soft knock on his door. Upon opening it, a large man under a slouch hat grunted something and handed him an envelope containing four tickets for that evening's performance and then quickly left without saying another word.

＊   ＊   ＊

Gambling played an important part in Costello's life. He gambled with a passion on anything from the outcome of an election to what part of town the first snowflakes of a blizzard would hit. A winning bet for him was reaffirmation of the superiority of his mental ability. Although he was a fan and had his favorite athletes, he tried not to let that influence his selections. He always maintained that he bet with his head, not his heart. Gambling was also important to him because he loved to rough house with the boys. He thoroughly enjoyed the male world of the gambling fraternity with its comradery and the intricate maneuvers everyone went through to try and gain an advantage.

The two sports he loved best were horse racing and boxing, and when he was barred for life from Belmont Race Track because he was a gambler, he made a point of calling on Joseph Widener in person to ask for reconsideration. The frosty old aristocrat who was head of the track was adamant, and Costello became angry.

"What the hell is the difference between you and me?" he asked. "You live in Philadelphia and run a gambling joint in New York — this track. I live in New York and run them in other states."

Each year he would take a vacation in Hot Springs, Arkansas, which was neutral ground for the mob. Racketeers from all over the country would meet in the wide-open town to frolic at the race track, night clubs, casinos, and the fights. They dunked themselves religiously into the famed sulpher baths. It was Hot Springs that Owney Madden, Costello's boyhood buddy who was a feared and notorious gunman in the twenties, had retired to. Madden had reformed and had married the daughter of a Hot Springs politician. Costello often remarked that he had never seen a man in his life who had changed so much because of a woman. In his later years, Madden, who had once borne the nickname of "Killer," evolved into a respectable citizen.

What Costello seemed to enjoy most about Hot Springs were the fights. He and Owney Madden and often Frank Erickson would bet each other on every bout. The highlight of the evening was a free-for-all, an impossible-to-predict event in which five black fighters would go into the ring and then be blindfolded. When the bell sounded they would swing wildly at each other until one man was left standing. He would be declared the winner. Costello loved the event and would bet wildly on the outcome. Years after the fact he would reminisce about its excitement and unpredictability.

Costello was fond of saying that lots of men have pissed away fortunes, but he was the only man who won a fortune pissing. During his salad days he would challenge friends to pissing contests. He would bet as much as a thousand dollars that he could maintain a steady stream the longest. He claimed to have a sure-fire method that enabled him to always emerge victorious. Most opponents, he explained, would drink huge amounts of liquid and refrain from urinating for hours

before engaging in the contest. This, according to Costello, was exactly
the wrong thing to do. The secret, he said, was to drink a moderate
amount of fluids and then pee shortly before you had to toe the mark.
This kept the pressure behind your stream minimal, and even though
your opponent would have a greater reservoir to tap, his bladder would
empty more quickly because of the force of his stream. He claimed
that he only lost one bet pissing in his life and that was for five thousand dollars. He retired after that on the theory that someone had
figured out a way to beat him.

✸　　　　✸　　　　✸

Although he preferred male companionship on most occasions, Costello got along quite well with women. He had a rather old-fashioned
view of the role of the female in our society, but in time this view
changed, and he was able to have a deep and serious platonic relationship with a famous woman writer.

The Costello's had a highly successful marriage. It lasted until death
did them part and was based on mutual respect and affection. Costello
was very much the head of the household, and Bobbie was content
to be pampered and indulged. While she occupied one of the main
compartments of her husband's life, he kept her separate and apart
from the many other areas he was involved in. She knew better than
to meddle in his affairs unless he invited her to do so.

The relationship was similiar to a benevolent despot or father figure
who generously provides status and the luxuries of life to the woman
of his choice. She, in turn, provided him with the stability and foundation stone upon which he could build his quest for respectability. It
was not unlike many upper-middle income marriages before the ad-
vent of women's lib.

Bobbie seldom cooked and spent her days following the traditional
pattern of the wives of the wealthy. She tended to social chores, shopped,
attended the theater, provided him with a lovely and tranquil home
and accompanied him when he needed her. Each year, for instance,
she personally addressed and sent out as many as a thousand Christmas
cards to their many friends. The Costello card was a harbinger of the
Christmas season; it was always the first to arrive. She also meticulously remembered anniversaries and birthdays and took the time to
choose thoughtful little gifts for friends at the appropriate times. She
was godmother to the two children of John and Cindy Miller and took
her duties seriously. Each year on their birthday, the children would
receive a card and a fifty-dollar bill from her.

Mrs. Costello, now in her mid seventies, was an attractive, medium-
sized brunette who dressed conservatively, used makeup liberally, and

had an eternal weight problem. Her bubbing spirits seemed infectious because of her high-pitched, little girl's voice. The combination gave her a scatter-brained Billie Burke quality which gave rise to the rumor that she originally was a show girl. Everyone who knows her agrees that she is an intelligent woman who has always conducted herself with charm and dignity.

Friends say that she was not only nice but concerned with being nice. She was noted for her sense of humor that was tempered by her sensitivity to the ungrammatical way she spoke and her husband's racketeer reputation. She loved to stay out late and attend the latest night club shows and had an insatiable curiosity about show business gossip. She was forever questioning Frank's newspaper friends about the inside story of a celebrity divorce or about who was having affair with whom.

The Costellos were childless, although they both related to children very well. (Frank liked to read nursery rhymes to the children of his friends.) The reason for their childlessness is unknown, but most of their friends are under the impression it was Bobbie's fault. This, of course, was in keeping with the highly masculine image Frank had of himself, and the opposite may be true.

Like so many childless women, Bobbie found an outlet for her maternal instincts in her two pets. No matter where she was, she returned home to cook dinner for her toy poodle and minature doberman at four P.M. Once she sent Frank a Father's Day card and signed the names of her dogs. He was highly insulted, and she never did it again.

Frank loved to tease her, and his favorite topics were her devotion to the pets and her weight problem. She didn't have his self control, and when the dessert cart was rolled around in a restaurant she would eye it longingly without making a selection. He would make the most of the situation and say, "Go ahead. Why not? You want it, so go ahead and have it." She'd look at him and ask, "Do you think it's all right?" He'd nod and encourage her some more, and after she had eaten the dessert he'd look at her and say, "How come you had that when you're not supposed to?" She would become furious, and Frank and everyone would laugh.

While she was not a prude and liked a mildly off-color story, she became upset by the ones that were crude or vulgar. Frank didn't like really dirty stories told in front of his wife, or any woman for that matter, but he couldn't always control things. Sometimes some of his underworld friends would tell stories that Bobbie found offensive. One particularly upsetting incident occurred at the Copa, and she complained to Frank who became mildly angry at her complaint.

"You're the one who always likes to come here," he reminded Bobbie, "and you never know who you're going to run into at these places. You've got to expect these kind of things to happen otherwise stop telling me to take you here."

Frank was very much the dominant figure in the relationship, and while she freely took part in the dinner conversations, he could cut her short with a look if he felt she was saying something better left unsaid. They never — at least in public — exchanged heated words although if Frank became really upset at something he would lapse into silence. Friends say he had the ability to make someone feel uncomfortable just by being quiet.

Like many women of wealth, Bobbie had a good deal of trouble with maids. They were constantly getting different ones, and Frank blamed that on the fact that Bobbie couldn't get along with them. He once jokingly said that if everyone had trouble with maids the way his wife did, then the maids should have a union, and he might look into organizing them some day. Bobbie, however, claimed that one of the main reasons for her maid problems was Frank's infamous reputation. She said that many of the maids were simply scared to death of him, and that anytime he had to tell a maid something, he had to tell it through her.

(One maid was fired, Frank confided to friends, because she propositioned him one early morning while Bobbie was asleep. He said that the maid, a young black girl from the South who had just been hired, asked him if he would like to "dip it." He told her he needed time to think about it because he was afraid his wife would wake up, and he'd let her know the next day. That afternoon he told Bobbie that he had caught the maid drinking liquor and told Bobbie to fire her immediately. It was typical of the diplomatic way he handled situations.)

Because of the many newspaper stories about his wealth, Costello was plagued by letters from people asking for money. A number were from young men who said that he was their father and that they wanted money to keep quiet about it. He simply ignored all mail requests for money. One London-born young man, however, was more persistant than the others. He used to hang out on Central Park West, across the street from where the Costellos lived, and when he saw Frank he'd rush up to him and claim he was his son. After a while it became embarrassing, and Bobbie suggested that Frank call the police and have the "London-born heir" arrested. Frank, however, wouldn't do that because he was afraid of what the papers might do with the story if they got hold of it. In time the young man gave up and disappeared, but Bobbie never let her husband forget him. It was a good way for her to get even with some of his kidding, and she'd ask in front of friends, "How do I know he was a fake?"

From the early thirties well into the sixties, Costello had a mistress. It was a long, discreet relationship in the French manner. They were never seen in public together, and even close friends were ignorant of her existence. She was an extremely beautiful brunette, a tall show-girl named Thelma Martin who was many years younger than Costello. He maintained her in a Fifth Avenue apartment directly across Central Park from the Majestic.

A detective who trailed Costello regularly in the thirties said that he would visit her every evening in those days.

"You could set your watch on that movement," the detective said. "Promptly at six o'clock he'd go into the apartment building at Seventy-second Street and Fifth Avenue, and at nine P.M. he'd walk out the lobby, hop a cab, and go home."

As he got older the frequency with which he would visit Thelma Martin slackened considerably. Nevertheless, the relationship continued to thrive, and detectives who guarded him after he was shot said that the only thing that would cause Costello to become angry was when they questioned him about her. He said that they had no right to interfere in his private business.

On a number of occasions police attempted to question Miss Martin to determine if she knew anything about her sponsor's affairs, but each time they looked for her she simply disappeared and didn't return to the city until interest in her had been forgotten.

Although Bobbie knew about Miss Martin, she never brought up the subject until the fall of 1957 when the Majestic became a cooperative. Her husband decided that he didn't want to buy the apartment and told Bobbie to look for a new one. She didn't want to move and planned her strategy. When he complained about all the money it would cost, she presented him with a carefully researched list of things he had purchased for the lady on Fifth Avenue over the years. The list was even translated into dollars and included an estimate of his total expenditures. Costello was astounded and impressed by the accuracy of his wife's information and after considering the matter hoisted the white flag. The Costellos didn't move.

Bobbie also left Frank once during their marriage, only he didn't know it until years after the fact. The incident occurred in the forties and was the result of his last-minute cancellation of a trip to California they had planned. He just called her up on the day they were scheduled to leave and said he had to go to Hot Springs on business. She blew her top, and as Frank flew to Hot Springs she packed a suitcase and drove all by herself to Atlantic City. The reason she chose the beach resort was because she and Frank had recently been there and had had a marvellous time. She was counting on him finding her easily when he came home because she knew that he had many friends there.

Things didn't work out the way she planned, though. To begin with, she arrived out of season, and the hotel was almost deserted. Secondly, the weather was miserable, and there wasn't a soul there she knew. The next day she drove home admitting to herself that her act of independence had turned into a disaster. Many years later she told Frank, and they both laughed long and hard.

The man (Part II)

An extraordinary thing happened to Miss Santha Rama Rau, the gifted Inian writer and playwright, in early summer, 1949. She met and became good friends with Frank Costello.

Meeting Costello was not unusual; becoming close friends with him was. One could search the world over and have difficulty in finding two people of more dissimiliar backgrounds. Miss Rama Rau is an intellectual, a member of one of India's most prominent families. She was educated in America but speaks English as if she had grown up in the Court of St. James. Her writing talents and perceptions have been hailed by critics everywhere. She is an incredibly accomplished and attractive woman.

Miss Rama Rau, who in private life is married to Gurdon Wattles, chief legal advisor to the head of the United Nations, was attending a party given by a wealthy friend in Sands Point, Long Island when she met Costello. She recalls that it was Jimmy Cromwell, one of the former husbands of tobacco heiress Doris Duke, who introduced her to him.

"I have to explain," she said, "that I was not only quite young at the time but not particularly well acquainted with America. I had been to college here, but that's really all — college life. I certainly was not acquainted with American affairs in particular and certainly not with anything involving the Mafia. So when I was introduced to

Frank Costello, it was just a name. The only Costello I had ever heard of was Costello of Abbot and Costello; and this surely wasn't that one."

Miss Rama Rau said that Costello arrived at the party in this "enormous grey Cadillac." He was dressed in sports clothes that struck her as odd because they just didn't seem to fit her initial impression of him.

"He seemed to me to be a typical city person, and even his sports clothes looked sort of like city sports clothes," she said. "If you saw someone else wearing the same clothes you'd say the man was in sports clothes. I remember thinking that the clothes didn't suit him, that he really shouldn't have been wearing those clothes. If you've seen really bad tennis players and very good tennis players wearing virtually the same clothes, you'll know what I mean. Somehow the bad players look entirely different because the good tennis players are used to having those clothes on.

"The first thing that really struck me about him was his voice. It was an astonishing voice. As a writer, one is always on the lookout for unusual personalities, and Frankie had that quality of the extraordinary. I mean, he seemed to know about a whole world that I knew nothing about.

"He was very much in command of himself and at ease with these particular surroundings. He asked me where I came from and what I did, and he seemed immensely interested that I came from India and was a writer. I had just published a book (*East of Home*) at that time, and he was very interested to know about the book, and mostly it was him asking me questions, and I really didn't get a chance to ask him anything. It never occurred to me to ask anybody about him. It seemed to me he was just somebody who was successful at whatever he did."

Before the afternoon was over, Costello asked Miss Rama Rau if she would like to have lunch with him some time, and when she readily agreed he took her phone number. She didn't give it another thought because she hardly expected to ever hear from him again. That same week he telephoned and invited her to lunch at the Waldorf-Astoria's Starlight Roof.

❈   ❈   ❈

"It was a lunch I'll never forget because I think never in my life have I felt like royalty quite so much as I did that day," she said. "You had only to walk in and say to the head waiter, 'Mr. Costello's table,' and you were instantly ushered in by a whole squad of waiters and seated. It was perfectly astonishing."

Miss Rama Rau even recalls what they had for lunch that day. When Costello asked her what she'd like, she said that she would have whatever he was having. He told the maitre d' "the usual," which turned out to be lamb chops.

"He was exceedingly polite and nice and in the course of lunch started talking about his early background. I was terribly interested why, in fact, he invited me to lunch, and the answer amused me. The way he talked, it was as though this was on orders from a shrink. You know, I have been advised to . . . and the gist of it was that his shrink was telling him that he was seeing too many of the same kinds of people, that he needed to broaden his horizons, that these moods of depression he suffered from had resulted from too much of the same kind of life and same places, and, of course, what could be more out of his line than this young Indian writer. I think it was really that that persuaded him to pursue the friendship at all, and I was absolutely enthralled because when he started to talk about his early days I gradually started to catch on to what sort of thing it was. I still didn't really know who he was."

Costello told Miss Rama Rau about his visit to his home town in Italy: how he had been hailed as the village boy who had made it, how he had met his sister there and had handed out handfuls of lire and had been driven to the railroad station in a decorated donkey cart when he left. He also told her about the extreme poverty of his youth and how his mother always nagged him, saying, "Frankie, go straight." He told her how the only people who seemed to have intelligence and a chance to get ahead in his East Harlem neighborhood were the gang members he got in with.

"By the end of the luncheon it became quite clear to me that his mother wasn't just talking about bullying other little boys," Miss Rama Rau said, "and that he wasn't just the conventional, successful businessman."

Leaving the Starlight Roof with Costello proved to be as unforgettable for the young writer as entering.

"I have often read about people carrying a roll of bills," she said. "I had never actually seen anyone with a roll of bills before, but Frankie had one, and he simply peeled them off and handed them to waiters or whoever happened to be in the vicinity. I thought it was a marvelous sort of gesture to leave in a cloud of tips. I was twenty-three or twenty-four and deeply impressed. It was a foreign world to me.

"When we got into the taxi, the taxi driver said the usual, 'Where to Mac,' or something of that sort without turning around, and it was the first time I realized what the effect of Frankie's voice was, and

the minute he said 191 East Sixty-second Street, which is where I
lived at the time, there was this sort of sudden double take, and up
went the flag again (so the fare wouldn't be recorded). It was really
a creepy experience because you had the feeling — I don't know
whether this is true or not for everyone — that you could break all
the laws and be protected (when Costello was there). You could go
through red lights, you could turn down one-way streets, and you
could do all sorts of things, and you'd be all right.

"He simply seemed to exude this feeling without, as far as I could
actually make out, without actually doing anything. He didn't tell the
driver to hurry, and he certainly didn't suggest that the flag go up.
Nevertheless, I think that the driver got paid at least twice what he
would have gotten paid.

"That happened often in taxis. Frankie was quite extraordinary in
how well known he was to people at this level."

*   *   *

From that point on the friendship flourished between the young
writer and the man reputed to be the head of the underworld. It was
all very proper with never a hint of anything tawdry.

Miss Rama Rau introduced him to her friends who were artists,
writers, and journalists, and they were as enchanted as she was with
his polite, impeccably correct, dignified manner that blended so strangely
with his heavy New York accent and fund of strange and interesting
stories. Costello, in turn, received from them a new vista of life to
contemplate.

After their first lunch, he ordered several hundred of Miss Rama
Rau's book from her publisher, Harper & Row, and distributed the
copies to his friends. Miss Rama Rau's editor at the publishing firm,
an extremely correct and proper lady from New England, was absolutely astonished when Costello ordered the books. That sort of thing
just didn't happen with Harper & Row authors.

"I often had to reach him to invite him to a cocktail party, and
this was where I became fascinated with the whole thing," Miss Rama
Rau recalled, "because to get hold of Frankie was marvelous in those
days. You called the barbershop in the Waldorf, and you asked if
Frankie was there. They always said 'no' and asked who you were
and what your number was, and you gave them your name and number
and hung up. It was never more than five minutes, usually less, before
Frankie would call back. This was absolute magic. I was enchanted
anyway."

Miss Rama Rau was given a complete fill-in on Costello's background
from a friend, Jane Rosen, who worked for the *New York Times*.

"Why on earth are you seeing people like that, and when are you going to invite me to meet him," said Miss Rosen in reaction to the news that her friend was seeing Costello.

"This was really the effect this friendship had on everybody I knew," Miss Rama Rau said. "They were first horrified that I should be mixing in company of this sort and also curious to meet him. I made it clear where I stood. I found him an exceedingly nice, very gentle, exceedingly courteous man, and all the time in which I knew him he was considerate in ways that I wouldn't have believed possible."

✿   ✿   ✿

Miss Rama Rau discovered that being Costello's friend had advantages other than being driven quickly from place to place by cab drivers. The merchants in her neighborhood were also impressed. It all started the first time she invited Costello for cocktails, and he had the local liquor store deliver a case of assorted whiskeys to her apartment.

"He himself never drank much," she said, "but he used to send a case of assorted bottles of liquor over everytime he came. And the result was that I got the most magnificent reputation in that neighborhood, and the cachet of being a friend of Costello's and being *known* to be a friend of Costello's was absolutely fantastic. It was very, very heavy stuff. I had no idea word would travel as quickly as that."

Miss Rama Rau suddenly found that the doormen on the block treated her with exaggerated politeness, the merchants waited on her immediately, the cleaners would promise fantastic service. All the normal little irritations one often has shopping were suddenly gone. It seemed everyone was falling over themselves to be pleasant and helpful to her.

✿   ✿   ✿

At the time of her friendship with Costello, Miss Rama Rau's uncle was the chief Indian delegate on the Security Council of the United Nations. This was at the time of the Korean War negotiations, and the Indian representatives were responsible for all business dealing with the exchange of prisoners. Her uncle, a painfully shy man who was a widower, had to give official receptions from time to time, and when he did he would call on his niece to act as hostess.

"I knew my uncle was bored silly at these official receptions," Miss Rama Rau said. "They were really extremely stuffy, and I thought it would be very amusing to have some people there who were in a completely different world and brighten things up.

"I invited Costello to come. Everybody that I knew in New York had been so terribly eager to meet him that I really didn't see what was wrong about it. It's not anything I would do now, but at that time, at that age, I thought it would make the party more interesting, and so I invited him, and he said he'd come, he'd be delighted. Then later on he called me back — in the meantime he made a few inquiries who my uncle was — and said that he wouldn't come to the reception because it would be very embarrassing for my uncle with all those foreign delegations there. The security police would be there on the spot, of course, and he said there was no question but that he would be recognized. He said my uncle's work was too important to jeopardize. I thought it was remarkably considerate of him."

✻   ✻   ✻

Costello was considerate in many other ways. Miss Rama Rau found that he was so sensitive that he was almost always able to anticipate what another person might want and that when he did something, it was done so nicely that there never was any sense of indebtedness.

She became aware of Costello's great influence in judicial and governmental business when she casually mentioned a problem that a friend was having. There was no attempt on Miss Rama Rau's part to get Costello to do something about the problem. It just happened that they met for lunch one day, and she told him about it as an item of gossip.

The friend, a foreign born young woman who was quite wealthy, had married a titled European who was a fortune hunter. After a couple years of marriage, she realized her mistake and wanted a divorce. However, because she had been married in New York, she couldn't get one because the law, which has since been changed, recognized only adultery as legal grounds. The husband wasn't guilty of that so the friend appeared to be stuck with her bad marriage.

"I told him the story, and he seemed very interested," Miss Rama Rau said. "We discussed how very unfair it seemed; because she was too young to know what she was getting into, she had to stay married to this man."

"Do you know the name of the judge?" Costello asked casually.

"DiFalco," Miss Rama Rau answered.

"That's one of my boys," Costello said brightly.

Sometime later, much to Miss Rama Rau's and her friend's astonishment, Supreme Court Justice S. Samuel DiFalco ordered the marriage annulled on the grounds that the husband had committed fraud when he entered into it. The miracle, obviously, had been performed by Costello because Miss Rama Rau's friend wasn't even aware that it was possible to get a marriage annulled on the grounds of fraud.

(S.Samuel DiFalco, now a Surrogate Judge in Manhattan, was sworn in as a Supreme Court Justice in 1948. He was a Tammany Hall and Reform Democrat candidate when he ran and also had the endorsement of the Liberal Party. Standing by his side during his swearing-in ceremonies were Generoso Pope, Manhattan Borough President Hugo Rogers, and Congressman Arthur Klein, all friends of Costello.)

         ❊   ❊   ❊

During the normal course of their many conversations, Costello occasionally mentioned a number of men whom he described as "my boys." Some were judges. Others were scattered throughout the legal, administrative, and legislative branches of the city and the state. Miss Rama Rau has forgotten most of the names, but even now, after all these years have passed, she often finds that while reading a story in a newspaper there will be a name that "rings a bell." It will be one of Frankie's boys.

Costello seldom mentioned his wife during the two years that they saw each other (which was usually once or twice a week). When he did mention her, it was with "great respect, great affection, and complete detachment."

"I never met her," Miss Rama Rau said. "She was just a separate department of his life, and it never occurred to him, and consequently it never occurred to me that I might ever meet his wife or ever be invited to his house.

"I think it says something about him that he made it seem absolutely ordinary, absolutely natural — because there was no reason why I shouldn't have met his wife. There was nothing remotely clandestine about our relationship. He was seeing me for pleasure and possibly instruction and possibly psychiatric reasons, and I was seeing him because I found him terribly interesting and very nice, and he was an introduction to a whole sort of America that I knew nothing about.

"He was very bright and very experienced. I had the curious feeling with him, had he not been a gangster, he would have been an exceedingly moral man. You know what I mean. I think he was a man of principles, and his principles may have been very different from other people, but he was very honorable about them. I had the feeling with him that he would never — within his code — betray a friend or do a dishonorable thing, and I can't imagine him acting out of meanness or spite or any of those things. He was exceedingly intelligent and I think that — but of course not an intellectual — and I think he suffered from, I know he suffered from, a lack of education. I think that probably preyed on him quite a bit.

"All the time that I knew him he was much more interested in getting to know what my life was like and who my friends were and what my interests were than talking about himself. He seemed perfectly open about things but not at all eager to talk. I don't think because he wanted to hide things so much as it didn't interest him. This was all stuff he knew. He was interested more in finding out about other people and how they functioned.

"What I saw was an amused kind of tolerant man with a great many regrets about his life, but not the sort of ones you'd expect. He didn't give the impression he regretted anything he had done. I think he regretted the things he missed in his life."

What do you think he was getting out of you and your friends?

"I don't know. I really don't know. Clearly he enjoyed himself. It couldn't all have been therapy. Somehow he wasn't finding in this very high-powered world what he wanted. I don't know whether he found it with all of us. I think that his feeling about not having had sufficient education himself, I think that had something to do with it because all of us had been to college and we were interested in the world and the life of the mind, and I think that all struck him as a terrific novelty. He would ask questions like what we thought one should seek in life or what one's life should be."

Did he think of himself as a benefactor?

"Not really, not in any pretentious ways. At least I never heard him moralizing about this, but I think he was very conscious of doing good when he gave to all the charities he gave to. I think that it was with the genuine wish to encourage young people and help them in small ways that he was so kind to me and all my friends. He approved of the sort of things we were trying to do. He was terribly willing to encourage that. Although nothing could have been further from the pattern of his life.

"Actually I really don't think that he would have understood it if you had suggested to him that, in his own way, that he was much more a threat to society than the overt gangsters. I don't think that he would have understood what are clearly the much bigger threats, the corruption of public officials."

❁   ❁   ❁

Miss Rama Rau was given an insight into how Costello regarded society in general when she introduced him to a stock broker who strongly disapproved of her relationship with him. Costello picked up the man's hostility immediately and asked him what he did for a living. When he heard the answer, Costello said, "Oh, we're in the same racket. We both gamble with other people's money."

"I don't think it was entirely a joke," she said. "I think that he saw an awful lot of society in general as legalized rackets. There was a touch of bitterness in what he said. I think he was exasperated by the fact that society insisted on considering him a racketeer because of an arbitrary line: if you're in gambling casinos, you're a racketeer; if you're gambling on the stock market, you're not."

When it became obvious to Miss Rama Rau during the Kefauver hearings that Costello would be going to jail, she said that she would write to him. He became agitated and asked her not to. He pointed out that her reputation could be damaged, and he would be very upset if their friendship resulted in her being embarrassed.

She recognized it as Costello once again being courteous, gentlemanly, and considerate, and because of circumstances she went back to India, and he went off to jail. They never saw or contacted each other again.

The man (Part III)

In his lifetime, Frank Costello became personally acquainted with scores of celebrities. Men and women whose names — over the course of the last fifty years — have become household words for most Americans.

Because he was sensitive to the fact that anyone linked to him suffered embarrassment, he was quite discreet about many of these relationships. He and Jim Farley, for instance, would meet on occasion in the steam room of the Biltmore's baths. There was nothing sinister about the relationship. Neither man ever asked each other for anything.

"I know some of the biggest men in the country," Costello once told District Attorney Hogan when he was being questioned about his friends.

Costello refused to name some of the people he knew, but if he had, President Harry Truman certainly would have headed the list. They met during the years the late President was an obscure senator from Missouri who headed a committee investigating war profiteering. Costello was a great admirer of Truman's earthy, straight-from-the-shoulder method of expressing himself.

Costello was fascinated with human motivation. He was always trying to understand the underlying cause that would explain a person's actions. One of his favorite games during dinner was to ask his

247

companions what person in all of history they would most like to
spend an hour in conversation with and why. His choice was Adolph
Hitler because he wanted to see for himself if the German dictator's
bestial acts were the result of insanity.

While much of Costello's attempts at intellectualism were mundane
and sophomoric, the fact remains that he did attempt to lift the subject matter of his conversations above the level of common gossip.
"Why do you think he (she) did that?" was his favorite question.

He had opinions on everyone and everything (many of them contra-
dictory). Like many men of the underworld, he was a political conservative and a flag waver. He responded to Senator Joe McCarthy's
rabble rousing accusations that there were Communists in high and
secret places, although he later realized he had been taken in as easily
as the midwest farmers.

He honestly believed that if the environment of his early life had
been better, he would have gone far. When he told District Attorney
Hogan that if circumstances had been different he might have been
on his side of the fence or remarked to a newspaperman the same
thought in regard to Estes Kefauver, he was being sincere. The breaks
in life, so far as he was concerned, were all that separated him from
those who were constantly attempting to put him behind bars.

Some of the famous people who Costello got to know over the years
were:

HOWARD HUGHES — Costello met America's most eccentric bil-
lionaire in the late thirties in California. Hughes was involved in making
pictures at the time and was quite accessible. In fact, in those days
he was often seen in Hollywood night clubs escorting one of the cel-
luloid glamour girls.

Costello was introduced to Hughes as a big-time gambler and financier from the East who was interested in oil, and Hughes — who was
having financial difficulties at the time — immediately attempted to
get Costello to invest $250,000 in a movie he was making. He told
Costello that he needed the money very fast to finish the picture.

Costello wasn't completely aware of just who Howard Hughes was.
He thought his family was in the oil business and didn't know that
his fortune rested on the very solid foundation of a bit which must
be used everytime anyone drills for oil. Hughes owned the patent
rights to the bit. Costello's first impression was that Hughes was just
a rich man's son who was running around throwing away all his money.
He, therefore, told Hughes that he wanted a little time to consider it.
Costello was seriously thinking of getting into the movie business in
those days, and he may very well have thought about investing with
Hughes.

That same night he ran into him at the Coconut Grove, Hollywood's most famous night club, and Hughes asked him if he had made a decision on whether to invest in the movie. Costello said he was still thinking it over. Hughes, who habitually went around without pocket money, then asked Costello to loan him a few dollars. Costello pulled out three hundred, but Hughes said, "No, no, I just want a few dollars. Ten will do." Costello gave him the ten and concluded that Hughes was in such bad financial trouble that he had to mooch ten dollar bills. Right then and there he made up his mind not to invest in any Hughes-produced movies. It wasn't until he got back to New York that he found out the importance of the money behind Hughes and the fact that he was just an eccentric. Hughes never paid back the ten, and Costello was fond of telling friends that one of the world's richest men was a deadbeat.

✳   ✳   ✳

BABE RUTH — They were good friends and used to play golf together occasionally at the Lakeville Country Club in Great Neck. Costello was fond of Ruth but recognized him for just what he was — a little boy in a man's body. Ruth, despite all the money he made, was often in financial trouble, and Costello would loan him money even though he knew there was little chance of him ever getting it back. Ruth was rather careless about his obligations.

Once when they were playing at Lakeville, Ruth asked to borrow five thousand. Costello didn't want to loan Ruth the money. He decided he was better off just giving it to him. So he proposed a five-thousand dollar bet on the hole coming up. Ruth, who played a much better game of golf than Costello, readily agreed.

The hole was a par five, and Costello's plan was to artfully lose, but to his astonishment he got off a magnificent drive which was followed by an equally magnificent wood that put him within putting distance for a possible eagle. In his entire life Costello had never made an eagle. He was torn between the desire to try and make it or three putt the hole to give Ruth a chance to win. The golfer in him won that struggle, and he went on to make what was possibly the only eagle of his life. He loaned Ruth the five thousand anyway and, of course, was never paid back.

✳   ✳   ✳

FRANK SINATRA — Much has been written about the real-life incident of how Costello got Sinatra the part of Maggio in *From Here to Eternity* when the singer's career was at its low ebb.

The bit about the thoroughbred horse's head being cut off never really happened, of course. It was just part of Mario Puzo's magnificent imagination that made the *Godfather* so fascinating.

The real facts were much less exciting. Sinatra knew Costello through Willie Moretti, and while they were hardly close friends, their paths had crossed many times. When Sinatra asked for help in getting the role, Costello simply contacted George Wood of the William Morris talent agency and some top movie executives on the West Coast. It was a favor they couldn't refuse because of favors received in the past. Costello acknowledged to close friends that he was the one who got Sinatra the part, but he never talked about the circumstances in detail.

❀   ❀   ❀

CHARLES LINDBERGH — Costello never actually met the famous flyer, but he became involved in the search for the Lindbergh baby when the infant was kidnapped in the early thirties. Lindbergh contacted him because it was thought that the crime may have been committed by someone well known in the underworld. Friends of Lindbergh advised him that Costello was the sort of man who would help. Costello was contacted and used all the resources at his disposal to try and find the infant. He was able to determine, to his satisfaction, that no one in the underworld was responsible and advised against paying the ransom. He had concluded that the baby was already dead. His advice wasn't taken, however, and the ransom was paid.

❀   ❀   ❀

MAE WEST — Costello took credit for dreaming up the publicity stunt that changed the brassy blond from an ambitous actress going no place into a sex symbol.

They were friends, and when she opened in 1926 in a shocking-for-the-times Broadway show called *Sex* — an immediate success that newspapers refused to accept ads for — they discussed ways in which she could exploit the play's notoriety. After a very respectable run of 375 performances, it was decided to put Costello's plan into action. He arranged through friends to have the cops raid the show and arrest Miss West on charges of corrupting public morals. Newspapers were tipped off to make certain there were lots of photographs of the event. Everyting went off just as planned, and Miss West was hauled off to jail. She pleaded "not guilty," and at her trial a police officer testified that he had observed her do a lascivíous belly dance in which she "moved her navel up and down and from side to side."

The judge found her guilty, and she happily spent eight days in jail which resulted in tons of free publicity. She emerged from her cell a superstar.

✵   ✵   ✵

BOBBY DARIN — The singer, born Robert Waldo Casado in the Bronx, blamed Costello for the poverty and misery of his childhood, and when he was a headliner at the Copacabana, studiously avoided meeting the man he knew was one of the club's owners. Darin's father was a soldier in the Costello family and was arrested and sent to jail when Bobby was just a youngster. During that period his family often went hungry because there wasn't enough money for food.

Darin hated Costello because he believed that he had reneged on the sacred underworld obligation which makes the capo of a family responsible for taking care of the family of a soldier in jail. It was a bum rap, though, for Costello. First of all, he wasn't obligated because Darin's father was not involved in family business when he was arrested. Secondly, Costello sent the entertainer his first piano when he heard Bobby was interested in music.

✵   ✵   ✵

J. EDGAR HOOVER — Costello met America's most famous cop through mutual friend Walter Winchell during the hunt for Lepke. It was hardly an intimate relationship, although they did treat each other in a civilized manner. Costello didn't like Hoover and considered him a "professional blackmailer" who used the information his agency gathered for his own personal ends. They would meet on occasion because they frequented some of the same places — the Stork Club and the Waldorf. One time they ran into each other in the Waldorf lobby and Costello complained to Hoover about the FBI following him into the hotel. "How do you know you're being followed here?" Hoover asked. "Everybody here's on my payroll," Costello answered. At another Waldorf meeting, according to columnist Earl Wilson, Hoover invited Costello to join him for a cup of coffee.

"I got to be careful of my associates," Costello told the FBI chief. "They'll accuse me of consortin' with questionable characters."

✵   ✵   ✵

JOE E. LEWIS — Costello was fonder and had more respect for comedian Joe E. Lewis than any other show business personality. He admired Lewis' personal integrity and style and appreciated the fact that he was a stand-up guy who had never turned his back on a friend in his life. These were qualities that Costello felt he had himself.

Lewis was a compulsive horse player and was always borrowing large sums of money from Costello which he would meticulously pay back. His entire philosophy of humor was built around life's losers. Costello appreciated this. "Every loser has a family," was one of Costello's favorite expressions. When the comedian died, a deeply saddened Costello attended his funeral.

❋   ❋   ❋

MARK HELLINGER — The Broadway columnist was Costello's favorite newspaperman in the thirties because he was the only one who would insist on paying his own way. All the others were shameless freeloaders. Once Hellinger broke his leg jumping off a ship, and Costello sent so many flowers to Hellinger's hospital room that the columnist complained to him that he was trying to make a gangland funeral out of a broken leg. In talking about Hellinger, Costello would say, "He had integrity."

The last years

In 1968, an American television producer who was in Yugoslavia on business noted that the members of the Government with whom he was dealing suddenly began to pay special attention to him. He was being wined and dined far out of proportion to the importance of his business — the importing of Yugoslavian-made cartoons for television. The independent Communist nation had a way of producing cartoons that were of very high quality, yet cheaper than those from anyplace else in the world.

The TV producer began to wonder what all the fuss was about when a high official invited him to dinner. During the evening the official asked him a rather surprising question. He wanted to know if he knew Frank Costello or had any way of reaching him. If he had, he was given to understand, the Government would not be ungrateful and all his cartoon deals would be given top priority.

The TV producer was absolutely flabbergasted. He wasn't certain he was hearing right. Did the official mean **the Frank Costello**? The American gangster? Yes, that was exactly the man. The official wished the TV producer to contact him on behalf of Marshal Tito. Could he do it?

By the sheerest coincidence, the producer happened to be a friend of columnist John Miller who he knew was close to Costello. Yes, he said, he could contact Costello through a friend, but what was this all about?

253

The official smiled happily and said that Marshal Tito wished to turn the Yugoslavian resort city of Zagreb into another Las Vegas to attract American tourists. The Marshal wished to have American-style gambling, coupled with top entertainment. Costello was to be discreetly approached with the proposal to see if he was interested in heading such an operation. The producer agreed to act as the intermediary.

He returned to America and told Miller about the offer. Miller became tremendously excited. The prospects sounded so fantastic. It was as if Frank Costello was being offered the whole country by Marshal Tito himself. However, before he thought it wise to approach Costello, he felt it was first necessary to find out more about the deal. Since his producer friend was going back to Yugoslavia soon, he asked him to talk to the official again and see if he could obtain more information.

"It took three trips," Miller said, "but finally it was all laid out for me. I was told that the Government would construct the gambling casinos, come up with the bankroll, everything. They had very ambitious plans and wanted Frank to run everything. The bottom line of the whole thing was that anything that the Government or Marshal Tito personally could do for him, he could have in addition to the financial aspects of the deal."

With visions of winding up in a public relations capacity for the entire project dancing in his head, Miller approached Costello at the Waldorf. He was breathless with excitement and told him he had something very big and important to talk to him about. They sat on a couch in the Waldorf's lobby while Miller told everything he knew.

"His initial reaction to the offer took five seconds," Miller said. "He just said, 'No,' and that was that. I was so excited about it that I couldn't help asking him why. Normally it wasn't protocol to ask Frank about his decisions, but I was burning up with curiosity and disappointment, and after all the conversations and running this thing out, it just wasn't enough to get one solitary word.

"So when I asked him why, he said, 'because you just can't trust the head of a government.' He said that it had nothing to do with where it was or who it was, just that you can't trust the head of any government. And if you trust the head, the army might come along and shoot him, and you can't trust them. You not only lose your business, but you become part of the guys who are doing the killing. Then he said that the deal sounded like it would be perfect for Meyer Lansky, and he asked me to send back word that he was retired and not interested, but he would be happy to have Meyer Lansky follow it up."

Miller said he didn't think of it at the time, but another reason Costello may have had for turning down the deal so quickly was his promise to Vito Genovese to stay retired for the rest of his life.

The TV producer delivered the message to the Yugoslavian official and came back with a message stating that they weren't interested in Lansky.

"When I delivered the message that they didn't want Lansky," Miller said, "Frank smiled and said, 'I thought Marshal Tito had only heard of me, and now I see that he knows me.' He took it as a terrific compliment that it was only him they wanted and no one else."

✿   ✿   ✿

In the last decade of his life, Costello came close to achieving the respectability and anonymity that he claimed he always wanted. The police were no longer interested in him — although they did spot check his activities from time to time — and the notoriety he had earned during the Kefauver hearings had begun to wear off. People just didn't seem to either know or care who he was.

The years had done little to alter his appearance. He still dressed impeccably and walked with the vigorous step of a much younger man. He had become much grayer, and the lines in his face had set more deeply, but otherwise he appeared the same.

Those closest to him were Miller, Gene Pope, and Phil Kennedy. After he was released from jail in 1961, Costello, Miller, and Pope continued their practice of dining together on the average of twice a week. After a while Pope dropped out when his publishing business started to consume all his time, and his close relationship with Costello was severed. Costello's estimate of the situation was that he had become an embarrassment to Pope.

He continued to maintain his life style and became even more rigid in his habits. Despite his retirement, it was obvious he wasn't in any financial difficulty. On the contrary, he told Toots Shor that he had a million in cash tucked away for emergencies. Friends would run into him at many of New York's finest restaurants where he continued to be greeted with enthusiasm by the head-waiters and waiters. (When he was with a large party, Costello habitually tipped headwaiters a hundred and waiters fifty.)

He stuck to his spartan routine of rising at five in the morning and breakfasting on coffee and a slice of toast with a smear of margarine. He then would breeze through the *Times* and follow this with a long

morning constitutional along Central Park West. He would have preferred walking in Central Park, but at that early hour he was concerned about street crime and didn't want to risk being mugged. About
ten A.M., he would head for the Waldorf, often walking all the way
in nice weather. He would walk across Central Park, cut through the
zoo, and emerge at Sixtieth Street and Fifth Avenue. If anything about
his habits had changed, it was that he now spent more time walking
in the park. In the afternoons, if he had nothing to do, he would wander
over to the Wollman Memorial Rink in Central Park and watch the
skaters. He also frequented the Central Park Zoo where the monkeys
fascinated him. Once one of the chimpanzees spat in his face, and
it promptly became his favorite. If the chimp was missing from its
cage, he would seek out one of the attendants to inquire about its
health. "That chimp's got real intelligence because it showed discrim-
ination," he told friends with an amused grin on his face.

On Fridays, Bobbie and he would drive to their home in Sands Point
where Frank would spend the weekend pruning his fruit trees and
tending to his rose bushes. He was proud of his gardening skills and
frequently entered local flower shows where on a number of occasions
he was awarded a blue ribbon for his roses. This seemed to give him
a great deal of satisfaction.

Sundays the Costellos would often entertain, and friends would
spend a quiet day with them watching TV or talking about old times.
Costello, as always, had center stage with his fund of interesting stories
about the past in which the names of well-known people he had known
would leap out of his conversation as from a page in a history book.

In his later years he was rarely seen out past ten P.M., although
once in a while he would treat Bobbie to an opening night at the
Copa. When they did go, they always sat at the center terrace table,
side by side, facing the entrance. Frank always sat so that he could
keep an eye on the door and spot whoever came in.

As all old men do, he spent more and more of his time attending
the funerals of friends. When journalist Quentin Reynolds died in
1965, reporters spotted Costello coming into the church by a side
entrance.

"The mass had just started when I spotted this guy with his hat
pulled down low over his forehead come in a side door," recalls Joe
Schroeder of the Associated Press. "I didn't know who it was at first,
and then I realized it was Frank Costello. He went over to the far
side of the church, away from the mourners. Then he knelt down on
the pew and got up about ten minutes before the mass was over. It
was obvious he wanted to pay his last tribute to the man, but by the
same token he didn't want to embarrass the family or anything like

that because he knew the photographers were around. He was just trying to be considerate.."

Sometimes in the afternoon he would visit Toots Shor's restaurant and spend a couple of hours kibbitzing with the garrulous proprietor. Other times he would meet Phil Kennedy who occasionally would bring a model or two from his agency for Uncle Frank to flirt with. It would never go further than that — just an old man gently teasing pretty girls young enough to be his granddaughters.

❋   ❋   ❋

His name came back into the news briefly in May of 1970 when he answered a subpoena and testified before a Manhattan grand jury investigating gambling. "He cooperated, he answered all the questions," Al Scotti, Hogan's chief assistant said in reply to inquiries.

The truth of the matter, of course, was simply that Costello had no answers of value to give. He was completely out of the picture and said as much to reporters who cornered him as he left the court building. "I'm retired. I don't know any more about this than you do."

❋   ❋   ❋

He was still regarded as a wise man by the Mafiosi, and the younger men who now headed the organization sometimes came to him for advice. Joe Colombo, a Mafia boss from Brooklyn, sought him out at the Copa lounge one day and asked him what he thought about the Italian-American Civil Rights League he had founded. The league was busy picketing FBI headquarters, proclaiming that the Federal agents were persecuting honest Italian-Americans and that the Mafia was a figment of the media's imagination. Colombo, in the spirit of the times, had proclaimed himself a civil-rights leader and, instead of shunning publicity, was busy giving interviews. Willie Moretti had been called crazy and was killed for much less.

Costello advised Colombo to change his tactics. He warned that publicity was a two-edged sword, and it was always best to try and maintain a low profile. Besides, the older, more conservative members of the organization didn't like what was going on, and this was bound to lead to trouble. Colombo listened and out of respect said nothing. He thought that Costello, who himself had had a hand in changing things in the old days, would approve of what he was doing. He continued on his course and held the league's first Unity Day Rally in Columbus Circle. A crowd estimated at fifty thousand showed up and listened as Colombo postured and made a speech. A year later the league held its second rally, and a black gunman, recruited by Crazy Joe Gallo, shot Colombo in the head. He survived but became a vegetable. The gunman was shot to death on the spot by Colombo body-guards.

Other Mafia leaders came to Costello for advice, and for a while the police and FBI thought he had come out of retirement. He was observed meeting with Carlo Gambino at the Waldorf. The law enforcement officials wondered what it all meant. Informers reported back that it was just Costello doing what he liked best — playing the role of the wise man. Gambino wanted advice on Mafia matters and Costello had obliged — nothing more than that. It was ironic, though, that the two met at all when you consider that Gambino rose to power when he backed Genovese in his attempt to have Costello killed.

When Genovese died in prison in 1969, the family that Costello once headed fell on hard times. At first Jerry Catena took over, but he was convicted on an obscure charge in New Jersey and sent to jail. Charley (The Blade) Tourine, a mob courier who police say is an illiterate, stepped into the power vacuum. Running the family was beyond Tourine's capabilities, and he turned to Costello for advice. Police noted that as often as two or three times a week, the pair would meet in Tourine's Central Park South apartment.

Why would Costello become involved again at this late stage of his life? Friends say that all he did was give the younger man some advice and that it flattered his ego to be remembered. There was nothing Costello loved more, his friends say, than dispensing the wisdom of his years to someone who would listen. Tourine not only listened, but he treated Costello with respect bordering on reverence.

*   *   *

On February 7, 1973, while sitting in his Central Park West apartment, Costello suffered a mild heart seizure. Because of his advanced age and history of heart trouble, he was hospitalized at Doctors Hospital on East End Avenue and Eighty-seventh Street. He didn't seem to be in any particular danger, but he must have had a premonition that he didn't have much time left. Through a friend he sent word to writer Peter Maas — after several months of considering doing a book — that when he came out of the hospital he would agree to spend the necessary time being interviewed so that his story might be told.

Costello had less time than he thought, and his willingness to talk became meaningless. Just what he might have revealed is open to a good deal of speculation. His friends say that they find it impossible to believe he would have talked about the Mafia and allowed himself to be remembered as another Joe Valachi whom he despised and regarded as "scum" for breaking his oath.

If his friends are right, what then did he have in his mind? Did he wish to leave behind a document filled with detailed and elaborate rationalizations to explain why he had become a racketeer? Or was it just a case of an old man intending to indulge his vanity? Costello regarded himself as being far above the Genoveses of this world and felt that his life reflected a unique bit of American history. Yet he had no illusions as to how he would be remembered — if he were remembered at all — after he was gone. If the Government could libel and slander a person while he's alive, he used to say, there's no limit to what they could do after he's dead.

From the window of his room at Doctor's Hospital, Costello could see the Triborough Bridge and follow the way it curved into Queens. "I can almost make out the houses I bought for my mother and sisters in about 1931," he told Phil Kennedy who was visiting him. "How much do you think I paid for those houses? They were brick, one family." Kennedy said he didn't know. "Five thousand," Costello said softly.

Staring out the hospital window he must also have thought about another site in Queens that he was familiar with and that lay just a short distance from the Triborough. It was St. Michael's Cemetery in Elmhurst, where the mausoleum that had caused him all that tax trouble stood. His mother, who had died in 1940, was interred there. So were his father and his sister Sadie who had traveled to America with him and who had helped raise him. Bobbie's parents, Cecelia and Jacob Geigerman, were there too. The disparity of religious backgrounds hadn't prevented Costello from burying his loved ones together. The mausoleum was where Costello's body would be placed when his time came.

Phil Kennedy visited Costello on the evening of February 17. They gossiped for a while, but Costello just didn't seem to have an interest in anything. He complained of being tired, and Kennedy decided to cut his visit short in order to give him time to rest. As he turned to leave, Costello smiled at him from the bed and said, "See you in the morning, champ." At seven-thirty A.M., on February 18, he suffered a coronary and died.

❋   ❋   ❋

Frank Costello would have been pleased to see that the *New York Times* began his obituary on page one and then devoted three full columns of an inside page to tell the highlights of his career. It was the sort of placement and space only persons of note receive. A one column picture showed him in his later years looking like everybody's favorite uncle. The obituary noted that he had been known as the "prime minister of the underworld" and that he was a symbol of the underworld's power in "politics, business and other phases of American life."

Bobbie seemed to take his passing quite well. Friends were amazed because her life was really an extension of his. She had no friends of her own and socialized only with Frank's friends. He had wrapped a protective cocoon around her life since the day they were married, and everything she said, thought, or did reflected his attitudes.

His death undoubtedly was cushioned for her by the countless details she had to attend to for his funeral. She knew that Frank would have wanted something quiet and dignified, and she was determined that the press not be given the opportunity to make a spectacle out of this solemn occasion. Phil Kennedy helped her with the arrangements, and all of Frank's friends with unsavory reputations were politely told that it would be best if they didn't attend the funeral because she feared unfavorable publicity. She also made it clear that there was to be no long cortege of flowerbedecked limousines following the hearse. Floral offerings were kept to a minimum.

She and Kennedy had a disagreement over whether to have the coffin opened or not. Kennedy wanted it closed because he felt Frank should be remembered the way he was in life and not the way he looked in his coffin. In Kennedy's own words, "He was not a very good looking corpse." Bobbie overruled him and insisted that it be open because she feared people might think that something was wrong. Kennedy attempted to talk her out of it, but she was adamant.

His wake was held in the Frank E. Campbell Funeral Home on Eighty-first Street, near Madison Avenue. In the entrance of a school, directly across the street from the funeral home, two detectives dressed in raincoats and looking inconspicuously conspicuous, as only detectives can on such occasions, stood watching to see who would attend. They had little to do because only relatives and a few of his legitimate friends came to pay their last respects.

The photographers and reporters were similiarly disappointed. Toots Shor was the only one newsworthy who showed up, and when he was asked why he was attending, he said simply, "Because he was my friend." He was shocked by the small turnout and apparently didn't know about Bobbie's request that everyone stay away.

Phil Kennedy, dressed in a black suit and tie, stood guard in front of the second-floor room where Costello was laid out. He knew most of Frank's friends and was there to prevent reporters and curiosity seekers from sneaking in. Inside, Bobbie, dressed in a two-piece grey suit, stood with her brother Dudley who had flown up from New Orleans. There were perhaps forty or fifty people in the room, and they formed little clusters, chatting quietly. Occasionally laughter could be heard.

The only one there who the police might have been interested in was Frankie Mario, the old friend of Costello's who supplied the linen to virtually all the top restaurants in the city. Mario, whose real last name is Bonfiglio, remarked that the only people he recognized were a few union officials.

Frank Costello's body reposed in a polished walnut coffin that had been placed on a raised platform against the far side of the room. He was dressed in a blue suit, a white shirt, and a blue tie. Death had contorted his features, and some had difficulty recognizing him. He looked much thinner than he had in life. Everyone agreed that he looked bad. A few modest sprays of flowers stood at the foot of the coffin.

There were no incidents to mar the dignity of the occasion. A small number of the curious attempted to get in, but they were quickly identified and agreed to leave without any fuss. One couple who managed to slip by the vigilant Kennedy decided that the whole thing was a bore and left without being told. They had managed a brief peek into the room.

"I thought it would be different than that. I thought it would be a real big thing," remarked the girl, about twenty and wearing blue jeans, to her escort as they left via the second floor elevator.

"Yeah, I figured they'd have food and drinks," her equally young and casually dressed companion answered. "It looks like they're taking it seriously."

A maroon hearse led the funeral procession over the Triborough Bridge to St. Michael's. At the burial site, Bobbie, supported by her brother, stood watching the coffin as a young Roman Catholic priest delivered a short prayer. It was over in a few minutes.

As she turned to leave, a cousin of Frank's, whom she either didn't know or didn't recognize, approached respectfully with his hat in his hand. She leaned forward to accept the expected words of condolence.

"What are you going to do with Frank's clothes?" the cousin asked.

She never bothered to answer.

Epilogue

The legacy Frank Costello left Bobbie included his tax problems with the Internal Revenue Service. Following his income tax conviction, the IRS slapped liens totalling between three and four million dollars against all his property. Bobbie didn't become aware of the liens until after his death when she found that her apartment on Central Park West, the estate in Sands Point, and various other parcels of real estate were tied up. This meant that if and when she sold the property, the proceeds would go to Uncle Sam.

Depressed and unable to cope with her problems, Bobbie fled New York in the middle of September, vowing never to return. Frank had been dead only seven months, but in that time she had changed from a still-vigorous woman to an old lady who had had the foundations of her life ripped away.

"She's lost without Frank," said her lawyer, Harold O.N. Frankel.

Friends described her as being a "broken woman," unable to forget the past and face the reality of the present. She stated that she intended to spend the rest of her life with her brother Dudley in New Orleans.

She also told friends that she was broke, with only five hundred dollars in cash to her name. The Government, she said, had taken everything.

No one believed her.

Index